EXCLUSION AND INCLUSION

Exclusion and Inclusion
The Gender Composition of British and Dutch Work Forces

LYDIA MARTENS
Department of Applied Social Studies
University of Paisley

Avebury
Aldershot • Brookfield USA • Hong Kong • Singapore • Sydney

© L. Martens 1997

Published by
Avebury
Ashgate Publishing Limited
Gower House
Croft Road
Aldershot
Hants GU11 3HR
England

Ashgate Publishing Company
Old Post Road
Brookfield
Vermont 05036
USA

British Library Cataloguing in Publication Data

Martens, Lydia
    Exclusion and inclusion : the gender composition of British
    and Dutch work forces
    1.Women - Employment - Great Britain 2.Women - Employment
    Netherlands 3.Sexual division of labor - Great Britain
    4.Sexual division of labor - Netherlands 5.Sex
    discrimination in employment - Great Britain 6. Sex
    discrimination in employment - Netherlands
    I.Title
    331.4'133

    ISBN 1 85972 458 2

Library of Congress Catalog Card Number: 96-079153

Printed and bound by Athenaeum Press, Ltd.,
Gateshead, Tyne & Wear.

Contents

Figures and tables

Acknowledgements

There are many people who have been great stimulants for me in my work on this project over the years. It started in the Department of Sociology at the University of Glasgow, and my special thanks go to John Eldridge and John MacInnes, who have both been closely involved in the various stages of the research. Over the years, I have also gained support from David Frisby, Harvey Ferguson, Bridget Fowler and others in the Department. Intellectual stimulation and emotional support was furthermore provided by the Women's Reading Group, which was set up during 1991 by a number of post-graduate and under-graduate students. I would also like to thank Alan Warde and Andrew Sayer for encouraging me to change this project into a book, and Wendy Olsen and Christof Armbruster for the many conversations which have aided the development of my ideas.

In the course of this doctoral research, there have been a number of people - some representing libraries and archives - who have helped me in bringing this project to its end. I would like to thank the library staff of the University of Glasgow; the KUB (Katholieke Universiteit Brabant) in Tilburg; and the IIAV (International Archive for the Women's Movement) in Amsterdam. Thanks are also due to the people who have provided me with access to the materials which have formed the backbone of the case-study on the British and Dutch banking sectors. In Britain, I would like to thank Pamela Anderson of Britbank for her help and co-operation; Charley Munn of the Scottish Institute of Bankers; Alan Scott of the Committee of Scottish Clearing bankers; archivists Elizabeth Ogborn and Vicki Wilkinson; and BIFU staff. In the Netherlands, my thanks go to Nicolette Engbers and Judith Wijnbergen of Dutchbank; the staff of the NIBE library and the Rijksmuseum Overijsel; Mr J.B. Kuyper of the Werkgeversvereeniging voor het Bankbedrijf; Geert Meiring and Dik Hamaker of the Dienstenbond FNV; and Eveline Ross and her colleagues at the historical archive of Dutchbank. As well as those mentioned here by name, there have been others who have been helpful during the data collection period of my research, and I would like to thank them too.

Most of all, I would like to thank all the former and current bank employees who have been so generous with their time, and who have been willing to share their work experiences with me.

Finally, I would like to thank my friends and family. My special thanks go to my friends Lisa Norris, Line Stevenson, and Rita Kempter, for giving me emotional support and companionship over the years. My parents Jeanne and Jo Martens have always encouraged and supported me in the various decisions and steps taken in the course of my life. This was, above all, the case during the years of research, when their home was always open for me on my research trips to the Netherlands. In this respect, my thanks also go to my sister Monique, who has always been willing to listen to, and respond to the stories about my work. Most of all, though, my thanks go to Steven Lucas. He has, over the years as friend and partner, encouraged me in the work I have set myself to do, and has shared the inevitable special and difficult moments which accompany a life of research and writing, with me.

Abbreviations

BIFU	Banking, Insurance and Finance Union
BO	The Bank Officer
BOE	Bank of England
BOG	Bank Officers Guild
CAO	Collectieve Arbeids Overeenkomst (collective bargaining agreement)
CBS	Centraal Bureau voor de Statistiek (central statistical office)
CDA	Christen-Democratisch Appel (contemporary Dutch centre-confessional political party)
CSCA	Civil Service Clerical Association
EC	European Community
EO	Equal Opportunities
HBS	Hogere Burgerschool (Dutch post-war secondary education) [6.25]
IOB	Institute of Bankers
KB	Koninklijk Besluit (Royal Decision)
KVP	Katholieke Volks Partij (Catholic People's party of the post-war years)
MULO	Meer Uitgebreid Lager Onderwijs (Dutch post-war secondary education) [6.25]
NCC	National Childcare Campaign
NHM	Nederlandse Handel Maatschappij (Dutch post-war bank)
NIBE	Nederlands Instituut voor Bank- en Effectenbedrijf (Dutch equivalent of IOB)
NMB	Nederlandse Middenstands Bank
NVV	Nederlandse Vakvereeniging (Dutch trade union council)
NUBE	National Union of Bank Employees
OR	Ondernemingsraad (works council)

PVDA	Partij van de Arbeid (Dutch contemporary Labour Party)
RB	Rotterdamse Bank (Dutch post-war bank)
TB	Twentsche Bank
TUC	Trade Union Council
UPOW	Union of Post Office Workers
VVD	Volkspartij voor de Vrijheid en Democratie (Dutch liberal political party)
WMA	Working Mothers' Association
WNC	Workplace Nurseries Campaign

Part 1
THE GENDER COMPOSITION OF WORK FORCES

1 Introduction

During the past two decades, there has been an increasing interest around the issue of women participating in employment in the formal economies of industrialized countries. This has been especially evident in the increasing attention given by the media; by - often, but not always - feminist academics; in discussions between women; women and men, at work and social gatherings alike, to a variety of topics ranging from women's presence in the managerial positions of the employment world, women's low pay and part-time work, to the recurring question of how women can combine employment with parenthood.

Looking at these issues from a comparative perspective has been part of this increased interest. The theme: how does women's position in employment compare in different societies, is increasingly becoming part of the work of many academics contributing to a body of knowledge on gender perspectives in employment and labour markets (e.g. Beechey, 1989, Dex, 1986, Jenson, Hagen & Reddy, 1988, Pfau-Effinger, 1995, Plantenga, 1993, Pott-Buter, 1993, and Rubery & Fagan, 1994, to name but a few). Dex (1986), for instance, in her work *the Sexual Division of Labour* looks at a number of features which characterize the gendered nature of paid work in the context of Britain and the United States. Others compare aggregate societies, like France and Britain (Beechey, 1989) or the Netherlands and Germany (Plantenga, 1993) on an aggregate level or specify their account to a particular sector of work within a specific time context (O'Reilly, 1992). Others again put forward a more general framework for explaining the gendered character of labour markets (Jenson, Hagen & Reddy, 1988, Pfau-Effinger, 1995, Rubery & Fagan, 1994, and Walby, 1989).

Certainly, as European countries continue their quest for greater European unity, increasing our knowledge of the differences in the gendered nature of employment in the various countries forming part of the European Community

(EC) is both warranted and necessary. On the one hand, because any policy aimed at the work forces of individual EC societies needs to be informed by such knowledge. On the other hand, because we (as European citizens and women in particular) would want to monitor the implications for women's employment of European legislation on work forces, taking into account the existing cultural specificities within societies.

This book will present, what can only be considered a small contribution to this knowledge, in that its subject matter is a comparison of changes in the gender composition of the Dutch and British work forces over a specific period in recent history, both on an aggregate level and specified towards the banking sector. As the examples shown above indicate, existing comparative work in this area has concentrated on the larger societies in the EC; like Germany, France and Britain. Consequently, the smaller societies are neglected. This work is an attempt to address this imbalance, by comparing a fairly small European country; the Netherlands, with a larger one.

My interest in developing a comparative analysis of gender composition changes in employment in the societies of Britain and the Netherlands was stimulated by a simple but surprising difference in the average participation rate of women in the labour markets of these two societies. The OECD figures which I looked at, a number of years ago, revealed this difference clearly; women's activity rate amongst the 15-64 years age-group was here shown to be 40.8 per cent for the Netherlands whilst being 58.5 per cent for the United Kingdom in 1984 (OECD Employment Outlook, 1986, p.140). More recent figures for 1993 still show a significant difference, but not as starkly as the 1984 figures provided by the OECD (53.0 per cent and 65.3 per cent respectively for the Netherlands and the United Kingdom).

At the time, this difference came as a surprise to me, and appears to trigger a similar reaction in others who first hear about it. The reason for this surprise, it seems, is related to the images of the two societies within Europe. There, the Dutch have the image of a 'progressive' people, whilst the image of the British as 'conservative' is rather the opposite. When these images are related to women's 'emancipation' and employment, they immediately conjure up the idea that there must be more women involved in employment in the Netherlands than in Britain. The notions of 'progressiveness', women's 'emancipation' and the number of women involved in employment get tangled up in a manner to produce this surprise reaction. In reality, however, as the figures just mentioned indicate, the reverse is the case.

But that is not all. The images of the Dutch as 'progressive' and the British as 'conservative' call for contrasts in other characteristics of women's employment in the two societies. On an aggregate level, similarities rather than contrasts seem to be more evident. So apart from the difference in the contemporary employment participation of women, there are several similarities in the gendered nature of employment in the two societies. Most notable here are (1) the relatively high ratio of part-time working amongst women in the two societies today, compared to some other European societies such as France (Beechey, 1989), and in conjunction, (2) the (still) limited availability of child care facilities in both countries. This begs the question how one can explain these - seemingly - strange social 'facts' and the apparent misconceptions surrounding them. The major task attempted in this book is to put these social 'facts' into their cultural and historical context. In order to explain the route I followed in the investigation of these matters, it helps to look briefly at some comparative employment statistics.

Trends in the gender composition of the Dutch and British work forces

When the contemporary figures just mentioned, are placed in the context of changes in the gender composition of the work forces and changes in the ratio of women's activity over this century, it becomes clear that we are not just talking about contemporary differences, but historical differences as well. In table 1.1 below, I have presented figures for the gender composition of the aggregate British and Dutch work forces over the century.[1] In table 1.2, similar figures are provided, though expressed differently as the ratio of women's employment activity. I want to draw out three features of comparative significance.

The Census material in table 1.1 gives us an overview of the recorded work force composition during this century. The first point to make is that during the first half of this century, the gender ratio of the work force remained rather stable for both societies. A point of difference is that at around 30 per cent for Britain and 23 per cent for the Netherlands, the Dutch female ratio of the work force lies below that of Britain during those years of 'stability'; a point noted by Dutch scholars (de Bruijn, 1989, Outshoorn, 1977, Pott-Buter, 1993). A second interesting difference between the two societies is evident when one looks at the Census figures for 1930/31 onwards. These figures indicate an end to the stability in the gender composition of the British work force over the Census dates 1931 and 1951 (as there is no Census for 1941 due to the war, it is difficult to indicate a moment of change, though it seems anyhow more constructive to look at these matters in terms of gradual change). It signals the much commented on increase in the female composition of work forces in the post-war years which has not been a peculiarly British phenomenon. Between 1931 and 1990, the female ratio of the British work force increases from 29.7 per cent to 42.8 per cent. In the post-war years, therefore, the British Census and the OECD Labour Force Statistics indicate a continuing increasing trend.

5

Table 1.1
Women as a proportion of the work force in Britain
and the Netherlands (percentages)

Year	Britain	The Netherlands	% difference
1901/1899[1]	29.1	22.5	6.6
1911/1909	29.7	23.9	5.8
1921/1920	29.5	23.2	6.3
1931/1930	29.7	24.0	5.7
1951/1947	30.8	24.4	6.4
1961/1960	32.5	22.2	10.3
1971	36.5	25.9	10.6
1975[2]	37.6	26.8	10.8
1980	39.2	30.4	8.8
1985	40.5	34.5	6.0
1990	42.8	39.2	3.6
1993	43.7	40.6	3.1

Sources:
1. 1901/1899 to 1971: British Census and Hakim (1979, p.25) for the British figures and for the Dutch figures the Dutch Census (Volkstellingen) as presented in CBS (Tachtig jaren statistiek in tijdreeksen: 1899-1979, p.66). When double years are mentioned, the first year refers to the British Census date, whilst the second refers to the Dutch Census date.
2. 1975-1993: OECD Labour Force Statistics.

This feature is somewhat different for the Dutch work force. There, the stability in the gender composition of the work force seems to continue into the post-war years. The *Volkstellingen* of 1930, 1947 and 1960 - with female ratios of 24, 24.4 and 22.3 per cent respectively - do not give an impression of a period of change in the gender composition of the Dutch work force. Change is only evident in the last 20 to 25 years. This is further supported by the figures provided in table 1.2. The change in British women's registered economic activity, and the lack of change in Dutch women's economic activity in the period just referred to is evident in the widening 'gap' in the activity ratios; reaching a difference of 25 percentage points in the 1971 census figures.

This brings us to the third point of comparative interest, which is that in more recent years, the 'gap' in women's activity rate in the two societies has closed somewhat. This is evident in table 1.2, which indicates a closure of the 'gap'

Table 1.2
Women of working age who are economically active in Britain and the Netherlands (percentages)

Year	Britain 15-59	The Netherlands 15-64	% difference
1921/09[1]	38	30.5	7.5
1931/30	38	30.1	7.9
1951/47	43	30.4	12.6
1961/60	47	26.1	20.9
1971	55	30.0	25.0

Year	United Kingdom 15-64	The Netherlands 15-64	% difference
1975[2]	55.1	31.0	24.1
1980	58.3	35.5	22.8
1985	60.5	40.9	19.6
1990	65.3	53.0	12.3
1993	65.3	55.8	9.5

Sources:
1. 1909-1971 are from Dutch and British Census data and Hakim (1979, p.3).
2. 1975-1993 are from OECD Labour Force Statistics.

from 25 percentage points to 12 percentage points in 1990. Whereas the years of change in the registered stability in British women's economic activity were the early post-war period, for the Netherlands the period of significant change were the years between 1975-1993. If the post-war years indicate a 'lagging behind' effect, the last 20 years would imply a 'recovering of ground'.

In this book I am mainly concerned with the last two points of comparative interest just discussed. This has allowed me to limit the time-period of the investigations to the years between 1940 and 1993. It also sets this study apart from two other comparative works which investigate the historical peculiarity of Dutch women's economic activity; those of Plantenga (1993) and Pott-Buter (1993). In these studies, a longer historical perspective is taken and the respective authors concentrate on the first point of comparative interest just indicated.

Trends in the gender composition of banking work forces

The elucidation of the culturally specific context underpinning the comparative differences and similarities in the gender composition of Dutch and British work forces will be developed at two levels of analysis; the macro-level of national trends and changes, and the middle-range level. A similar approach has recently been taken by Janneke Plantenga in her study of women's work in the Netherlands and Germany (1993). Her work is one which combines an examination of the national level with case-studies at a local level. Two cities; Tilburg in the Netherlands and Mönchengladbach in Germany, serve as case-studies through which her theoretical analysis is consolidated. Our work differs in the sense that the case-study explicated here concerns one sector of work instead of specific localities, even though the industrial histories of the two towns discussed in Plantenga have historically been dominated by the textile industry.

The benefits of this kind of methodology mix are evident in both studies. Aggregate level analysis enables the researcher to develop a view of general developments whilst avoiding the danger of being bogged down by the complexity of specificities. Case-studies, on the other hand, enable the researcher to develop a more detailed history around the themes which are studied, and also allows for the examination of cultural patterns at the level of the individual experiences of men and women (Plantenga, 1993, p.8). The banking sector is studied here as a specific case in its own right. However, a further major purpose of this case-study is the comparison of the banking sector with the aggregate analysis in an effort to strengthen the theoretical framework. The following examination of the gender composition of the Dutch and British banking sectors shows that banking provides the possibility to examine questions similar to the ones which I introduced with respect to changes in the aggregate work force. One important theme which is examined here is whether explanations of gender composition changes in the aggregate work force and the differences which are found between the Netherlands and Britain, are also explanatory for banking employment?

The choice of the banking sector as a case-study has been an informed one. Investigating banking employment in the context of the period between 1940 and 1993 is interesting for a number of reasons. First because there has been a radical change in the gender composition of bank staff in both societies in this period. Secondly because the change in the gender composition of bank staff has gone accompanied with an absolute growth in bank staff and radical changes in the nature of banking employment. The increase in the absolute number of men and women occupied in Banking and Insurance[2] between 1930/1931 and 1971 is evident in table 1.3. The number of persons involved in

Table 1.3
Banking and Insurance staff in Britain and the Netherlands
by gender

	Britain			
Year	Total	Female	Male	F/M%
1931	262,471	57,501	204,970	21.9
1951	334,952	117,163	217,789	35.0
1961[1]	43,242	17,777	25,465	41.1
1971[1]	55,538	26,406	29,132	47.5

	The Netherlands[2]			
Year	Total	Female	Male	F/M%
1930	48,2	8,3	39,9	17.2
1947	67,6	16,2	51,4	24.0
1960	100,1	27,5	72,6	27.5
1971	145,0	49,6	95,4	34.2

Sources: the Census and CBS, 80 jaren statistiek in tijdreeksen 1899-1979, p.66.
1. Census material from 1961 and 1971 is from a 10% sample.
2. Figures need to be multiplied by 1000.

Banking and Insurance in the Netherlands tripled in this period and the British Banking and Insurance work force doubled. The increase in the number of female employees forms an important part of this absolute increase, though there are some interesting cross-national differences here. Whilst the British finance sector sees a larger absolute increase for female employees than for male employees, in the Netherlands the reverse is the case. There, even though the ratio of female employees increases, the absolute increase in male employees over the Census years exceeds that of female employees. Consequently, the gender ratio of Banking and Insurance staff changes in favour of women in both societies, but in the Netherlands this feminization does not take place to the same extent as in Britain. Prior to the war, in 1930/31, about 20 per cent of employees in this sector are female in both societies (the Netherlands at 17.2 per cent lies somewhat below Britain at 21.0 per cent). The important difference in the extent to which feminization occurs between the two societies is clear from the figures for 1971. The female component of Banking and Insurance staff in Britain in 1971 is nearly 50 per cent, whilst in the Netherlands only a third of employees are female at this stage.[3] Today, this disjunction in the female ratio amongst bank staff is still evident (see chapter 7 for more detailed figures). In Britain, the female ratio amongst bank employees has continued to increase since the 1970s. In some British banks this means that the female to male ratio amongst staff is now around 60 per cent. In the Netherlands, the female ratio has also continued to increase, but has not reached the 50 per cent level in most Dutch banks by 1987 (Tijdens, 1989, p.236).

The lay-out of the book

The arguments in this book are developed in three parts. This general introduction chapter and chapter two form Part 1 of the book. In the current chapter, as must be clear, the general reasons and rationale for this study are explicated. Chapter 2 is a discussion of the theoretical literature which relates to the research questions developed in chapter 1. These include explanatory perspectives on post-war changes in women's economic activity; perspectives on the peculiarity of Dutch women's economic activity; theorizations on the (historical) construction of gendered labour markets; and perspectives on the feminization of sectors/types of work. In these two chapters an agenda for investigation is established for parts 2 and 3 of the book. Part 3 finishes with the concluding chapter 8.

Part 2 of the book shall concentrate on the historical period between 1940 and 1965. Here, a processional account of the socio-economic and ideological-cultural context of the period will be presented in an effort to explain the later increase in Dutch women's participation in remunerated work, compared to their British counterparts. In Chapter 3 the presence and decline of marriage bars in the two societies is discussed. This is an interesting topic to look at in its own right, since research on this employment feature - like so many aspects of history which affected women - has been relatively neglected; though more so in Britain than in the Netherlands. Marriage bars are furthermore of interest here because gender relations perspectives on post-war changes in women's economic activity (chapter 2) have emphasized the importance of the increase in the employment of married women in this period, whilst some (e.g. Walby, Glucksmann) have even linked the latter directly to the occurrence and timing of the abolition of marriage bars.

There is, however, a third reason why attention is given to this institution. Chapter 3 records the comparative variations found in the occurrence of such bars in the Netherlands and Britain. And whilst I argue that they undoubtedly constituted one form of patriarchal exclusion, the cross-national differences point to some important cultural differences between the two societies. This theme is further explored in chapter 4, where ideological notions of gender exclusion are related to a discussion which traces the relative tightness of the labour markets in the two societies in the period under consideration. Firstly, divergent war-time experiences and the implications for labour market tightness are discussed. This is followed by a consideration of the direct post-war years and leads into my argument that changes in ideological thinking about women's societal roles is linked to economic/political changes.

The changing gender composition of banking work forces in the two societies between 1940 and 1965 will be under discussion in chapter 5. Taking the empirical feature, that feminization amongst British banks is more extensive in this period, as starting point, I argue that this period sees the development of a particular gendered organization of banking work, in which the operation of a marriage bar accompanies the expansion in female recruitment and employment. This development, I will argue, is partly related to the peculiarity of banking employment, but it is also related to what is occurring on an aggregate level. The evidence presented in these three chapters is used in the construction of a theoretical framework which characterizes the gender relations histories of the two societies.

The contemporary period (1965-1993) will be under consideration in part 3. Here, I will return to the research question introduced in chapter 1. That is: how can we account for the 'recovering of ground' in Dutch women's economic activity, compared to British women, in the contemporary period (1965-1993). In chapter 6, this question is addressed at the aggregate level. A processional approach is presented, in which the economic/political and ideological-cultural context of the time is described. I argue that neo-conservatism on the political level is adopted in different ways in the two societies, which is related to historical differences in the respective political systems. This, in turn, carries two implications for gender inclusionary efforts in remunerated work. On the one hand, it leads to distinct differences in understandings around, and the quality of part-time work available in the two societies. On the other hand, it leads to differences in the ways in which second wave feminism impacts on a national state level. This is explained through a discussion of campaigns for childcare facilities in the two societies.

In the final empirical chapter, change and continuity in the gender composition of banking staff is subject for discussion. Here, I discuss the implications of a changing economic environment on the employment operations in two banks: Dutchbank and Britbank. I also trace the incorporation of feminism into the employment policies of these two banks in the form of equal opportunities policies. These take various forms of retaining women employees (e.g. career-breaks, part-time working, childcare facilities). By linking these two developments, I outline the position of women in banks today. The analysis of the banking sector in the contemporary period is then related to the aggregate level analysis of chapter 6.

In the conclusion (chapter 8), I will develop, by way of a critique of existing explanations of change and continuity in the gender composition of work forces, a processional characterization of a gender relations history. This should, in addition, provide the basis for returning to, and explaining, the contradiction with which I started this book.

Methodological concerns

Before going further, I will identify the materials I used to develop this comparative study of two societies. We have already been confronted with one of these sources; the gathering of employment statistics. I feel the need, at this point, to address my use of employment statistics in this work. First of all, it has often been intricate work to gather figures; like those presented in table 1.1 and 1.2, keeping in mind the degree to which they are comparable. Table 1.2 forms a good example of this difficulty. The activity ratios for Dutch women over the Census years 1909-1971 were calculated to 'fit in' with those for Britain. Dutch calculations of these figures (e.g. CBS, 80 jaren statistiek in Tijdreeksen, p.66) typically include the total population, whilst the British equivalent which one finds in Hakim's work (1979, p.3) only include the population of working age.[4] In gathering employment statistics of this sort, I had to be very aware of what was included.

In addition, to bring the figures of table 1.2 up-to-date, I have supplemented the Census material for earlier years with OECD figures for the last 20 years. This limits comparability further, because the definitions used for who is, and who is not included in the collected figures differs between the Dutch Census, the British Census, and the OECD Labour Force Statistics, and within each of these over time. The OECD figures, for example, have breaks between 1982/83 and 1986/1987. Sociologists often use statistics as a source which trigger research questions. However, and at the same time, they have emphasized that statistics are not facts, but constitute social constructs (a recurring example here is the discussion on Durkheim's usage of suicide statistics) in their own right. Employment statistics are no exception to this; it is people who take decisions about the definitions involved in the collection and calculations. And the figures which we are presented with reflect these decisions.

In this, and further chapters, I will incorporate tables with 'comparative' figures. This is not a study of statistical intricacies, however, and as such I have accepted figures without always tracing definitions. I therefore recognize the limitations in the comparability of these figures. Nonetheless, I believe that they will be useful to indicate trends. In addition, where this is relevant, I will discuss the issue of social construction and its implication for women's employment. Statistics are part and parcel of the social fabric which provides the source for understanding changes in women's economic activity over time and between societies. And investigating these, after all, is the aim pursued in this work.

Apart from statistics, various other sources have been used. In general, however, I have limited myself to the gathering and comparing of secondary literary sources in relation to gender composition changes of the aggregate work forces. The materials collected for the banking case-study were varied. These included research of banking archives and banking journals for the early research period and for the contemporary period, in both societies. These sources were supplemented by semi-structured interviews with former bank employees, current bank employees, bank managers and equal opportunities staff. I also talked to some representatives of trade unions covering banking employment.

With the employee interviews, I intended to gather stories of the work history of bank employees, including their experiences of their work and their colleagues and the relation of this to their domestic lives.[5] I did go out with a set number of questions, which were designed to draw out the gender differences found in banking employment, and changes therein over time. They were also designed to see whether and/or how these gender differences related to the employment structure in the banks. Furthermore, I tried to find out how the informants' work history was related to the domestic relations within their households. Throughout, I have remained open for additional comments and stories. This proved very informative, especially in the accounts of former bank employees, because so much of their histories were unknown to me before I started on the interviews. In the appendix some further information on the interviews has been brought together.

In this case-study of changes in the gender composition amongst bank staff, some practical decisions had to be taken regarding the scope of the research. It was, for example, not possible to research a number of banks in both countries over the period between 1940 and 1990. I therefore made the decision to concentrate the research on two banks, one Dutch bank (referred to from now on as Dutchbank) and one British bank (here referred to as Britbank). In the interest of anonymity, in particular with respect to the bank employees and personnel staff who co-operated in this study, I will refrain from providing the reasons why these specific banks were chosen. Having said that, I have to make it clear that where this seemed desirable, I have ventured into researching certain aspects in relation to other banks.[6]

In work of a comparative nature, particular words, phrases or concepts have meanings which are unknown to a section of the readership. It is important for the researcher to acknowledge this, and explain problematic concepts. In my discussion of the historical context around the development of Dutch women's economic activity, two terms; pillarization and confessionals, recur, of which this is true. These terms first appear in chapter 3, and they are related. Pillarization (pillar; pillarized) is the English translation which I have used for the Dutch term *verzuiling* (*zuil; verzuild*).[7] The terms confessionals and confessional are the translations I have used for the Dutch terms *confessionelen* and *confessioneel*.[8] When using the term confessionals I talk about those who belong to particular religious groups. In the context of the Netherlands at the time, these included Catholic and various Protestant groups.

During the beginning of the 20th century, the Netherlands sees the socially specific formation of a *verzuild* (pillarized) sociality, which gives the socio/political organization of Dutch society its unique character. Stuurman (1981, 1988) has argued that the formation of a pillarized social order was driven by the emancipation of the Catholics. During the early 20th century, the Catholics established a foothold in 'alle lagen en instituties van de samenleving' ('all layers and institutions of society'), and the institutionalization of the other two pillars; the Protestant and the socialist pillars, needs to be seen, in part, as a result of the Catholic expansion drive (de Bruijn, 1989, p.119).

De Bruijn uses in her discussion (1989, pp.118-9) a description of Dutch pillarization by Bax, E.H. (1988), *Modernization and cleavage in Dutch society. A study of long term economic and social change*, Groningen: Universiteitsdrukkerij Groningen. Pillarization is described by Bax as:

> Een subsysteem in de samenleving dat politieke macht, sociale organisatie en individueel gedrag verbindt en dat, zowel in concurrentie als in samenwerking met andere sociale en politieke groepen, is gericht op doelstellingen die worden geinspireerd door een gemeenschappelijke ideologie die door de leden van de zuil wordt gedeeld voor wie de zuil de voornaamste bron van sociale identificatie is. (1988, p.25) (A subsystem in society which links political power, social organization and individual behaviour, and which, in competition as well as co-operation with other social and political groups, is directed by aims which are inspired by the communal ideology which is shared by the members of the pillar, and for whom the pillar forms the most important source of social identification.)

In effect, then, pillarization meant that the Catholics as well as the Protestant and socialist sections of the population took on politically and culturally distinct identities, which pervaded all aspects of life. The Catholic pillar, for instance, consisted in Catholic political parties, Catholic schools, two Catholic universities, Catholic trade unions and employers' federations and a number of other specifically catholic groups and organizations. One consequence of Dutch pillarization, outlined by de Bruijn, is that the pillarized order in Dutch society overshadows other social oppositions; like those between labour and capital; liberal and conservative; and between the sexes (de Bruijn, 1989, p.119).

Notes

1   Aggregate figures for women's employment participation are mostly presented in two ways. The first of these is an expression of the share of women (or men) found in the total work force. I have here called this expression the gender composition of work forces. The common term used for the share of women in the work force is women's participation rate. The second way in which women's employment is statistically expressed is through, what is often called, women's activity rate. This reflects the ratio of active women in the female population. One difficulty for comparing aggregate figures between societies using the activity rate is the question which age-group is included.

2   The Dutch *Volkstellingen* only report an Industrial Classification which combines figures for Banking and Insurance. For comparability, I have added Insurance to the classification of Banking and Bill-Discounting for the British figures, though figures for Banking and Bill-Discounting alone are also available (see note 3 below).

3   British figures for Banking and Bill-Discounting alone are presented in table 1.4. Compared with the British figures of table 1.3, it is clear that Insurance must have had a higher female ratio than Banking in 1931. In 1971, however, the reverse is the case and the female ratio amongst banking staff alone is over 50 per cent. There is evidence to suggest that the inclusion of the sector of Insurance causes a similar diminishing effect on feminization in banking employment in the Netherlands (1960 *Volkstellingen* and Tijdens, 1989, p.234).

4   In the end, the Dutch figures are still not totally comparable with the British figures, as the age-groups are different. Even so, they are 'better' than the available Dutch activity rates, as these figures include the oldest and youngest female population (amongst whom economic activity is very low), which reduce the overall figures. The significance of this statistical point is evident, as the female activity ratio for 1930

which the CBS gives is 19.5 per cent, whilst my calculation comes to 30.1 per cent.

Table 1.4
Banking and Bill Discounting staff in Great Britain

Year	Total	Female	Male	F/M%
1931	99986	19856	80130	19.9
1951	142695	52708	89987	36.9
1961[1]	18908	8413	10495	44.5
1971	27754	14779	12975	53.2
1981	36779	20714	16065	56.3

Source: Census for England and Wales, Scotland and Great Britain.
1. Census material from 1961-1981 is for a 10% sample.

5   The methodology used here is one akin to that used by other researchers (e.g. Cockburn, 1983, Burns, T. & Stalker, G., 1961).

6   See for further explanation of these issues chapter 1 of Martens (1994).

7   In the dictionary Van Dale, handwoordenboek Nederlands-Engels, *verzuiling* is translated as '± denominationalism ⇒ sectarianism, compartmentalization (along socio-political lines) ... 'pillarization''. *Zuil* is translated as '0.1 [pilaar] pillar ... 0.2 [groepering] sociopolitical group/block ... 1.3 de zuilen van de staatsmacht ... foundations on which the power of the state is based ...'.

8   In the Van Dale, handwoordenboek Nederlands-Engels, *confessionelen* is translated as '(supporters of the) religious parties'. *Confessioneel* is translated as '0.1 [overeenkomstig een geloofsbelijdenis] confessional ⇒ [ihb. mbt. onderwijs] denominational ... 0.3 [pol.] confessional ⇒ religious, denominational 1.3 de confessionele partijen ... the religious parties'.
For further consultation on Dutch pillarization see the following sources:
1. Bax, E.H. (1988), *Modernization and cleavage in Dutch society. A study of long term economic and social change*, Groningen: Universiteitsdrukkerij Groningen.
2. Stuurman, S. (1983), *Verzuiling, kapitalisme en patriarchaat. Aspecten van de ontwikkeling van de moderne staat in Nederland*,

Nijmegen: SUN (diss).
3. Lijphart, A. (1968), *Verzuiling, pacificatie en kentering in de Nederlandse politiek*, Amsterdam.

2 Gender, exclusion and inclusion in employment

This book deals with the gender composition of work forces at two levels of comparative analysis; the aggregate level of national work forces, and the middle-range level of banking work forces. Theoretically, the analysis of the gender composition of work forces has been approached in different ways, relating to the specific empirical issues which are investigated. In the first instance, approaches relating to aggregate labour forces may be distinguished from those pertaining to specific sectors of work. But there also exists great variety in the kind of themes pursued in relation to aggregate work forces.

This chapter starts with a discussion of alternative explanations of aggregate changes in the gender composition of work forces. Interested scholars have asked such diverse questions as how the post-war increase in the female ratio of the work forces of Western industrialized societies may be explained, and how the peculiar economic activity patterns of Dutch women may be accounted for. These approaches will be discussed with the aim to delineate the commonalities in these approaches. Furthermore, national accounts (British and Dutch) identify some culturally specific trends and features, which this study will have to take account off.

In the last section I argue that there is a distinct literature on the feminization of sectors of work, distinguishable from the approaches discussed above. If the latter concentrate on aggregate economic, cultural and institutional themes, approaches to the gender composition of specific occupations or sectors of work come close to analyses of occupational segregation.

Given the comparative nature of this work, I have consulted both British and Dutch commentaries. It is clear that there exist distinct differences in the theoretical tools used. British accounts, in particular, are closely related to conceptions of the character of gender relations, such as patriarchy or 'gender order' (Connell, 1987). In Dutch accounts, such conceptualizations are absent, though this does not mean that gender does not constitute an important aspect of the analysis. Below, I will show due sensitivity to these differences, though it is true to say that in the accounts which do theorize class and/or gender relations, clear conceptions of gender exclusion and inclusion in employment are present.

The feminization of Western industrialized work forces

The increase in the ratio at which women in industrialized West European and North American countries, on average, participate in paid work over the last 50 years or so, has not gone unnoticed. Mostly, comments which have been made on this refer to the post-war period, and this feature is remarked upon by commentators from various societies. During the 1950s and early 60s, a number of studies appeared which address the changing nature of women's work in Britain (see Le Gros Clark, 1962, Myrdal & Klein, 1956, Jephcott et al., 1962). As early as 1956, for example, Myrdal & Klein comment on *Women's two Roles* in British society, and with that recognize their role as paid workers. In 1969, the French Sociologist Sullerot compared various industrialized countries on the increase in women's economic activity. This study, however, described patterns but provided little explanation of them. Braverman (1974) was first in theorizing the increase in women's employment by making it part of his analysis of post-war capitalist accumulation.

'Development of capitalism' approaches

Explanations of women's increased activity in employment roughly vary between those which emphasize the development of capitalism as being the explanatory causal factor behind this increase and those which argue for the inclusion of a gender relations perspective in some kind of combination with the development of capitalism. Braverman may be regarded as belonging to the first group. His argument is that post-war capitalist accumulation gives rise to the increased size of businesses which in turn entail larger administration units. Overall, there is an increase in service sector work and a declining significance of manufacturing production and work. Rationalization (with which Braverman means deskilling and new technology) in these larger capitalistic enterprises means the increased significance of low-paid and low-skilled work relative to other work. In addition, there is an expansion in the demand for labour.

Post-war capitalist expansion has created a demand for labour so great that 'alternative' sources of labour are drawn on. This is how the post-war increase in the employment of women and migrant labour is explained. In his argument why there has been an increase in women's employment, Braverman draws on a somewhat confusing combination of two features: women's lower pay and their membership of a reserve army of labour. On the one hand, by their entry into employment, women are argued to become part of the stagnant and floating forms of the reserve army of labour.[1] On the other hand, they are employed in the increased number of low-paid and low-skilled jobs, since their employment has always been characterized by low pay. The process of women's integration into paid work is further facilitated by an expansionist universal market; i.e. by capitalist production taking over a part of the work which was previously done by women in the household. This trend, so the argument goes, provides further stimulus in releasing women from domestic work, and enables them to join the labour market.

Subsequent to Braverman's thesis, there has been - what often seems to be - an endless debate about the theoretical explanations he puts forward (Beechey, 1977, Siltanen, 1981, Power, 1983, Dex, 1984, Lever-Tracy, 1983, Walby, 1986, to name but a few). Some of the commentators who have criticized him offer alternative explanations which remain within the same theoretical framework; i.e. placing emphasis on the development of capitalism, whereas others have argued for the necessity to transcend the 'capitalism only' approach.

One example of the former is Power's (1983) argument that if women are to be considered part of a reserve army of labour, the appropriate form is that of the latent form, where women are regarded as a new and permanent source of labour which may be utilized by an expanding capitalist economy in times when the labour supply is tight. Her argument that women form a part of the latent reserve attempts to deal with the problem associated with seeing them, as Braverman does, as part of the floating and stagnant reserve. This attaches a push-pull notion to women's employment, which means that they are pulled into employment when labour supply is tight, but are pushed out again when labour supply is plentiful. Power argues that women's inclusion in remunerated work is not of a temporary, but a permanent nature.

In Braverman's push-pull account of post-war labour force feminization as well as Power's revised version of the latter, we find a conception of exclusion and inclusion in remunerated work, based on the gender of workers, and generated through the 'forces' of capitalism. In the post-war years, the 'forces' of capitalism (which include tight labour markets, the creation of more service sector employment, and the cheapening of work more generally) result in a shift from the exclusion of women from remunerated work towards their increased inclusion. Before considering the critics of this position, I shall first consider a 'second generation' of accounts, which may be subsumed under 'development of capitalism' approaches.

In *Feminization of the Labor Force: Paradoxes and Promises* (1988), Jenson, Hagen and Reddy do not discuss post-war labour force feminization. Instead they take the contemporary period under the loop. In their introduction, Hagen & Jenson argue that the rising aggregate female activity rate, in the context of rising unemployment in OECD countries in general, is one of the main paradoxes of post-war labour force feminization. In their attempt to explain the causes of this paradox, Hagen and Jenson argue that, in the last 20 years, we have seen the demise of Fordism and Keynesianism (which characterized the direct post-war years), the latter making way for, what has been called, neo-liberalism or new-conservatism.

Hagen & Jenson point to the fundamental difference between the early post-war years and the last two decades, in terms of the expansion in women's formal employment. In the former period, this expansion was facilitated by tight labour markets and large government expenditures, in the latter period the reverse appears to be the case. In the latter period, they argue, the

> ... important point to note is that the very process of response to economic crisis came to involve an increased dependence on high rates of female employment. (Hagen & Jenson, 1988, p.6)

Exactly why this should be so is not explained very well in Hagen and Jenson's account. They merely point to the historical fit between the changed employment requirements of business and the type of labour supplied by women (1988, p.10). Hence:

> Business strategies for restructuring have involved cost-cutting, shortening product-cycles and increasing flexibility in the production process to be better able to respond to unstable market conditions. This search for flexibility involves a demand for a new type of labor. Women have emerged as very desirable employees in these circumstances because their relationship to the labor market has traditionally displayed the characteristics of flexibility so much wanted in the current conjuncture. (Hagen & Jenson, 1988, p.10)

The conjunction between changed business/economic 'needs' and women's 'flexible' labour supply, is further facilitated by the political shift towards neo-liberalism/conservatism. Second wave feminism is brought forward as an analytic category of explanation, but how this is related to the paradox is not elaborated. On these grounds it may be argued that this account of contemporary labour force feminization is mainly a 'development of capitalism' approach.

As such, it has further affinities with earlier versions. One of these is the linkage between the rise in cheap work places and women's employment. Hagen & Jenson argue that the increase in women's employment participation in the last 20 years has been mainly directed by demand-side influences, the implication of which has been a downward trend in the quality of women's employment. Their conclusion is, therefore, that 'there is not ... much to cheer about in this achievement of record levels of female participation in the paid labor force' (1988, p.11). Unlike earlier versions, though, in this account the rise in part-time working and other 'non-standard' forms of employment take a central position in the discussion of the flexibilization and cheapening of work in industrialized societies. Because British and Dutch work forces are characterized by high ratios of part-time working, this perspective shall be taken up again in chapter 6.

Gender relations and 'development of capitalism' approaches: British perspectives

A second group of critics of Braverman's thesis have argued that the development of capitalism is not sufficient as an explanatory framework for explaining why there has been a shift from the exclusion of women from remunerated work towards their inclusion. One forceful critique outlines the economic inconsistency in his argument that women's lower income explains their increased employment in the low-paid and low-skilled employment which was a result of the post-war expansion in capitalistic enterprise. Indeed the question is why, if women's work may be characterized historically as requiring lower pay as compared to male employment, entrepreneurs have not taken advantage of this by employing more women in the past? One could argue that this issue is especially pressing for employers during times of recession when the need to reduce labour costs are greater than in boom times. Certainly an added question to this is why women's work has been historically regarded as cheaper than that of their male counterparts.

It is questions like these which have led British critics, in particular, to argue that an analysis of changes in women's employment in the post-war period requires the integration of a gender relations perspective with the 'development of capitalism' approach. Dex (1985) has criticized the application of Marxist concepts, like the notion of a reserve army of labour, for leaving 'obvious cracks' in the analysis of women's employment. One of these cracks is the neglect of women's own efforts; i.e. changes in their labour supply, in the increase.

Women have played an active role in bringing about these changes by the purchase of new consumer goods, by desiring to have greater control over family resources and their own independent means, by preferring in Britain part-time jobs in order to be able to satisfy their list of desires, ... alongside shouldering domestic responsibilities. (1985, p.187)

She argues that an important aspect of an analysis of women's increased economic activity must consist in linking 'women's position in the home and their position in the labour force to men's positions in both of these spheres' (Dex, 1985, p.198). Although she does not provide such an outline herself, she does point out that in order to explain the post-war increase in the number of women involved in employment, one can not fail to look at the significant increase in married women being employed in the context of an increase in part-time employment; features of women's post-war employment in Britain, which are ignored in the earlier 'development of capitalism' approaches.

These two aspects of British women's increased economic activity are also brought to the fore in two other accounts, each with its own conceptualization of gender relations. Crompton and Sanderson (1990) express gender relations in terms of the concept of 'gender order' (Connell, 1987). Their argument is that the increase in women's economic activity in the post-war period may be understood in terms of Connell's emphasis that 'the structure of gender relations may be internally contradictory' (1990, p.47). In the context of post-war demands on labour resources, this is explored in the contradictory state policies on women as mothers and workers at the same time. On the one hand, the post-war years saw a move towards the fuller citizenship of women, as demanded by liberal feminism and the liberalism of post-war thinking. Evidence of this trend are the abolition of discriminatory practices in employment - such as the abolition of the marriage bar and the equal pay debate - and an increased access to education. This opened up the way for women to 'enter' employment.

At the same time there was a strong current which laid the responsibility of childcare with mothers, providing strong motives for women with children in need of care to stay at home with them. This recurring motherhood ideology, according to Crompton and Sanderson, explains the characteristics of post war married women's employment; i.e. its part-time nature. This perspective, then, argues for the interrelation between the factors of labour demand and gender struggles (at the level of liberalism/egalitarianism), and puts the rise in part-time working in the post-war years into its historical and culturally specific context.

The work of Walby (1986, 1989 and 1990a,b) provides another forceful critique of 'capitalism only' approaches. Her challenging alternative to the issues at hand is a dual systems approach. In dual systems analyses, it is argued that class relations and gender relations are interrelated, but that these two systems of social relations need to be seen as independent from one another. One commonality in this approach is the development of a gender relations model utilizing the concept patriarchy. Whilst Dutch feminist scholars gave up 'attempts to formulate an all-encompassing explanatory theory of women's oppression ...' (Brouns, 1988, p.39) long ago, amongst British feminists this certainly has not been the case. This has not meant that British scholars have accepted earlier formulations of patriarchy uncritically, and to date a significant number of British scholars work with a patriarchal conception of gender relations (e.g. Alexander and Taylor, 1981, Cockburn, 1983, 1986, Lown, 1990, Summerfield, 1984, Walby, 1986, 1989, 1990, and Witz, 1992).

Walby's macro-theoretical model of patriarchal social relations is interesting to look at here in more detail, because she addresses similar questions to the ones with which this research is concerned. For example, her analysis is based upon the idea that patriarchal gender relations pervade all spheres of life; including the domestic sphere, employment, and the state, and that relations in different spheres interrelate with each other. The corollary is that Walby's analysis contains an explanatory link between gender relations in the domestic sphere and gender relations in employment. The relationship between home and work seems certainly relevant in a comparative analysis of the rise in women's economic activity, especially when one considers that the post-war increase in women's employment in Britain must be seen mainly as an increase in the employment of married women. More importantly, though, is the centrality of the concept exclusion (and consequently inclusion) in Walby's analysis of patriarchal relations in employment, as well as the opportunities offered by her analysis to understand variations in historical shifts and cross-national variations in the gendered character of sociality. So let us consider her analysis in a more detailed fashion.

Walby endeavours to get away from the much criticized variety of dual systems analysis, where patriarchy is 'based' in a different sphere from that of the capitalist mode of production. The solution found by Walby is to introduce a domestic mode of production as one structure of patriarchal social relations which together with other structures of patriarchal social relations characterize the nature of patriarchy. The latter is defined as:

> A system of social structures, and practices in which men dominate, oppress and exploit women. (Walby, 1989, p.214)

Apart from the domestic mode of production, Walby extracts another five social structures as being the most important here. They are, respectively, patriarchal relations in paid work; in the state; male violence; patriarchal relations in sexuality and cultural institutions (Walby, 1989, p.220).

According to Walby, these structures of patriarchal social relations interact with one another. One example of this is the relationship between patriarchal relations in employment and those in the domestic sphere. A pressing question which needs addressing is why, if women get oppressed within the household, they do, by marrying *en masse*, go into this relationship voluntarily. Following Walby, this can be explained by the fact that in the sphere of paid work - the alternative to a life in the household - women are not on an equal footing with male workers. Finding themselves at the bottom of the occupational hierarchy, with low wages and bad conditions, the alternative of the relative autonomy of the household can be quite appealing.

An interesting insight in Walby's conceptualization of gender relations in employment is that she sees the closure of access to paid work by men against women as the key feature of patriarchal relations in paid work. Over the years, this strategy has changed emphasis from one where closure of access was established through a strategy of exclusion to one of segregation. The latter may be regarded as a form of inclusion (see also Witz, 1992). The outcome of the struggle between capitalists and women for employment and of men (in Walby's case the emphasis is placed on male-dominated trade-unions) against female employment has given rise to a shift from exclusion in most areas of work to occupational segregation in most areas of work. In short, then, Walby argues that the increase in women's activity rate in Britain in the period under consideration may be attributed to two interrelating factors; capitalism's demand for labour on the one hand and women's demand for employment (feminist activity) on the other. The reasoning behind men's resistance to the employment of women is their fear of women's competition, but more important for Walby are the benefits they receive from having a wife at home producing household services for them in what she conceptualizes as the patriarchal mode of production.

Within this theoretical framework, changes in women's activity rate in Britain are traced from the Second World War onwards. According to Walby, the increase in women's employment is mainly due to an increase in the number of married women who are engaged in employment. One significant patriarchal strategy of exclusion, the marriage bar, disappears as a result of feminist activity against this and as a result of the escalating demands on human resources made by the war-time emergency. In addition, the war-time experience means 'the institutionalization of part-time working' (Walby, 1986, p.188), another lasting feature which facilitates women's entry into employment after the war. A continuous increase in the number of women employed in Britain in the post-war years, she argues, can only be explained by acknowledging the interrelation between capitalism's demand for labour and patriarchal relations in employment.

Although Walby's analysis of patriarchal relations in employment is tightly argued, it leaves a number of questions unanswered.[2] One of these is the unquestioned assumption that all women want to do remunerated work. Evidence suggests that not all British women have wanted to do paid work in the past, and the question is what changed this situation. Moreover, Walby states that part-time working became an institutionalized form of employment in Britain during the Second World War, but she does not explain why this should be so. In this respect, then, Crompton and Sanderson's analysis, discussed above, appears to provide a more accurate analysis of British history.

I have here discussed theoretical models of the increase in women's economic activity in industrialized countries. Though earlier explanations lay emphasis on the 'development of capitalism' in the post-war period in explaining labour force feminization, subsequent contributors have argued that there is a need to integrate a gender relations perspective in order to get a clearer understanding of this aspect of social change. The latter have also pinpointed some culturally specific characteristics of British post-war feminization ignored in the early 'development of capitalism' approaches. These are that labour force feminization in Britain has mainly been caused by changed economic activity amongst married women. This is related to the decline of marriage bars and the increased prevalence of part-time working.

Lastly, a major shortcoming embodied in the work of Braverman and those who have theorized about contemporary feminization, is their neglect of cross-national variations in the patterning of gendered labour markets. This is an obvious problem for a study like this, which has identified significant variations in the extent of feminization of the national work forces of the Netherlands and Britain. In the next part of this chapter, then, approaches are discussed where cross-national variations in gendered European labour markets are not ignored.

Cross-national variations in the gender composition of work forces

In this section I discuss accounts in which cross-national differences in patterns of labour force feminization are acknowledged, and seen as important enough to demand attention and explanation. Dutch accounts which address the peculiarity of Dutch labour force feminization are considered first.

The peculiarity of Dutch labour force feminization

The two most comprehensive studies of the peculiarity of Dutch women's economic activity to date are undoubtedly the work of Hettie Pott-Buter (1993) and Janneke Plantenga (1993). These two studies take remarkably different approaches to the issues at hand. Pott-Buter's study, which covers the period 1850-1990, is a seven country comparison, in which an examination of employment related statistics (on participation rates; occupation by industry and status; economic activity by life cycle stage and marital status; and fertility rates) in conjunction with a historical comparison of state regulation, leads to an evaluation of the relevance of economic theories in the explanation of the issues concerned.

Plantenga's study is also historical in its approach (covering the time-period of 100 years), though her aim to investigate Dutch women's lower economic activity compared to women in surrounding countries is translated into a two-country comparison featuring the Netherlands and Germany. This study of the gender composition of Dutch and British work forces has more in common with Plantenga's work, in particular because our studies are informed by sociological as well as feminist academic influences. However, in contrast to the work of Pott-Buter and Plantenga, this study spans a shorter time period (1940-1993), the consequence of which is that the specific aims pursued in our respective research are different. Given the shorter historical period of this investigation, I have indicated a specific interest in explaining the later increase in Dutch women's employment participation in the post-war years compared to British women, and the subsequent 'recovering of ground' in Dutch women's economic activity. This difference, I would argue, has some implications for the course taken in our analyses.

I agree with Plantenga that little concrete research on the peculiarity of Dutch women's economic activity preceded her efforts, but that there do exist a number of suggestions and speculations on how to explain the historically lower economic activity of Dutch women. These speculations may be found in the work of de Bruijn (1989) and others (e.g. Blok, 1989, Morée, 1992, and the Social Cultureel Planbureau, 1988). Taken together, three themes recur in these commentaries, which are:
1. Cross-national variations in socio-economic conditions.
2. Variations in the war-time experiences of the Netherlands and surrounding countries.
3. Differing ideologies on women's work outside the home, related in the Netherlands to pillarization.
Each of these themes will briefly be addressed below.

Variations in socio-economic conditions. Various themes fall under this heading. One of these is de Bruijn's (1989) argument that one reason for the historically low economic activity amongst women is the late industrialization in the Netherlands. As this theme relates specifically to the question why the female activity rate was lower over this century compared to, for instance, the British female activity rate, it falls strictly speaking outwith the time-period of our concerns. Plantenga, however, for whom this theme is relevant, throws

27

doubt on the suggested link between late industrialization and low economic activity amongst Dutch women (1993, pp.2-4). Under the all-encompassing term socio-economic factors she is instead specifically concerned with the relative productivity of the Dutch labour force, which, in turn, becomes the backbone of her explanatory account. In effect, little attention is given by her - or other Dutch contributors - to a third socio-economic aspect, which has been a central element in explanations of post-war labour force feminization in the 'development of capitalism' and dual systems approaches discussed above; the relative tightness of the labour market over time.

In addressing the question why no aggregate rise in Dutch women's recorded economic activity can be observed until the 1970 *Volkstelling*, the issue of the relative state of Dutch and British labour markets is of considerable interest. Some observations made by de Bruijn already indicate that the relative tightness of the Dutch and British labour markets may have varied at different points in time. The latter, for instance, points out that rationalization in the agricultural sector in the post-war years results in a significant decline in the number of people employed in agriculture. Presumably this entailed the release of significant numbers of people to be employed elsewhere.[3] In comparison, only a tiny fraction of the British work force was employed in agriculture by 1945, so any reductions here could not entail a great displacement of labour resources.

Diverse war-time experiences. In both countries some research has been done into the issue how wars have affected the nature of gender relations in the two societies. Given the research questions identified in chapter 1, we would here in principle be interested in the Second World War and its implications. The war-time experiences in these two societies were quite different, and are linked to the German occupation of the Netherlands. Britain remained a 'free' country during the war and literally utilized all its resources and powers to remain that way, and work towards the defeat of the 'enemy'. Practically, this meant that in Britain, a vast war economy drew upon the labour resources of a large number of its citizens. Occupation by German forces, very soon after the war started, meant that no war-time economy was developed in the Netherlands. This suggests that certainly in the short-term (the actual war years), the labour implications were quite different.

It is true to say that considerably more research and commentaries exist in Britain on the more specific concern with the short-term as well as long-term implications of World War II on women's remunerated work patterns. Even so, in both societies speculations about this relationship have abounded from the day the war finished. This makes it difficult for the researcher to delineate speculation from 'reality', and to justify the continued interest in a topic, which, following Plantenga and others, has outlasted its usefulness by far

(Plantenga, 1993, pp.6 and 193). Nevertheless, there are two distinct reasons why the Second World War years will not be ignored here. Firstly, as one of my research aims is to investigate the cross-national difference in the timing of the rising trend in women's economic activity, the World War II years are important. Secondly, during the 1980s, a number of British feminist studies (Summerfield, 1984, 1988, Walby, 1989, 1990a,b, Crompton & Sanderson, 1989) have reconsidered the World War II period in terms of the implications on the position of British women in society, and it would be presumptuous to ignore them here without further ado.

Gender ideologies and women's remunerated work. This brings me to the third theme which recurs in reasonings about the peculiarity of Dutch women's economic activity; that of dominant ideological ideas on women's paid work outside the domestic sphere. The ideological contention in the Netherlands has historically been one which did not look upon the employment of certain groups of women, such as married women, in a positive way. Plantenga has pointed out that such a climate was not specifically Dutch, as a similar ideological climate could be found in Germany. It would seem that the same was the case for Britain (see for instance Crompton & Sanderson, 1990 and Wilson, 1980).

Even so, various Dutch commentaries voice the opinion that this ideological climate was stronger in the Netherlands than in surrounding societies. Wiener & Verwey-Jonker have, for instance, argued that domestic ideology was so strong that, even when families found themselves less well off, the married woman of the household would try out all sorts of measures before, and in favour of, deciding to go out to work (1952, p.17). The latter is supported by Morée (1992), who argues in favour of a strong relationship between the later increase in the Dutch female economic activity rate after the war and Dutch ideological contentions during the 50s.

> Meer dan in de omringende geindustrialiseerde landen en de Verenigde Staten heeft men hier altijd veel waarde toegekend aan mannelijk kostwinnerschap en de voortdurende aanwezigheid van moeders bij hun kleine kinderen. (Morée, 1992, p.15)
> (More so than in surrounding industrialized countries and the United States much value has always been attributed here to the male breadwinner and the continuous presence of mothers with their small children.)

Whether or not the 'male breadwinner and female dependent' ideology was stronger in the Netherlands compared to surrounding societies is something which is hard to establish. Yet, Plantenga has offered a variation on this theme

29

by suggesting that it was not the ideological message *per se*, but the structures through which the message was dispersed, which explain why this ideology pervaded Dutch society more (1993, pp.5 and 189). The structural context she speaks of is pillarization. In contrasting Germany with the Netherlands, she argues that German society was characterized by a horizontally layered class sociality, whilst the Dutch pillarized social order vertically cut through the class structure of society. The consequence was that middle class gender ideology could more easily be imposed onto the working classes. The relevance of this thesis for the comparison of Britain and the Netherlands seems worthy of further consideration.

Cross-national variations in gendered labour markets

The availability of European based comparative employment statistics (i.e. Eurostat and OECD labour force statistics) now make it possible to compare gendered employment patterns across European national societies (see, for example, Paukert (1985) and subsequent OECD reports). These statistics, in conjunction with an increased scholarly interest in European cross-national analysis, have stimulated the generation of several cross-national studies related to European gendered labour markets (examples include Drew, 1992, Fagan et al., 1994, Lane, 1993, Pfau-Effinger, 1993, Rubery and Fagan, 1994 and the *International Journal of Sociology* special 1995 edition on 'European Labour Markets in a Gender Perspective', Vol. 25, No. 2). As these studies have multiplied, it is increasingly recognized that set against a background of 'strong and certainly more than superficial similarities in the position of women across countries', there are 'surprising variations in the experience of women between countries' (Rubery and Fagan, 1994, p.141). The corollary has been the start of efforts to theorize 'cross-national differences and universal social trends ... within a single (theoretical) framework' (Lane, 1993, p.275).

Although the number of studies which can be included here are still limited, some common themes are evident. One may identify those who have emphasized, or concentrated on, the role of the state in the causation of cross-national variations in the gender patterning of labour markets (e.g. Lane, 1993, Plantenga and van Doorne-Huiskes, 1993, and Walby, 1990a). In her article *From Private to Public Patriarchy* (1990a), for instance, Walby theorizes about the differences which are found in the position of women in contemporary industrialized societies. These societies have seen a shift this century from private to public patriarchy. Although women can now be found in the public spheres (i.e. employment, politics, etc.) in these societies, they are subordinated within them. Differences in the position of women in these societies depend on whether the state or the market has been more significant in drawing women into the public sphere. Western Europe is seen as having a 'mixed state/market' form of public patriarchy. In effect then, Walby emphasizes the sameness of the public form of patriarchy in West European societies as opposed to the USA or East European societies, though ultimately, variations in this form of patriarchy in these societies are:

> Caused by the difference in state policy which itself is an outcome of various struggles between opposing forces on both gender and class issues. (Walby, 1990a, p.95)

Pfau-Effinger, I believe, rightly points out that these accounts centre too much on the role of institutions. One of the resulting problems is evident in the accounts of those who have emphasized the role of the state. Exemplified, for instance, in Lane's statement that:

> National patterns of female labour force participation and labour market situation ... are due to the different gender regimes at the level of the state. (1993, p.291)

Such approaches speak a certain mono-causalism in explaining cross-national variations, which, I would argue, can not do justice to the intricacies involved. Another issue to address is whether West European nation states are indeed characterized by a 'mixed state/market' form of patriarchy, or whether there is a need to acknowledge greater variation in the latter, in order to account for cross-national differences in the gender patterning of their respective work forces. I think that Pfau-Effinger (1995) and Plantenga (1993) go some way in addressing this issue by arguing for the inclusion of a consideration of culture as an integral aspect of cross-national work of this kind.

Feminization in the banking sector

Theoretical perspectives on the feminization of types of work, the sex-typing of work and explanations of occupational segregation are intimately related. It is clear that conceptually, the sexual division of labour in the home and in the work place can be seen as distinct from each other, without ignoring that they are related. The sexual division of labour in the workplace has been termed occupational segregation by Hakim (1979), who has pointed out that one may distinguish further between two forms of occupational segregation: the horizontal and vertical forms.[4] Another dimension of the sexual division of labour in paid work is pointed out by Walby and the Dutch *Sociaal and Cultureel Planbureau*. They include the distinction between full and part-time work (Walby, 1989, p.223, Sociaal en Cultureel Rapport, 1988, p.354).

31

Explanations of occupational segregation vary with regards to the disciplinary background of the theorists (economists, sociologists) and the area of concentration (socialization, labour market segmentation, gender and class debate). In recent British discussions on explanations of occupational segregation, there is agreement that in order to get to a comprehensive analysis of occupational segregation, a multi-factor approach to the problem seems most helpful (Dex, 1985, Bradley, 1989, Crompton and Sanderson, 1990). In addressing the issue why, in banking, women were included into clerical work at the time and in the form which this occurred, I am going to follow the distinction which Crompton and Sanderson have proposed between theoretical perspectives or explanations of occupational segregation on the one hand, and perspectives on the processes which bring occupational segregation about (Crompton and Sanderson, 1990, chapter 2). It is a concentration on the latter which is required for our purposes here. A number of perspectives have been developed on the processes of sex-typing (or the processes whereby women become integrated into work which was previously mainly done by men). Hakim (1979) and others have pointed out that once occupational segregation is established, it is relatively stable and resistant to change. It is therefore of considerable interest to consider what triggers change. In the perspectives discussed here, there is agreement that in the processes which give rise to changes in the gender composition of certain types of work, the agents who are present in the sphere of employment need to be considered to see in which way they interrelate to bring these changes about. These include in first instance employers (capitalists or entrepreneurs); employees (male and female; skilled and less-skilled); and employer and employee organizations. With respect to the latter, the trade union which covers that sector of work is often cited. Furthermore, it may be the case that certain other institutions need to be included here. One such example is the state.

Gender exclusion and segregation, and the role of trade unions

Current perspectives differ in respect of how effective or significant they argue these different agents to be. At the same time, a number of these accounts are again phrased in terms of the capitalism/patriarchy debate. This is the case with Walby's analysis of gender segregation in employment which was discussed above. According to Walby, gender segregation in employment may be explained by looking at the interrelation between patriarchal and capitalistic forces within employment. The sex-typing of work becomes established by a struggle between different agents who have different interests in the employment of women. Working in favour of women's entry are capitalists' interests in cheap labour and women defending their right to work. Working

32

against women's entry are male workers who regard women as competition, but who also desire to keep them in the home. Though she argues that:

> Particularly important institutions which affect gender relations in the paid workplace include trade unions as well as employers and the state (Walby, 1986: 243),

in effect much emphasis is placed by her, in her analysis here, on the role which male-dominated trade unions play in the gendering of the labour market by means of the two main strategies indicated by her; those of exclusion and segregation. This is backed up by her in the case-studies on engineering, clerical work and the cotton industry. To a lesser extent, she gives attention to the role of the state and employers in these processes. In relation to the former, she discusses the creation of policies which work against women's interests in employment.

That trade unions have had an influence on women's exclusion and segregation in some sectors of work is clear. Indeed, the printing industry, as discussed by Cockburn (1983), is a good example of a sector of work where trade unions had the power to influence the staffing of the industry. But that does not mean that the same is the case in different types of work. Indeed, in relation to clerical work, one of the three sectors of work researched in *Patriarchy at Work* (1986), Walby argues that the relative weakness of the clerical trade unions in fact meant that they had to resort to the weaker patriarchal strategy of segregation as opposed to exclusion. Yet, the history of gendered employment relations in banks in undoubtedly one of gender exclusion, followed only relatively recently by inclusion.

In banking employment, I would argue, the trade unions were so weak as to have no influence on employer decision taking whatsoever in the crucial period when more women were engaged in clerical work there. In Britain, the trade unions in the banking sector are relatively young, being established after the First World War. In Scotland, the then called NUBE (National Union of Bank Employees) was accepted by bank employers as a bargaining partner in the 40s. But in England and Wales, bank employers refused to acknowledge NUBE until the late 1960s. Dutch banks were not positively inclined towards trade unions either, as is clear from Dutch commentaries (Tijdens, 1989), and my discussions with former bank employees (see chapter 5). This gives one a certain premonition as to the influence these unions could have had on employment policies. So in banking, there is no or little trade union influence at the time when feminization in clerical bank work occurs. But this can not be taken to mean that banking employment has historically not been shaped by the influence of patriarchal strategies, for this runs against the available evidence.

It is not surprising to find that Walby concentrates in her account on the role which male-dominated trade unions have played in bringing about and maintaining gender exclusion and segregation in employment. The direction which her analysis here takes is influenced by some of the controversies of the capitalism/patriarchy debate. Since one of Walby's main aims is exactly to 'prove' the 'independence' of the operation of patriarchal forces, as opposed to capitalistic forces, in the sphere of employment, concentrating on trade unions at least does not make her analysis vulnerable to the critique that women's closure of access to employment is fuelled by capitalist forces. Walby's discussions here, then, have an important point to make. Nevertheless, as such, Walby's analysis contributes to the fact that relatively little attention has been given in research on gender relations in employment, to the way in which patriarchal forces, as well as capitalist forces, have an influence on employers' strategies. As such, the tendency in explanations of women's position in labour markets to see patriarchy and capitalism 'as two distinct systems' with different agencies, where employers pursue 'capitalist' interests and male workers 'patriarchal' interests' (Witz, 1992, p.26), is not sufficiently challenged by her.

What this means is that no comprehensive analytical tools are available to understand the historical trajectory of women's employment in some sectors of work. In the banking sector specifically, the history of gendered employment relations has seen three distinct phases. The first phase was a period when women were excluded from clerical bank work in both societies. This phase is followed by their formal - though partial - inclusion. Partial, on the grounds that for a time period, marriage meant the end of women's clerical bank work (and married women were not considered as possible new recruits). The third phase is one of formal inclusion. During this phase, no formal exclusionary practices remain, though this does not mean that informal exclusionary practices ceased.

So there is a need to work towards an analytical framework, which better suits the historical specificity of banking feminization. Such a framework, I would argue, departs from previous approaches on gender exclusion and inclusion in the sphere of employment in three main ways. Firstly, more attention needs to be given to the interrelation of capitalist and patriarchal forces in employer decision taking. Secondly, there is a need to give more attention to the interplay between class and gender. Lastly, whilst Witz has argued that social relations may manifest themselves differently depending on whether working class or middle class work is being studied, the same may be applicable for different types of middle class occupations. This last theme involves the comparison of exclusionary and inclusionary gendered tactics in the medical professions (which form the subject matter of Witz' work) and in clerical bank work. Though such a comparison is certainly of significant interest in a study which investigates the different ways in which patriarchal gender relations have materialized in different types of work, it will not be attempted here.

Exclusion, partial inclusion and formal inclusion in banking employment

In Walby's scheme, employers very much represent and embody the interests of capitalism. On the basis that women have historically offered cheaper labour than men, this leads her to argue that employers have been a force pushing for the inclusion of women in employment, as opposed to men (who have embodied patriarchal interests and pushed for the exclusion of women from employment). By arguing that the employer or manager who makes employment decisions is himself subject to two opposing influences, 'either to indulge his taste for patriarchy and exclusionism, or to economize on his labour costs' (1985b, p.1062), Cohn acknowledges that employers themselves form part of the gender order. This creates the possibility that employers have historically engaged in exclusionary practices on the basis of patriarchal influences.

In the history of clerical work, he discusses various instances (in the British Post Office and the Great Western Railway) where managers have indulged in their patriarchal attitudes, by conjuring up reasons as to why their discriminatory employment policies made 'economic sense'. On the other hand, he suggests, a number of conditions may operate together to trigger off a change in employers' decision taking in favour of the employment of women. One of these is the state of the labour market which a particular firm faces (an aspect which Walby and others have also pointed to). Apart from this 'external' factor, Cohn points to a number of firm specific factors which may stimulate feminization.

A number of these conditions were present in the internal labour market which characterized banking employment. Bank employment included a considerable amount of relatively low-skilled routine work, and in fact, the extent of this was on the increase in the post-war years. At the same time, banks operated tenure-based salary scales and offered their employees a job for life. These together would have formed an economic rationale behind feminization in conjunction with the operation of a marriage bar. They provided banks with the opportunity to limit the years of employment of a percentage of its work force, which could then be replaced by a younger and cheaper work force; an employment strategy called 'synthetic turnover' by him (Cohn, 1985a, p.95). In short, Cohn puts forward an argument which points specifically to the economic factors at work in triggering a change in the patriarchal attitudes amongst a firm's management.

But apart from such distinct economic motives, in relation to banking employment other motives may have driven employer decision taking as well. The first point to be made here is that the character of social relations between employer and employee differ, depending on what sector of work is considered (see also Witz, 1992, p.35). For instance, it seems rather straightforward that social relations between printing trade workers and their bosses have, historically, been rather different from social relations between bank employees and their managers. Bank employers and their employees did not espouse to a 'them and us' ideology to the same degree as was present in occupations where no career ladders of this kind existed. Savage has pointed out that because of the internal labour market in British banks, male bank managers and male bank employees have historically had 'their fortunes tied up through the significance of career mobility' (1993, p.197). One implication of this for patriarchal gender relations is that the interests of male bank employees and their male employers have coincided (Lown, 1990, Witz, 1992), firstly in the exclusion of women from clerical bank work and, following on from that, their partial inclusion.

Several reasons may be indicated as to why bank employers and their male employees had their 'fortunes tied up through the significance of career mobility' (Savage, 1993, p.197). The idea that the male career path is facilitated by the employment of women in routine clerical work only, is not a new idea (see e.g. Crompton & Jones, 1984, p.3). Indeed, it has been argued that such a strategy was used in the British Civil Service from the time they first employed women in clerical work; i.e. the late 19th century (see Parliamentary paper (1946, Cmd. 6886) *Marriage Bar in the Civil Service*). But until the post-war years, most British banks had not thus far used such a strategy. However, under certain historical conditions it may have been in the interests of both bank managers and their male employees if the career progression of male bank employees was speeded up. In a comment made by Savage and Witz, in relation to Lloyds Bank's decision to employ more girls in the 1920s and 1930s, this is hinted at (1992, p.11).

This leads us onto a further point. In the time-period which concerns us here, the relations between bank managers and their employees (men and women) were paternal in character. In models of employer interests/behaviour in explanations of gender exclusion and inclusion, this feature has been neglected. Even Cohn - who acknowledges that employers may not just be 'driven' by their 'capitalist' interests - seems to assume that employers operate with a 'modern rationality'. In the time period of this case-study, the prominence of a paternal traditional ethos amongst bank employers was reflected in the social relations within its institutions. Acknowledging these relations enables one to recognize how the management of both British and Dutch banks was actively and autocratically involved, not just in running their financial business, but also in the shaping of the lives of their male, and - once present - also their female employees. In the banking case-study, which starts in chapter 5, the process of shaping employment relations in banks in both societies was one in which 'gender and class intersect in the construction of identity' (Witz, 1992, p.26).

Conclusion

Explanatory accounts which consider continuity and change in the gender composition of national work forces and specific sectors of work differ considerably, though in both approaches one may indicate a concern with gender exclusion and inclusion. In turn, aggregate approaches differ because the objectives on which the analysis is based vary. In addition, I have identified cross-national variations in the theoretical concerns of the contributors discussed. More specifically, in the work of British commentaries (and that of Pfau-Effinger) there is an explicit concern with theorizing the character of gender relations, whereas Dutch contributors have not done this. Nevertheless, a number of common concerns may be elicited. These include the significance of the socio-economic, political and cultural-ideological context around the empirical themes being investigated.

As indicated in chapter 1, I will adopt a similar mode of investigation at the aggregate level in this book. This, however, does not mean that the themes pursued, and which pertain to each of these contexts are chosen at random. Rather, they are informed by the themes and time-periods identified as carrying some significance in explaining change in the gender composition of British and Dutch work forces. Consequently, in chapters 3, 4 and 5 there is a continuing interest in the Second World War period and marriage bars in employment. As indicated above, the socio-economic context I will investigate is the relative tightness of the respective labour markets.

Notes

1   Those who are unfamiliar with the meanings of the three forms of the reserve army of labour; the floating, the stagnant and the latent forms, may refer to Braverman (1974, pp.386-88).

2   See for a more general critique of Walby's dual systems analysis Bradley (1989), and Crompton and Sanderson (1990). For a more subtle critique of aspects of Walby's analysis of patriarchal gender relations in employment Witz (1992).

3   This may be supported by figures. Whereas in 1947, 19 per cent (or 747,100) of the total Dutch work force were engaged in agricultural

work, by 1960 this had declined to 11 per cent (or 446,800) (CBS, *80 Jaren Statistiek in Tijdreeksen*, p.66).

4   Horizontal occupational segregation points to the existence of women's occupations and men's occupations, by which is understood that of the various occupations which can be distinguished (Hakim looks, for example, at the Occupational Classification of the British Census), there are occupations in which predominantly women can be found, whilst there are other occupations in which predominantly men can be found (see further Hakim, 1979, Bradley, 1989, Walby, 1986, and Crompton and Sanderson, 1990). Vertical occupational segregation points to the phenomenon where in the hierarchical work structure of a particular type of work, a gender division can be found. Clerical work in banking employment is one example of this. Female bank employees can be found mainly at the bottom of the job hierarchy.

Part 2
GENDER EXCLUSION IN WORK FORCES
1940-1965

3 Marriage bars in employment

During the first half of the 20th century, marriage bars - restrictions preventing women[1] from participating in paid work when they are married or get married - were not an uncommon feature of employment relations in both societies under consideration. The presence of such bars in employment has become increasingly rare from the Second World War onwards, and today they do not exist anymore in Britain or in the Netherlands. Since the period of decline of such bars falls in the research period, it is interesting to look at this in relation to some of the main research questions considered here.

Marriage bars must be considered as an aspect of gendered employment relations and looking at them is interesting for a number of reasons. The first of these concerns an exploration of the link between the presence of such bars and the activity of women in employment. More specifically, in relation to our concerns here the question is what the link is between the increased decline of the bar during the post-war years, the increased activity rate of women in the post-war years - which has been argued to be mainly an increase in the number of married women in employment - and the cross-national difference which was found in this respect. In table 3.1, the economic activity of married women in the two societies is traced over the period 1900-1971. It shows that the recorded increase in economically active Dutch married women starts later than is the case for British married women. In the light of this, I will examine here whether marriage bars in employment were more common in the Netherlands than in Britain, and whether such bars were a common feature of employment at a later date in the former society.

But such an investigation is not an easy task. The source material on marriage bars is rather fragmented, and no proper mapping of patterns has so far been attempted. The first necessary task to gain an insight into the questions just posed, therefore, is to map the presence of marriage bars in the two societies, and to draw out comparative similarities and differences in the patterns found.

41

However, the worth of such work might be challenged. Many commentators - Dutch ones in particular - hold the opinion that the relationship between marriage bars and the extent of women's economic activity is very weak. Some notable exceptions to this stance can be found in the work of Cohn (1985a) and Walby (1986, 1989, 1990a). The latter has argued that the decline of the marriage bar is invaluable in explaining the increased participation of women in paid employment in the post-war period (Walby, 1986, 1990a). There is furthermore a cross-national difference in the extent to which marriage bars have been investigated. British scholars tend to agree that the marriage bar is a neglected feature of gender relations in employment, which is in need of analysis (Walby, 1990a, Glucksmann, 1990, p.300, and Roberts, 1988, p.73). In the Netherlands, the social circumstances surrounding marriage bars has been researched more fully. I shall link this to cross-national variations found in the existence of marriage bars later in this chapter. This suggests that certainly from a British point of view, further research into marriage bars would be considered worthwhile. In addition, given that this is a comparative study, I think that this project is relatively immune from such objections. A cross-national comparison of patterns of marriage bars has not been attempted before, and such an exercise might, at least, aid the understanding of cultural differences between the two societies under investigation. Nevertheless, at the

Table 3.1

Economically active married women as a proportion of the married female population in Britain and the Netherlands (percentages)

Year	Britain 15-59	Netherlands 15 and over
1901/09*	10	7.5
1921/20	10	4.7
1951/47	26	9.9
1961/60	35	6.7
1971	49	15.2

Sources and notes:
Britain: Hakim (1979, p.3). These figures have been calculated from the Census, for England and Wales only, and include all women between the ages of 15-59.
The Netherlands: These figures have been calculated from the Dutch Census and include all women from the age of 15 and over.[2]
* With the exception of 1901 for Britain, these figures exclude the group of divorced and widowed women.

end of this chapter, I will come back to the disagreement about the relationship between marriage bars and women's economic activity.

Lastly, because marriage bars have not been investigated comprehensively in a British context, I will address another view which has become 'common' knowledge, though the question is whether enough is known about marriage bar patterns to support it. This is that formal marriage bars have affected middle class women more than working class women on the grounds that such bars were more prominent in occupations which attracted middle class women. Since Dutch accounts have little to say in this respect, cross-national comparisons will also be made.

Mapping the presence of marriage bars

> Differential treatment in regard to Insurance is not by any means the only disability encountered by married women who seek work. Their first trouble is to get any work at all. (Strachey, 1937, p.59)

> Den vrouwelijke ambtenaar - 't staat heusch zo in de wet,
> Wordt als hij trouwt onmiddelijk de keien opgezet!
> Droomt hij dus van zijn echtvriend of van zijn trouwjapon,
> Dan komt hij onverbiddelijk op een afvloeiingsbon'
> (The female civil servant - it truthfully says so in the law, will be out of a job as soon as she marries! So if she dreams of a husband and marriage gown, she will relentlessly be put on a redundancy list! Poem by Mevr J. Veeken-Bakker cited in Posthumus-van der Groot et al., 1977, p.196)

This effort to map patterns of the occurrence of marriage bars shall begin with an overview of the types of variations which I have come upon, apart from cross-national variations. There are many facets to this variation, and I therefore think it is more appropriate to talk about marriage bars in the plural. There is not one marriage bar, there are many.

The first variation concerns a variation in the presence of a bar in different types of work. In some firms or sectors of work, marriage bars have never existed, in others they have. A second facet to this variation concerns the time period in which various bars existed. Some were introduced before the First World War, some thereafter. Some were abolished during the Second World War, some thereafter. But even when such bars existed, some bars existed formally, as explicit employment policies, whilst others were more implicit. The bar in the British Civil Service is an example of the former; it was a formal bar, written down in the Service's employment regulations. Other bars were more implicit, in the sense that they were either a verbal or even a non-verbal understanding between employees and their managers that marrying female staff would be expected to leave.

The next aspect of variation concerns those types of work where a formal bar existed. Where this was the case, like in Dutch state employment, the vigour with which the bar was implemented varied over time. So from the 1920s, married women were officially barred from state employment, but even so, for a large part of the time in which this was the case, marrying female employees would be dismissed on the day they married, and reinstated the day thereafter. In both societies, a certain realism meant that often divorced and widowed women, or women who were the sole breadwinners in a family, were exempted from the rule.

Further variation could be found in the character of the bar. In some sectors of employment where the bar was introduced, the so-called phasing-out (or dying-out) system was used. This meant that married women who were already employed could stay on, but any marrying woman would be sacked, whilst no married women were taken on. Variation also occurred as to who policed the bar. Often, this would be the employer. But in the Netherlands, the state and Catholics appear to have played a prominent role in getting bars instated and implemented. Glucksmann (1990), on the other hand, cites examples of women who really left employment on marriage because of their husband's wish that they should stop, and women are even known to have policed the bar on each other (Taylor, 1977, p.55). Furthermore, trade unions often took a specific position on the marriage bar, though the question is how effective they were in policing the bar. Lastly, the presence of marriage bars appears to have varied in relation to the state of the labour market. This is put forward as a major causal factor for the rise in the existence of bars in the inter-war period, and has also been argued to be important regarding the decline of the bar.

The relevance of the main facets underlying the various patterns found in marriage bars will be illustrated in the following discussion which maps in more detail the presence, timing and abolition of marriage bars in different sectors of employment. In turn, the Civil Service, teaching, white collar work in private employment, the professions and private industry, will be considered. Because of the nature of this enquiry, this discussion will necessarily take me outside the periodization of the book. In figure 3.1, an overview is given of the variations discussed in this section.

The Civil Service

One commonality between the Netherlands and Britain is that in both countries there existed a marriage bar in the Civil Service and in teaching. In Britain, a marriage bar applied virtually from the beginning that women were employed

Sector of work	MB present?	Time variation	Variation in implementation
Britain			
Civil service	yes	lengthy <1900-1946	little, though in W.W.II
Teaching	yes	inter-war years 1920s-1944	little, during W.W.II
White collar	yes; probably complete	lengthy; from first female employees till 1950s - early 1960s	little, during W.W.II
Other professions	variable; many exceptions	variable	not known
Industry	variable	variable	some

Sector of work	MB present?	Time variation	Variation in implementation
The Netherlands			
Civil service	yes	<1907 and 1924-1957	many
Teaching	yes	<1913 and 1925-1957	many
White collar	yes; probably complete	lengthy, into 1960s	some; after W.W.II
Other professions	variable; exceptions	not known	not known
Industry	often	variable	some

Figure 3.1   Overview of marriage bars in different sectors of work in Britain and the Netherlands

in the Civil Service,[3] right through till 1946. The National Whitley Council Report on the *Marriage Bar in the Civil Service* (Cmd. 6886, 1946, p.3) states that the first official document indicating a marriage bar in the Civil Service dates from 1894. Cohn indicates that the first women were employed in the General Post Office in 1870, whilst a marriage bar became enforced here at the end of the 1870s. It is clear from the Report by the National Whitley Council (1946) that the formal marriage bar in the Civil Service was enforced with virtually no exception on all women who married, over the whole period of its existence. The only exceptions which seemed to have been made, applied to women who worked in the higher ranks of the Service and of whom it was expected that dismissal would be against the interests of the Service. This constituted to only one exception during the 1920s. It is notable that at the end of the 1930s and during the Second World War years more exceptions were made to the rule than ever before (National Whitley Council, 1946, p.6).

Since the war had as a result that marriage bars in various types of work were not implemented (though often with the understanding that this was a temporary measure) it was a time in which there was a lot of debate about the pros and cons of marriage bars. So too in the Civil Service, where there was discussion as to whether a marriage bar should continue to apply in the post-war period. The Report by the National Whitley Council (1946) was meant to evaluate this debate concerning the bar in the Civil Service. From the opinions expressed in the Report it is clear that in 1946 - the year in which the marriage bar was abolished - there still existed a lot of support for the bar in the various departments of the Service and amongst the staff associations. Significantly, the Union of Post Office Workers was against its abolition, and though it was not successful in keeping the bar in place in the Post Office, it did continue to implement the bar amongst its own staff until 1963 (Boston, 1980, p.252). In addition, whenever redundancies were threatened in the Civil Service during the 1950s, members of the Civil Service union CSCA brought up arguments for the reinstatement of the bar. In view of Walby's assertion that the Second World War saw the end of marriage bars in Britain, this evidence indicates that support for the bar had not disappeared after the war, and that, indeed, bars still existed after the war.

In the Netherlands, the first marriage bar in the Civil Service, affecting women in the Post Office, was instituted in 1904 and can be directly related to the increased influence of confessionals on a state level.[4] That the issue of the marriage bar was a contentious one at this time, is clear from the fact that this marriage bar was abolished again in 1907 when the liberals took over government (Schoot-Uiterkamp, 1978, p.193). Between 1907 and 1924, there existed no formal marriage bar in the Civil Service, though there were attempts to push one through the legislature. In 1924, a Civil Service marriage bar became law again; this time the right-wing government - led by the Catholic

Minister *Ruys de Beerenbrouck*, was responsible (Posthumus-van der Groot et al., 1977, p.196, and Blok, 1989, p.119). From 1924 onwards a formal marriage bar existed, though the enforcement of the bar varied over time. At first marrying female staff could be reinstated the day after they married, but during the 1930s depression, even this was not a possibility anymore. It seems, then, that its enforcement was most complete during the years of the depression in the 1930s. During the war, the Civil Service suffered a shortage of staff because some of its male employees had to take up employment in Germany and the implementation of the marriage bar was consequently relaxed in 1942, only to be imposed again at the end of the 1940s (Vries-Bruins, 1948, pp.16-18). The war and post-war period support the view that the implementation of the bar in Dutch state employment varied with the state of their labour market. The marriage bar on state employees was finally abolished, by law, in 1957.

From this discussion, two significant cross-national differences are evident. The first concerns state involvement in the marriage bar. In Britain, the actual government (or the state) was never much involved in discussions about the bar, with the exception of the abolition of the bar in 1946. In the Netherlands this was quite different. From the moment that the confessionals gained power on a national level, national efforts were made to regulate married women's employment through marriage bars. The other difference concerns the timing and enforcement of the bar in the Civil Service in the two countries. In the British Civil Service, the timing and enforcement were rather homogenous. The bar was instituted during the 1880s, and implemented almost completely (except during World War II) till 1946. In the Netherlands, the bar in the Civil Service is characterized by a series of introductions and abolitions, as well as variations in its enforcement over time. This gives one the impression that the reasons behind the institution of the bar in the two countries were different.

Teaching

In both countries a marriage bar was enforced during the inter-war period in teaching and commentators on this in both countries associated it directly with a downturn in the economy and reductions in government spending (Oram, 1983, Bakker, 1982 and others). In both countries, local authorities were the major employers of teachers and it is for this reason that there is not a situation, like in the Civil Service, where there is either a marriage bar in this employment or not. The extent of a marriage bar in teaching depended on the number of local authorities which decided to enforce a marriage bar. The exception to this were certain time-periods in the Netherlands, when national law either prohibited local authorities from operating marriage bars or enforced them to curtail the employment of married and marrying female staff.

Before the inter-war period, marriage bars in teaching were not so common in Britain. It has been argued that overall many female teachers would leave their employment when they married on their own accord, though there is evidence that some marrying female teachers stayed on (Davidoff & Westover, 1986, p.108, and Bradley, 1989, p.211). The extent to which this happened seemed to have been different over the regions. In London, it seems that it was relatively common for women to stay on. Bradley estimates that in 1908, 39 per cent of headmistresses and 23 per cent of female assistants were married, whilst the Census average for England and Wales was 7 per cent (1989, p.211). So in Britain, before 1922, only a small number of local authorities carried a marriage bar. This changed when, with the depression of 1921, many local authorities introduced a marriage bar.

But the situation was more complex than that. As local authorities moved to introduce marriage bars, national government did not act against these decisions, neither did it actively encourage the action. The Sex Disqualification (Removal) Act of 1919 is brought up by a number of commentators in relation to this (Oram, 1983, Spender, 1984, Lewis, 1984, and Hunt, 1988). Though in theory, this legislation was to protect women from discrimination in employment, in practice it was not interpreted by the legal establishment in that way. Hence during the 1920s, it became increasingly difficult for female teachers to remain in work after their marriage or for married female teachers to find work. This situation continued throughout the 1930s, though the abolition of the marriage bar on teachers by the London County Council in 1935 signalled a change. Even so, the presence of married women amongst teachers did decline over those years. After having reached a peak in World War I of 15 per cent, by 1930, only 10 per cent of female teachers were married (Silverstone, 1980, p.185). In the 1944 Education Act, the enforcement of a marriage bar in teaching by local authorities was legally abolished, after married female teachers had been employed by many local authorities during the war years.

In the Netherlands, the history of the marriage bar in teaching is somewhat different again. Here, some local authorities questioned the employment of married female teachers already in the 1880s, but they were challenged by national government (led by the liberals who were against intervention of any kind) when they tried to introduce a marriage bar through additions to the existing employment law for teachers. As the influence of confessionals on a state level increased during the first decade of this century, there was a short period between 1910 and 1913 in which national government instituted a bar in teaching. The next action against married female teachers occurred in 1925, when through a law amendment local authorities were given the power to enforce a marriage bar if they so wished. During the 1930s, further law amendments actually required the dismissal of all state employed female teachers on marriage.

Bakker (1982), in her article on changes in the occupational segregation in teaching during the inter-war period, questions the relationship between the bar in teaching and the ratio of married female teachers. This is underpinned by figures. In 1920, only 5.4 per cent of female teachers in primary education were married; i.e. considerably lower than for British female teachers. Further figures reveal that this rate declined from 6.0 per cent in 1929, to 5.5 per cent in 1932, 4.4 per cent in 1935 and 2.6 per cent in 1938.[5] The enforcement of the marriage bar decreased again after the war. Due to labour shortages married women were employed again to a certain degree, though the actual abolition of the bar in law only occurred in 1957, together with the abolition of the bar in the Civil Service. The *International Labour Review* indicates, though, that at the beginning of the 1960s, marriage bars still applied in some private schools (*International Labour Review*, 1962, p.372).

So in Britain, it would be accurate to call the inter-war period the 'epoch of the marriage bar' (Bradley, 1989, p.211) for the teaching profession only. In the Netherlands, there is more variation in the presence of a bar in teaching over time. In all, a marriage bar in teaching and Civil Service employment in the Netherlands was present more than a decade after its abolition in Britain.

White collar work in the private sector

> In the business and commercial world dismissal on marriage is very usual, and the proportion of married women who succeed in getting clerical or secretarial work is noticeably below the proportion in any other occupation. (Strachey, 1937, p.60)

In tracing the history of marriage bars in private sector white collar work and the professions (see below), one comes upon a problem also present in researching the marriage bar in industry. This problem is worth mentioning because it has consequences for any analysis of the occurrence of marriage bars. In the discussion of the Civil Service, we only dealt with one employer; the state. In teaching, the number of local authorities involved as employers was greater, and this already made it difficult to trace the extent in which marriage bars had been present. In industrial and white collar work, by virtue of the fact that we deal with a large number of institutions, this problem is exacerbated.

The number of institutions involved, and their size contribute to a further problem for researchers of the marriage bar; the availability of evidence. In certain types of employment, like teaching and the Civil Service, evidence of the marriage bar is relatively readily available, because written records are available. One may expect to find written employment records for the larger employment institutions, particularly those bureaucratic in character. For smaller establishments or industry at the time, written records are rare, partly because records were not kept, and partly because, even with regards to the private large bureaucracies, written records have often been lost or destroyed over time. This makes research into marriage bars rather difficult. Where written records are not available, the researcher needs to consider other ways of attaining information. Oral historical accounts have been useful in revealing the presence of marriage bars in industry (see below).

The consequences of these methodological issues are the following. The evidence which I have been able to find on the presence of the bar in the types of work still to be discussed is much more sketchy than that discussed for teaching and the Civil Service. More importantly, although evidence might not always be available, this does not mean that marriage bars did not exist in certain types of work. I will come back to this issue in the section where industrial work is discussed, as I feel that this issue is even more pressing there.

Work in the Civil Service and other white collar work, as well as work in a number of the professions only became acceptable employment possibilities for women of the upper and middle classes during the second half of the 19th century. The historical development of the so-called 'white blouse revolution' is well documented for Britain (e.g. Silverstone, 1976, and Anderson, 1988). The same is the case for the Netherlands, where the last decades of the 19th century saw the opening up of the *'nette vrouwen beroepen'* (respectable women's occupations), amongst which were: nursing, teaching, telegraphy, office work, shop work and childcare.

It can be said with certainty that in banking and insurance; sectors of work where increasing numbers of women found employment during the 20th century, marriage bars were common, though it is hard to say when these came into existence for the individual institutions. In the Bank of England, one of the first banks to employ women in 1893, a marriage bar accompanied the bank's decision to employ women (Bank of England Archive). Similarly, it would seem that in Lloyds Bank, a marriage bar was certainly present when, in the second half of the 1920s, the bank actively started to recruit more women (Savage, 1993, p.210). But the entry of the first female employees varied between different banks (see chapter 5), and whilst this at first entailed the employment of typists and secretaries, the feminization of clerical work came even later.

White collar employment in the private sector in Britain provides further support to doubt that the post-war period were marriage bar free years. This is apparent from evidence collected by the International Labour Office (1962). In 1962 it reported that though the Bank of England had abolished its marriage bar, there still existed one in three of the *Big Five* banks. The same, the report goes on, was the case in some local authorities - though these are not named, and in some insurance and shipping companies. Details about the operation of marriage bars in Dutch banking and insurance are also sketchy. For banking specifically, commentators seem to hold to the idea that a marriage bar was common, though when this started to be the case is not clear. Clearer is when the bars disappeared; this was during the 1960s.

In British banking, marriage bars remained as an employment policy well after World War II, and in that sense stands out from equivalent middle class types of work, in teaching and the Civil Service. In the Netherlands, marriage bars in banking also outlasted the bar in state employment (abolished in 1957), though not by as many years as was the case in Britain.

The professions

Next to white collar work in the private sector, an increasing number of women were able to find employment in such occupations as shop-work and nursing, and also in the more prestigious professions like medicine and law. Did a marriage bar exist here too?

About nursing not much is said in British commentaries, except that there did indeed exist a marriage bar here (Silverstone, 1980, p.12). Others apply the broader term of medical staff (Spender, 1984). But apart from these remarks, little details are available as to when it was introduced and why, nor what the reasons were for its introduction or when married women were allowed in. Ray Strachey does indicate that only those medical staff who fell under the control of the public authorities suffered from a marriage bar, but she commentsL

> There are a number of professions in which the question of a marriage bar does not arise. In law, medicine and accountancy, etc., nothing is heard of it. (1937, p.61)

The presence of marriage bars amongst medical staff controlled by local authorities seems to mirror teaching, in that its presence was dependent on the politics of the specific local authority involved. For instance, it should be noted that at the same time as the London County Council abolished the marriage bar for teachers in 1935, it did so for medical staff as well (Lewenhak, 1977, p.226). Other evidence suggests that some medical staff (often midwives, health visitors etc.) were exempt from the bars which many local authorities carried before World War II, but this was not applicable to all local authorities (National Whitley Council Report, 1946, pp.20-21). One reason why so little is known about marriage bars in the medical professions may be that they were not exactly common there. Following Witz (1992), it would indeed appear to be the case that closure strategies, other than the marriage bar, were used in the medical professionals.

That there were exceptions to these examples in the professions is indicated again by Strachey, who gives a comprehensive guide on the possibilities for women in employment at the end of the 1930s. The professions where there is no talk of marriage bars are politics, and:

> Curiously enough no marriage bar exists, and no arguments to support it are ever adduced in the professions connected with the arts. Women musicians, painters, actresses and writers may marry as much as they please, and do in fact marry without abandoning their careers. (Strachey, 1937, p.61)

Despite the fact that a number of studies[6] exist on the new *'nette vrouwen beroepen'*, I found very little information which could be used to map marriage bars in the professions in the Netherlands. Two small references were found. First, a comment in the *International Labour Review* (1962) suggests that in 1962, some department stores still carried a marriage bar. Second, a comment in *Mercurius* (the journal for the Dutch white collar union *Mercurius*) was found about the exclusion of doctors and accountants from the proposed nation-wide marriage bar on women (*Mercurius*, 1939, p.228) in the inter-war period.

From the evidence provided here, it would seem that marriage bars in banks and insurance companies were very common, and lasted longer than in other middle class types of employment. Certainly an interesting question to examine is why this should be so. In addition, not all professions carried a marriage bar. In explanations of such bars, one issue which needs to be addressed is why such bars were common in some occupations for middle class women, whilst in other occupations they were not.

Marriage bars in industry

Evidence of marriage bars in industrial work is much more patchy and harder to find than in the areas of work already discussed. Apart from the large number of firms in industry, and the issue of written records, another problem for investigation may be given. Many of the firms which were operating in the first half of this century no longer exist (because of bankruptcy or merger) and their records are difficult to trace. In all, most information available on marriage bars in industry concerns larger firms, and has often been brought to attention through oral historical accounts, rather than through written evidence of this. However, to argue, as Cohn has done, that larger industrial firms are more likely than smaller firms to have carried marriage bars may be misleading

(1985a, p.112). For the reasons just given, it is likely that marriage bar evidence for larger firms is more likely to have survived; and there is a distinct possibility that lack of available evidence may generate a bias in this respect.

In both societies, a marriage bar could be found in various industries and at various time periods. Though the evidence is sparse, I will here present a picture of the occurrence of the bar in industry in chronological order.

The period prior to World War I. In both countries, there is evidence that a marriage bar existed to a certain degree in the 19th century. There are some general remarks about the existence of a marriage bar in private British industry before World War I.[7] But there are also some references to its presence in specific firms; like the biscuit factory Huntley and Palmer, and in Cadbury's Bournville factories (Lewis, 1984, p.186, Braybon, 1981, p.28). There are also some clear examples that a marriage bar was not an uncommon feature of employment relations in Dutch industry before World War I (for some back-ground information concerning types of industry and the employment opportunities of Dutch women around the turn of the century see Martens, 1994, cht. 4). One well known firm, Philips, which was founded in the south Dutch town of Eindhoven in 1891, did not employ married women from the start, even at times of great shortage in cheap non-married female labour.

Around the turn of the century the issue of married women's employment took on the form of a national debate in both societies.[8] The crucial theme of this debate was whether married women's employment should be banned. In Britain, the lady commissioners of the Royal Commission of Labour supported a ban on married women's work, but no national legislation of the kind was ever developed. In the Netherlands, a Mr P. Aalberse attempted to instate a national marriage bar via an amendment to the 1911 labour law (van der Molen, approx. 1938, pp.25-7). Parliament rejected this amendment because of a recognition that many married women had to go out to work out of economic necessity.[9] A bar would prevent such women from supporting their families independently and/or push them into financially less lucrative work, like the various forms of hidden home work which were available to them; forms of work which were not covered by 'protective' legislation.

It is difficult to gauge the influence of this ideological climate on industrial employers. Some seemed to have operated marriage bars because they believed strongly in the ideals of the time (Braybon (1981, p.33) mentioned Edward Cadbury as a British example). In some Catholic regions in the Netherlands, employer practices must have been influenced by the local Catholic establishment.[10] Other employers will have based decisions on perceived economic motives. But even then there was diversity of opinion. Some firms thought that a marriage bar made economic sense because it enabled the employer to keep a young and cheaper work force (Lewis, 1984, p.186). Other firms considered it an advantage to employ married women because they were seen to work solely out of economic necessity, and were hence expected to be more docile than the average work force (Glucksmann, 1990, p.117). Given this, it is difficult to give an indication as to how common marriage bars in industry were.

World War I. According to Lewenhak (1980), the marriage bar was relaxed in Britain during the First World War, but evidence to support this assertion is lacking, even in Braybon's (1981) *Women workers in the First World War, the British experience.* She does discuss the expansion in the ratio of married women working during the war:

> Married women made up 40% of all working women throughout the country: in Leeds 44% of women in the four main engineering firms were married, although in 1911 only 15% of women workers in the area had been married. (Braybon, 1981, pp.49-50)

This is significantly higher than the Census average for married women, before and after the war, which lay between 10 per cent and 15 per cent of the total female population.

No evidence of a decline in marriage bars in Dutch industry was found. Blonk indicates that, because of expansion in production in the textile industry in *Twente*,[11] significantly more labour cards were issued to married women. But since it was not uncommon for married women to be employed in the textile industry in *Twente*, it would be wrong to generalize from this that married women's employment rose in other areas of the Netherlands as well.

From the inter-war period onwards. There is evidence both of firms which operated a marriage bar amongst its female staff, and firms which did not, in the inter-war years. Some of the firms which did operate a bar in Britain during this period include the biscuit factories; Kemps and Peek Frean (Glucksmann, 1990, pp.30 and 107, Jephcott et al., 1962, p.66), Courtnaulds, Boots and Players, Unilever and Imperial Chemical Industries Ltd., Cadbury Brothers Ltd. and Rowntree (Glucksmann, 1990, p.223, and Report of the National Whitley Council, 1946, pp.21-22). Others have indicated the existence of the bar in the more traditional types of industry, like in coal mining (John, 1982, p.16), in the tinplate industry in Wales (Owen Jones, 1987), and in some of the lace and hosiery industries in Nottingham (Taylor, 1977, p.53). Lastly, in the cotton industry in Lancashire, in which historically many women - married and unmarried - had found employment, a marriage bar was introduced during the 1930s, when due to the decline in the industry, unemployment in the area increased (Lewenhak, 1977, p.215 and Walby, 1986, p.180). This was a marriage bar in the form of a phasing-out system. On the other hand, there were also specific firms who did not operate a marriage bar on their female staff. Amongst these are a number of the firms researched by Glucksmann, like Hoover, Morphy Richards and the EMI company.

During World War II, all of the British firms mentioned in the National Whitley Council Report withdrew their marriage bar (1946, pp.21-22), though most firms voiced the opinion in 1946 that they would probably return to their pre-war policy. Indications are that when the labour market remained tight after the war in many areas of the country, the bar disappeared in a number of firms. One point in case was the biscuit factory Peek Frean. There are a number of important indications that the operation of marriage bars in British industry had not completely vanished by the 1960s. When private industry is discussed in the report on the marriage bar in the *International Labour Review* (1962), it is remarked that:

> In the Philippines and the United Kingdom also the practice of requiring women to resign on marriage appears to be followed in some undertakings. (*International Labour Review*, 1962, p.375)

Equally, a bar could be found in the latter years of the 1960s in certain areas where the employment opportunities women enjoyed had historically not been good, like in Northern Ireland and South Wales (*International Labour Review*, 1962, p.374 and Lewenhak, 1977, p.292). Some evidence exists, then, that the presence of marriage bars in Britain varied by region.

There is no doubt that marriage bars prevailed in certain sectors of employment and in certain regions in Dutch industry, in the inter-war period. In industry in *Brabant*, a marriage bar was employed virtually by all employers. It is difficult to see this as unrelated to the influence of Catholicism in this area (e.g. Brand (1937), Kooij & Pley (1984), and de Bruijn (1989) discuss its presence in the electronics firm Philips; the textile industry and the tobacco industry. See also *International Labour Review*, 1962, p.374). In the new industries, like diamond production and tailoring in the cities, married women were also barred (Bruijn, 1989, p.31), though Catholicism did not have a great influence here.

But just as one can indicate in which industries and regions marriage bars could be found, one can indicate in which types of work and regions married women were not barred. Examples here are not as numerous as in British industry. In fishing-net weaving, 70 per cent of weavers were married women (Doorman, 1948, p.211), though this was a declining industry which had virtually disappeared by the 1940s. Doorman cites the town of *Maastricht* where married women were found in the ceramics industry, the tobacco industry, tailoring and in the retail trade; where they often managed prestigious establishments, including hotels (1948, p.212). Furthermore, unlike the textile industry in *Tilburg* (a town in the Catholic province *Brabant*), in the province of *Twente*, married women did go into the textile factories (with the exception of the town *Hengelo*) (Blonk, 1929, p.229).

Marriage bars in industry continued their presence as employment relations in the post-war period. And though the Dutch state had agreed to stop the bar on its female employees in 1957, the *International Labour Review* Report makes it clear that Dutch Industrial employers had not all followed suit.

> The Netherlands reply indicated that in various private undertakings the general rule holds good that female employees are dismissed on marriage. (*International Labour Review*, 1962, p.370)

The presence of marriage bars in Dutch industry is also likely to have been affected by national efforts to regulate women's employment. As discussed above, there were heated national debates on this topic during the depression years. During the 1930s, three attempts were made to establish national laws to regulate the extent of women's remunerated work, two of which affected married as well as unmarried women (Schoot-Uiterkamp, 1978, p.197).

Cross-national variations in industry. There exists concerted evidence that marriage bars existed in both societies considered. It would seem, though, that marriage bars were more widespread in industry in the Netherlands than in Britain. If not for the whole period under consideration, then certainly from the inter-war years through to the post World War II years. In Britain, one can see changes in the attitude towards the employment of married women by industrial employers before the end of the 1930s. A point in case is the biscuit factory Peek Frean, which started to employ married women during busy periods in 1937, after it had operated a vigorous marriage bar during the 1930s. This firm, after the war, made a radical U-turn in its employment policy towards married women, when they found themselves facing a considerable labour shortage problem. The force of unmarried young women from which they had drawn their labour before the war seemed to have shrunk, as young women were increasingly able to enter into white collar jobs, which they considered as more desirable than factory work (Jephcott et al., 1962). The question is to what extent other British firms came to suffer from this same problem at this time. The example of Peek Frean, however, indicates - an area of comparison and possible difference between the two countries - that the relative labour supply at specific times, must be considered in order to explain variations in the continued presence of marriage bars in industry.

In the Netherlands, after the large scale attack on the employment of married women during the 1930s, which took place both at a state level as well as in other areas of social life, married women were not, for some considerable time, regarded as a possible work force which employers could draw labour from (Blok, 1989, p.62). Even when they faced, like Philips, extensive labour shortages. Following the Report by the *International Labour Review* in 1962, one has to concede that in private industry one could still find marriage bars to a certain extent in both societies. To this we may add with some certainty that they were more extensive in the Netherlands than in Britain by this time.

Similarities and variations: how to explain marriage bars?

Having mapped marriage bars by considering their prominence and timing in different sectors of work and cross-nationally, it is time to return to the main questions raised at the start of the chapter. The discussion begins with the claim that marriage bars were more common in middle class types of work in Britain. I shall then move on to consider possible explanations for cross-national variations in the occurrence of marriage bars. This discussion will take place in the context of the various explanations which have been brought forward to explain such bars. Three factors seem to recur in explanations about the occurrence of this phenomenon. These are:
1. The tightness of the labour market,
2. The importance of ideology, and
3. The economic or other interests of various interest/power groups.
I will take a look at each of these factors in turn.

Labour market tightness and gender ideology

There is no dispute amongst contributors that the tightness of the labour market influenced the occurrence of marriage bars. However, about the reason why the tightness of the labour market influenced the occurrence of the bar, not every contributor is clear. Some merely state that the demand for labour is important, like Lewenhak (1977, 1980) and Hunt (1988). Others, like Oram (1983) and Blok (1978/1989), go further than that. They argue that as unemployment increased during the inter-war recessions, there was increased debate about who in society had most right to the available work. Married women, for several reasons, were argued not to have the right to work under such circumstances. These arguments were closely related to ideologies around gender roles, as is evident in the types of arguments which circulated during the 1930s depression in the Netherlands, when unemployment was high. The ideology of the male breadwinner and his female dependent at worst assumed

57

that married women who worked during the 1930s Dutch depression, were benefiting from a double income, whilst others did not have an income at all. This was considered selfish and immoral; these working married women took the bread out of the mouths of others. So the slackness of the labour market obviously brought out certain reactions in people, which a tightness of the labour market did not, or to a lesser degree.

Ideology has been mentioned by many as an influence on the occurrence of the bar. Summerfield, for example, explains the marriage bar as:

> One of the most concrete ways in which the ideology of the male breadwinner and female dependent was expressed. (1984, p.14)

Lewis also indicates the importance of ideology in her explanation of the increased occurrence of marriage bars in the early 20th century. Yet, she talks in terms of 'the ideology of separate spheres' (1984, p.77) and 'the ideology of motherhood' (1984, p.102), and argues that the heyday of marriage bars was the early 20th century.

> During the early 20th century and increasingly during the inter-war years the ideology of motherhood was reinforced legislatively by the marriage bar, *which was chiefly applied to professional women* and which served firmly to delineate the world of married women from that of men at a time when it was becoming widely acceptable for single middle class girls and women to go out to work. (Lewis, 1984, p.102. italics my emphasis)

Lewis does not deny that working class women were to a certain extent affected by marriage bars, but her arguments imply that middle class women were more affected than working class women, and it is this which she seeks to explain. Lewis suggests two reasons why middle class women were affected more by marriage bars than working class women. The first of these is that unlike working class women - who, the argument goes, had always engaged in remunerated work - it was becoming more usual for middle class girls to go out to work. The second reason (also mentioned by Glucksmann, 1990, p.224), is that middle class women were most likely to be found in work which was enjoyable to do, whilst they at the same time were more likely to be in a position to work, since their double burden was not as heavy as that of working class women. The latter could not rely on domestic help or benefit from the relatively expensive newly developing domestic work aids. These changes are argued to have posed a threat to the established patriarchal order, which firmly placed a woman within the confines of the home. Lewis' explanation of the increased presence of marriage bars in British middle class occupations is that they were the means by which the patriarchal order of sexual segregation could be maintained at a time when it was threatened. The slack labour market is attributed little importance in the explanation; the increased presence of marriage bars in the inter-war period was merely 'exacerbated rather than explained by the economic depression' (Lewis, 1984, p.200).

A number of questions confront Lewis' arguments. Firstly, as is clear from Strachey's comments, not all professions where middle class women could be found carried a marriage bar. Surprisingly, the ideology of separate spheres does not appear to have applied to all middle class women equally. Furthermore, a time variation factor is evident in the occurrence of the bar in those sectors of work affecting middle class women. Lewis regards the inter-war years as the period of increased occurrence of such bars, but the previous section has shown that there exists considerable variations between occupations as to when bars were introduced, and when they were abolished. Lewis' argument is one which generalizes at the expense of empirical detail. Rather than assuming homogeneity in such patterns, it would be rather interesting to find out why marriage bars in various middle class types of employment were abolished at different times.

Secondly, it seems to me that Lewis' argument presents gender ideology in a uni-dimensional way, whilst it does not do justice to the importance of slack labour markets. Lewis looks at the problem from the angle of the domestic sphere; i.e. the increased employment of middle class women might upset the sexual division of labour in the household, if left to its own devices. I would suggest that there are different ways in which gender ideology talk pops up in relation to marriage bars. In the sphere of employment, a slackening of the labour market may generate discourses on proper gender roles, either by male employees who feel under threat, or by employers who regard the marriage bar as a means to reduce labour costs.

Lastly, there is the question whether it really was the case that British middle class women were more affected by the bar than working class women? To come straight to the point, given the methodological problems involved in researching the marriage bar (see previous section) one runs the danger of falsely generalizing that middle class women were more affected because more is known about the bar in sectors of work where middle class women were employed. In all, given the evidence which I presented whilst mapping marriage bars in British employment, I tend to agree with the view that in Britain, the bar was more prominent in middle class types of employment. I would argue, however, that this is not the case for the Netherlands. Below, I shall return to this aspect of cross-national difference.

Having said that, the explanatory accounts just discussed are not sufficient to explain the variations found in middle class types of employment in Britain. A further route to explore is to consider more closely the way in which these two; the state of the labour market and gender ideology, influence or are influenced by the economic and social concerns of the various 'parties' involved in the employment sphere. Parties which are directly affected are women and married women in particular, employers and men. Their interests have often been pursued by institutionalized bodies, like trade unions, the confessional establishment, the state, employer's organizations, women's groups, and the family. I will first consider those who examine employers' role in the institution and maintenance of marriage bars. Then, trade unions will be put under the limelight. Finally, I will look at the interests of the state in influencing women's paid employment.

Employers and their Associations

The most elaborate account in which the interests of employers in marriage bars is discussed, is provided by Cohn in *The Process of Occupational Sex-typing* (1985a). His arguments are well worth considering because of their elaborate nature, though his analysis contains helpful as well as misleading elements. Nevertheless, it is an argument which brings us closer to an understanding of the patterns found.

Cohn's starting point is that under certain conditions of employment a situation exists in which it becomes economically beneficial for a firm to artificially increase turnover amongst its employees. This occurs, so Cohn argues, when there is a situation in which (1) the labour market is slack, (2) when the firm follows a payment policy which increases over time periods by way of providing incentive, and (3) when the firm has a large percentage of low-skilled work on offer. When a firm facing this situation is involved in increasing its turnover, the firm is involved in, what Cohn calls, 'synthetic turnover'. One strategy of 'synthetic turnover' is the marriage bar, which enables the employer to:

> Place maximum tenure limits on positions with short learning curves. After a given number of years, the employee is forced to resign. Tenure bars provide effective limitations on career lengths, but they may create fundamental problems of legitimation. (Cohn, 1985a, p.95)

Hence following the three conditions mentioned above, he furthermore argues that where a marriage bar is used as a means for turnover, there needs to be a:

> Normative climate that will tolerate overt sex discrimination. (1985a, p.109)

This condition is crucial to the extent that if it does not hold, a marriage bar can not exist. Cohn, hence, acknowledges the importance of the two factors which were considered earlier; those of the tightness of the labour market and gender ideology concerning married women's employment (though the latter under the name of 'normative climate'). But he does so on the level of the employer, considering how these two factors and some specific characteristics of the employment structure in firms, make it financially interesting for an employer to institute a marriage bar. Having said that, Cohn does not consider the issue of a normative climate, which is favourable towards the discrimination against married women in employment, any further. This is rather a pity since it entails that he neither considers how this normative climate might be affected by the tightness of the labour market.

Cohn's argument seems to be that a marriage bar is most likely to be found in clerical work, since here one is most likely to find the combination of conditions which make such a bar economically viable for the employer to enforce. As examples, he looks at the British General Post Office (Civil Service) and the Great Western Railway as companies which had a marriage bar for a long period of time; the Post Office (as has already been discussed) from the decade in which it started to employ women in the 1870s, until 1946.

Both firms, so Cohn argues, faced the situation discussed above in which it became economically rational to increase turnover rates. In both companies, employment was guaranteed till retirement age (a condition which somehow seems more important in the formation of employer interests, than Cohn gives it credit here). In the Post Office, there existed a lot of low-skilled work and in order to facilitate employee morale, the payment structure contained time-based increases. By introducing a marriage bar, flexibility was created at the lower skill levels and career paths of male employees were facilitated. This at the same time meant a reduction in the number of employees who were paid above their level of productivity. So by introducing a marriage bar, direct financial gains, as well as indirect gains could be made. The latter included facilitating male employee morale. The National Whitley Council Report, when looking at the arguments for the retention of the bar in the Civil Service, touches on this same aspect when stating:

> Where there is a large amount of routine work to be done, it is a real advantage to employ women who stay only a few years and leave on marriage. The amount of routine work in the Civil Service is so great that the Service cannot provide adequate careers for all the young persons recruited to the lower grades: it is essential, therefore, to have a fairly rapid turnover, and marriage wastage is a highly important factor in this. (National Whitley Council Report, 1946, p.12)

This manner - rarely openly acknowledged - in which the male career has been facilitated in some types of work, provides the basis upon which a number of characteristics of female white collar employment can be explained. I will return to this in chapter 5.

Cohn's account provides a convincing reasoning of the conditions under which the operation of a marriage bar is in the interests of certain employers. And whilst this analysis provides useful aspects needed in any analysis of marriage bars, he then continues to 'explain' general marriage bar patterns. It is here that the argument becomes less coherent. It seems to me that in his effort to explain sectorial variations in the prominence of the marriage bar, Cohn runs into problems because he extends his hypothesis, which is shaped in accordance with evidence on the British Civil Service, rather insensitively to other areas of work. The presence and decline of the marriage bar in teaching, for example, is explained by the changing state of the labour market (1985a, p.114). Interestingly enough, he does not link his hypothesis to the case of teaching. Presumably, if he did, he would have to conclude that since teaching is not a low-skilled profession (where learning curves are not short with early peaks), that there is little economic incentive for engaging in synthetic turnover.

Considering Oram's discussion and Cohn's analysis, it seems likely that the marriage bar in teaching was an economic cost rather than a benefit to employers. Training costs for teachers compared to other types of work were quite substantial and the same for all training teachers, regardless of gender. And Oram comes to the surprising conclusion that, though local authorities claimed that the reason behind the instatement of the marriage bar was 'economic', no local authorities researched this matter thoroughly. In 1935, London County Council established that not much support could be established for these argued economic benefits (Oram, 1983, p.139). This then, may be the reason why, even though Oram argues that the marriage bar in British teaching can not simply be ignored, the bar in teaching was relatively short-lived compared to other middle class types of work.

The work of Cohn and Lewis together may go some way in explaining the time-variation factor in marriage bars in British middle class occupations. The main reason behind the marriage bar in teaching may indeed be 'the anti-feminist backlash' Oram has suggested (1983, p.136). This is equivalent to Lewis' argument on the threat to the ideology of separate spheres. In other middle class types of employment, like white collar work and work in the Civil Service, where internal labour markets were operational, the marriage bar presence may be explained more in terms of Cohn's hypothesis.

Further problems arise in relation to industrial work. Cohn states that because tenure-based payment structures are not common in blue collar work, problems with over-annuation do not occur. Wages are here likely to be piece-rated or set through collective bargaining, and

> Therefore, in manual occupations there is no need to engage in synthetic turnover. (Cohn, 1985a, p.111)

In Britain and the Netherlands, and probably many of the other countries mentioned in the Report by the *International Labour Review* (1962), marriage bars did exist in much blue collar work at various time periods. One might further suggest that employers could realize economic interests through the selection of workers. Tenure-based payment structures may not have been common in industry, but they certainly did exist. In addition, it is a well known feature of industry in the first half of this century that wage variation existed between different types of employees. Often this took the following order; adult men could demand the highest wages, followed by adult and married women. Generally speaking boys earned more than girls. So in principle, firms could save on their wage costs by selection of workers. In addition to the issue of wages, in many industries low-skilled employment features highly. This makes one think that Cohn's conditions work to some extent in some industries.

Cohn, in his analysis, provides us with the conditions under which the operation of a marriage bar is of economic interest to employers. A decisive condition is that there needs to be a normative climate in which discrimination against married women in employment is acceptable. If this is so, the desirability for employers of operating a marriage bar depends on the state of the labour market; when this is slack, employers can be more choosy, than when this is tight. Given these circumstances, one may expect to find marriage bars in firms which have a fair percentage of low-skilled work and which operate internal labour markets.

Trade Unions

Some contributors to the debate on gender relations in employment have emphasized that patriarchal exclusionary practices have often been pursued through trade unions (Walby, 1986, 1989, 1990, Glucksmann, 1990, p.193). The marriage bar in employment is one such patriarchal exclusionary practice. These contributors hence stress the idea that trade unions have, in the past, often pursued aims and strategies which were against the interests of female workers and to the benefit of male workers. Especially in the craft unions, but also in white collar unions, women were either excluded from membership in an attempt to keep them out of industry, or organized with the aim to control their presence in specific sectors of employment and hence prevent them from undercutting male wages.

Though I agree that historically seen, there is enough evidence in support of this, when considering the marriage bar in employment and the reactions which can be found amongst trade unions towards these, one striking factor is that trade union support for and against (and fight for and against) marriage bars in the various occupations which they represented, has been varied. This counts both between unions, over time and within unions.

A number of trade unions were supporters of a marriage bar. The Union of Post Office workers (UPOW), for example, is known to have been a staunch supporter of the marriage bar. It was against the abolition of the bar in the Civil Service, when the matter was discussed at the end of the war. And when the bar was abolished in 1946, it continued to carry one amongst its own employees till 1963 (Boston, 1980, p.252, Lewenhak, 1977, p.265). Equally, in the Netherlands, the *R.K. Tabaksbewerkersbond* (Catholic tobacco workers union) campaigned vigorously to get the bar accepted and implemented in their sector of work, during the 1920s (Kooij & Pley, 1984, p.74).

In addition, a number of trade unions were somewhere in between being actively in favour or against the bar. One can speculate about why this was so. As pointed out above, Glucksmann and Walby have stressed that where trade unions did organize women, this was often done out of the interests of the male workers (as well), since unorganized female employees posed the threat of undercutting male wages. Certainly with respect to the marriage bar it needs to be borne in mind that the exclusion of married women from the union, or campaigning in favour of their exclusion on the side of the union, created this same possibility. So all unions faced this dilemma in their decision taking. Here, the fact that trade unions do not constitute one coherent body of thought, but are themselves institutions in which dominant interests are constituted through the weighing up of the interests of the various agents involved, is clear. And as trade unions organized women employees, there was also a need to address the interests of their female members, or to give the impression that these were taken into account. It is not surprising to find, therefore, that trade unions often did not seem to either be coherently in favour, or against the bar.

There are a number of cases, then, of trade unions in which the executive was officially against the marriage bar, whilst many members were in favour of it. This was the case in the Bank Officer's Guild (BOG), which was officially against the bar. During World War II, when BOG served the interests of bank employees in England and Wales, the issue of the marriage bar was actively discussed (as is clear from their journal: *The Bank Officer* in 1941. See chapter 5). Even so, the stance of the union leadership was challenged on various occasions by voices of dissent within the union in support of the bar. Interestingly, these voices were not just those of men. The same occurred in the Civil Service Clerical Association (CSCA). Here, whilst the leadership of the union was officially against the bar, there was still support for it amongst its members (Boston, 1980, p.253).

Certainly, where opinion within a union differed on the topic of the marriage bar, the leadership had to tread carefully. So even when the official stance of a union was against the bar, this does not mean that the union also actively fought against it. This, it may be argued, was the case for the National Union of Teachers, when the bar was introduced on married female teachers in the early 1920s (Oram, 1983, p.143). Oram is clear about the conflicting interests within this union. This also counts for the *Bond 'Mercurius'* (which covered Dutch white collar employees, including banking) in the post World War II years. The bar was included in the banking *CAO* until the 1960s and the union may either be accused of merely paying lip service to its stance (which according to their journal *Mercurius* of 1939 had been an opposition to the bar), or in being ineffective in their attempts to get the bar rescinded in Dutch banking. I suspect the latter was the case.

One of the rare examples, where a trade union did fight against the marriage bar in its sector of work, concerned the National Union of Women Teachers. Not surprisingly, according to Oram, this self-confessed feminist union contained active members, who were willing to go further in their objectives (Oram, 1983, p.145). There are other examples, too, where separate women sections were set up by women employed in a sector of employment, often out of discontent with the 'male-dominated' trade union in looking after their interests (Walby, 1986, p.152). This does not mean that all women were against the marriage bar in employment. Support for it was often present amongst unmarried women in certain sectors of work. Lewenhak provides examples of this from the 1850s, when working class women supported the payment by employers of a family wage (1977, p.51). And also later on, during the 20th century, when the presence of married women in, for example, white collar work, was regarded as defeating unmarried women's claim for equal pay (Lewenhak, 1977, p.225).

In explaining why trade unions were for or against marriage bars, one is confronted with issues of competition and membership interests. And just as was the case with employers, trade unions and their members often resorted, in order to support their arguments for the bar, to patriarchal ideologies around the family and women's proper role in life. Similarly, it is easy to see how, when unemployment was on the increase, unions laid more stress on these ideologies, in an effort to influence the outcome of 'who gets the jobs which are left' or 'who should be the first to leave'. Examples about this include the debates in the CSCA during the 1950s, and the numerous examples from the 1930s.[12]

But how effective were those unions which favoured the bar? Some examples of trade unions not getting their way have already been brought forward. In the light of this it is important to point out that the power unions have been able to wield has historically varied over time and between unions. The latter is a matter not often directly considered by those who have commented on patriarchal attitudes within trade unions, particularly where it concerns the marriage bar. In chapter 5 this matter will be pursued in relation to the marriage bar in banking employment.

The state, pillarization and marriage bars

Let us now turn to cross-national differences in marriage bar patterns. Cohn's marriage bar analysis works well for the British Civil Service, on which the explanatory model was based. However, given the cross-national variations found in the time-period of its existence and its implementation, his analysis must be acknowledged as culturally specific, and further investigation is necessary. Moreover, if it is true that marriage bars were more common in working class types of work in the Netherlands than in Britain, how can this be accounted for?

The relation between the presence of marriage bars and the state has been at the forefront of discussions on marriage bars in the Netherlands. This is not surprising, since the Dutch state, mainly through confessional influences, appears to have played a leading role in the institution of marriage bars. Here, I will look at state activity and policies with respect to married women's employment more closely. State activity and policies will here be seen as the result of a process; as the outcome of struggles between the different interest groups involved at the level of the state (following e.g. Walby, 1990, p.95). This necessarily requires an outlining of the interest groups involved in the state, their concerns, and the relative strengths of these groups in pursuing their interests.

With respect to the British state, this exercise shall be attempted in chapter 4, whilst the discussion here will be limited to the state and marriage bars. As Walby has pointed out, the state and its policies have on many occasions worked against the interests of women workers. Significantly, during the inter-war period, unemployment policies increasingly discriminated against married women seeking financial support after dismissal (Walby, 1986, pp.172-173). But there was no effort on a national level to limit married women's employment. This is supported by the report on *Women in Industry* (1930: Cmd. 3508). Here, the effects of restrictions on women's employment in industry as stipulated by the Factory Acts are discussed, but no mention is made of a marriage bar (or of discussions to impose such a bar as part of state policy). So although state policy during the 1930s implied that the costs of married women's unemployment were to be borne by themselves or their families (hence reinforcing the idea that married women were dependents), no efforts were made to keep them or take them out of the sphere of employment.

In contrast, in the Netherlands, the inter-war period may be regarded as the pre-eminent period in which efforts to curtail women's employment were made on a national level. Married women were often implicated in these efforts, but during the 1930s, various attempts to limit the employment of unmarried women were also made. In order to explain which interest groups were active at the level of the state, reference needs to be made to the socially specific formation, during the beginning of the 20th century, of a *verzuild* (pillarized) society in the Netherlands (see also chapter 1). With the emancipation of the Catholic section of the population in this period, the Catholics as well as the Christian and Socialist sections of the population took on politically and culturally distinct identities. These pervaded all aspects of life, so that e.g. the Catholic pillar consisted in Catholic political parties, Catholic schools, Catholic trade unions and employers' federations and a number of other specifically Catholic groups and organizations. This implies that the political parties which were active at the level of the state held the views and ideological beliefs of the specific pillars. So there was a Catholic political party and a Christian party, as well as a liberal and socialist party. During the 1930s, the confessionals were in government, and their 'solutions' to the main social problems of the day, such as unemployment, were put into practice.

One recurring answer to the question, why so many efforts to curtail women's employment were made during the inter-war years, has been that the confessionals argued that limiting women's employment was the means to solve the country's rising unemployment (Kooij & Pley, 1984, de Bruijn, 1989, Schoot-Uiterkamp, 1978). The details of these attempts were already discussed to some extent. In first instance during the 1920s and early 1930s, efforts to limit women's employment affected married female state employees only; i.e. teachers and Civil Servants. But the official marriage bar on state employees was not implemented strictly at first. This only happened when unemployment started to rise at the beginning of the 1930s. Then leading politicians in the state, in their self-confessed efforts to deal with unemployment, decided to put their own stance on dual income families; that these were undesirable in a society in which there existed high unemployment, into practice amongst its own staff first. As such, the state set an example to other Dutch employers. As unemployment rose in the early 1930s, the marriage bar on state employees first became more severely implemented. Thereafter, not just married women's employment in state employment became implicated in political debates, but a general employment ban on married women was sought, and also unmarried women became the target for employment curtailment efforts through the state. Though these policy proposals were never passed, it is impossible to see these efforts as unrelated to the power groups which held government at this time. Without exception, the 1930s proposals were made by confessionals in government. The differences in the presence and enforcement of the marriage bar in state employment in Britain and the Netherlands, can not be understood without reference to the influence of the state in this. The British state interfered little in the employment decisions made by employers, whilst the Dutch state did.

But that is not all. The preceding suggests that Dutch female Civil Servants and teachers were, in practice, mostly affected by national legislation. But the debates at the end of the 1930s also indicate that confessional ideology did not distinguish between middle class and working class types of work; working married women in general were targeted. Dutch pillarized reality further entails that the presence and influence of confessionals on a local level is important. In industry, confessionals had an influence at a local level in those regions where they were prominent. There are numerous examples of this in relation to married women's industrial work (Kooij & Pley discuss the Dutch tobacco industry in the inter-war years. See Martens (1994, cht. 4) for discussion).

Marriage bars and women's economic activity

We have now arrived at the stage in the discussion where we can return to one main objective; that it, to speculate on the relationship between the presence of marriage bars and women's relative economic activity. It was pointed out that there already exist some conflicting views on this matter. On the one hand, there are those who argue that there is a strong link between the presence of the bar in employment and the absence of married women from those types of employment, like Cohn (1985) and Walby (1986, 1989). Cohn's analysis, for instance, takes it very much for granted that marriage bars were implemented by employers interested in putting a limit to the tenure of a certain group of employees; i.e. that of marrying women. On the other hand are those who argue that this link is not so strong (Schoot-Uiterkamp, 1978, Bakker, 1982, Braybon, 1981, Lewis, 1984, Glucksmann, 1990). Some of the marriage bar evidence discussed here does not sit easily with the first assumption.

In the discussion below, I shall limit myself to a review of a Dutch study of the 1930s, which is well-known amongst Dutch scholars. I have chosen for this study in particular, because I stated in the introduction that Dutch contributors have tended to argue for the limited influence of marriage bars on recorded employment rates, and this study shows that the reason for this is both historical and political. This will furthermore highlight the role of some interest groups which have so far been left out of the discussion; namely feminists, the family and husbands.

So far, reasons which work in favour of marriage bars have been discussed. But marriage bars were certainly not always implemented with the consent of those affected or interested. Some examples of women opposing marriage bars have already been mentioned. Now that we are familiar with the main cross-national variations in the occurrence of the bar in the two societies discussed, it is also possible to understand cross-national variations in the nature of resistance against the bar in the two societies. Apart from individual opposition to the bar, which has, for instance, been voiced by women through oral historical accounts (Glucksmann, 1990), evidence of British women fighting against marriage bars can be found at the level of specific occupations and industries. A good example of this is the National Union of Women Teachers vigorously opposing the bar on teachers in the inter-war period. In contrast to the Netherlands, however, no national campaign against the bar existed in Britain. The Netherlands knew a committee of Dutch feminists; the *Comité tot Verdediging van de Vrijheid van Arbeid voor de Vrouw* (Committee for the Defence of the Freedom for Women to Work),[13] which campaigned against the marriage bar at a national political level.

Some of the research criticizing the 1930s attempts at curtailing women's employment originated from this committee. Schoot-Uiterkamp remarks in her article that the debate around married women's employment during the 1930s was accompanied (as is often the case) by a use of available statistics on women's employment. Following these figures over the early decades of the 20th Century, the conclusion drawn by protagonists of the marriage bar was that women's employment had undergone a tremendous expansion at the expense of men's employment.[14] Despite the government's efforts, married women's employment had also increased, and the protagonists called for more severe legislation to curtail this trend in times of unemployment.

The challenge to this interpretation of the Census figures came from the feminist economist Posthumus-van der Groot. She argued that this so-called increase in women's employment (and the slower increase in men's employment) was not caused by a rise in married women's work, but was instead attributable to a number of factors which were related to changed Census techniques and population changes. To adjust for these influences she argued that one should look instead at the female/male ratio amongst the labouring population; i.e. investigate how many men, women and married women worked on average amongst every 100 people employed. The conclusion she came to was that in the Netherlands, a very small percentage of the work force, that is 2 per cent, consisted of married women.

In addition, she provided a cross-national perspective on women's economic activity. Dutch married women's employment, it turned out, was well below that in its surrounding countries. Following the figures calculated by Posthumus-van der Groot, at a level 2.2 out of every 100 people in paid work, Dutch married women worked less than their counterparts in other countries. In Britain, 5.5 married women could be found amongst 100 persons employed, whilst in France and Belgium, at 13.4 per cent and 10.1 per cent respectively, the difference was even stronger (Schoot-Uiterkamp, 1978, p.189). How, this lobby wondered, did the government expect to tackle male unemployment by the curtailment of married women's employment, given that so few married Dutch women were engaged in remunerated work outside the home?

This issue has been taken up by de Bruijn (1989) and Plantenga (1993). The former concludes that married women and the marriage bar in employment were used as a scapegoat in the government's anti-unemployment policies (de Bruijn, 1989, p.116). As unemployment increased, the public contention against married women's employment increased, and the attack on married women was an easy means by which the government could appear to be tackling unemployment. In the meantime, of course, no real solutions were found to stem the lengthy period of severe unemployment, which was caused to a large degree - as argued by de Bruijn (1989), Brand (1937) and others - by the extensive mechanization which took place during these years in Dutch industry. The case of Philips was a telling example of this phenomenon. Its work force more than doubled in the latter half of the 1920s, only to decline again by 50 per cent in the early 1930s (Brand, 1937, p.37).

Publications, like that of Posthumus-van der Groot, were intended to highlight the inadequacy of the unemployment policies of the Dutch confessionals, and defend the right of married women to work. The political stance of Dutch feminists has therefore historically been one which states that marriage bars were not needed, because Dutch married women left employment out of their own accord. They were even considered harmful, because they prevented those women who needed to work from gaining an income. A similar line of argument may be found in British accounts, to which I will now turn.

The tip of an ideological iceberg

Braybon has asserted that the imposition of an *official* marriage bar in the post World War I period was hardly needed given that 'such social pressure was brought to bear in wives by husbands, relatives and employers at once' (Braybon, 1981, p.218). Though Braybon is not explicit about what she means by an *official* marriage bar, she does indicate a point which is emphasized by others as well (Glucksmann, 1990, p.224). This is that many women chose to leave employment when they married. Some did this because of their own convictions, some left employment through pressure from family or husband.

One of Glucksmann's interviewees left employment when she married in 1939 because of her husband since:

> The men didn't like their wives working in those days. The attitude was if you were a man, you should be a man enough to keep your family. (Glucksmann, 1990, p.32)

On the other hand, social pressure might also come from family. Taylor sights the example of a mother who refused to look after her daughter's child so that she could go out to work, on the grounds that she thought that married women should not work (Taylor, 1977, p.55).

So amongst many British as well as Dutch people, there existed an ideological resistance towards the employment of married women. One could argue that these are examples of a marriage bar operating in an implicit, informal or unofficial manner at the level of the family and the individual. Two things are of major importance in this discussion. The first is that the ratio of marrying women who left their employment when they married (more or less out of their own accord) must not be underestimated. The second one is that the line between an implicit marriage bar and the absence of a marriage bar in an ideological environment which opposes married women's employment, is thin indeed.

In the end, it seems to me that the exodus of so many young women from the British and Dutch work forces upon marriage (even if there was no formal marriage bar stipulating that they had to leave), and the existence of formal marriage bars, were part and parcel of the same dominant ideological thinking about women's employment. Marriage bars were the visible tips - where they were explicit - of the ideological iceberg which surrounded married women's employment. And though the interests in having such bars may have varied, to include the more economist concerns of employers, the existence of such bars was nevertheless dependent on this ideology.

Conclusion

In conclusion, we may note that it is hard to indicate a direct correlation between the introduction of marriage bars and changes in the relative significance of married women's employment. However, two points may be added to this. Firstly, we may say with some certainty that there exists a correlation between the more intense presence of marriage bars in Dutch employment (when this is compared to Britain) and the lower employment participation of married women on an aggregate level. Secondly, the co-occurrence of longer lasting marriage bars and the later increase in married women's registered employment in the Netherlands on the one hand, and the earlier increase in married women's employment in Britain together with the earlier decline of marriage bars on the other hand, can hardly be considered a coincidence.

This chapter has furthermore provided us with the empirical evidence from which we can start to construct a picture of the particular cultural formations which have characterized the two societies studied here. This theme will be elaborated on in the next chapters.

Notes

1   I am here concerned with marriage bars which applied to women. In the history of employment, marriage bars have also affected men. One example is banking employment. Prior to World War II there was a ruling in some British and Dutch banks that young male employees were not allowed to marry before they had reached a certain age (see chapter 5). The form and implication of this type of marriage bar is obviously different from the bars that are discussed in this chapter.

2   Compare with Plantenga, 1993, p.52.

3   In 1946, British Civil Service employment included employment in the various Ministries and the Home Office, but also employment in the Inland Revenue, the Board of Trade, the Post Office and various national museums, galleries and libraries (National Whitley Council Report, 1946, p.8).

4   Posthumus-van der Groot et al. (1977, p.193). They point out that this decision was made through a so-called *Koninklijk Besluit (K.B.* or Royal Decision). Royal Decisions were argued to be particularly difficult to fight against since, unlike normal law proposals, they were not debated in parliament. They could therefore not be fought against before implementation, but only afterwards.

5   These do not include all forms of primary education and the percentages are calculated from figures provided by Bakker (1982, p.110).

6   Amongst these are: Bakker, 1984, Bakker-van der Kooij, 1981 and Morée, 1982.

7   See for instance Hunt (1988, p.5), Lewenhak (1980, p.5) and (1977, p.51).

8   Evidence of this debate in Britain and the Netherlands is discussed in the undated (approx. 1938) publication *De Beroepsarbeid van de Gehuwde Vrouw* written by the Dutch female politician Gesina van der Molen. See pp.20-27.

9   Dutch liberals, socialists and feminists opposed the views of Dutch

confessionals in relation to the marriage bar. The views of Dutch feminists have been documented in publication by the *Nationaal Bureau voor Vrouwenarbeid* (the National Bureau for Women's Work) which had been set up after the national exhibition in 1898 on women's work. The *Nationaal Bureau voor Vrouwenarbeid* was very aware of class differences in relation to employment. In an early study done by the *Bureau* in 1901, the extent of hidden home work amongst poor working class women is recorded. Whereas the Dutch Census of 1899 indicates that only 9.5 per cent of all married women (including divorced and widowed women) were economically active, the Bureau found that of the 200 poor families they investigated, 50 per cent of the married women contributed the whole year round to the family income by doing hidden homework. It was for this reason that the *Bureau* advised against the further limitation of married women's work.

10 A quote by Brand illustrates this well

'Toen mijn vader omstreeks 1895 een filiaal begon in C, was het eerste (!) bezoek aan den pastoor. Wie bende gij? was de pastoor zijn vraag. En toen het onderzoek gunstig uitviel, was het beschad "als ge het vrouwvolk buiten de fabriek houdt, dan kunde gij op mijn medewerking rekenen".' (Brand, 1937, pp.62-3) ('When my father started a business in C around 1895, the first visit was to the priest. Who are you? the priest asked. And when the enquiry turned out positive, the priest said "if you keep the womenfolk out of the factory, you have my blessing".') This was also quoted in de Bruijn (1989, p.101).

11 The Netherlands had taken on 'neutrality' during the First World War. During this time, Dutch industry was booming, because closed borders meant a monopoly market.

12 See Martens (1994, cht. 4) for an illustration of the way in which rising unemployment and patriarchal ideology interrelate together in bringing about a marriage bar in the organized section of the Dutch tobacco industry during the 1930s.

13 This committee became later known as the Committee 'with-the-long-name'. It was set up in 1935 with the aim to fight against the various proposals which were formulated just then to curtail women's employment further than was already the case. And after the war it continued its fight to get the bar abolished amongst state employees (see chapter 4).

14 Between 1920 and 1930, there had been a 21.5 per cent increase in the number of women employed 'outside the home', whilst the increase for men had been 15.7 per cent. In addition, the Census figures showed a

small increase in the 'outside the home' employment of married women, from 7.53 per cent to 7.93 per cent in this period (Schoot-Uiterkamp, 1978, p.185).

4 Ideological exclusion and labour market tightness

In this chapter the socio-economic and the ideological-cultural context of the period 1940-1965 will be related to the different cross-national developments around women's recorded economic activity. Within this period, the war years will be considered in their own right, as distinct from the period between 1945 and 1965. This was a conscious decision rolling forth from the discussion in chapter 2. Rather than ignoring these years, as some Dutch contributors have done (de Bruijn, 1989, Plantenga, 1993), I intend to present evidence on which an informed evaluation may be made with respect to the significance of this period for the main issues under investigation. Starting with the comparative socio-economic conditions, there are strong indications that the British labour market was under more stress than the Dutch labour market between 1940 and 1945. The question asked here is whether this had a long-term impact on dominant cultural values around women's role in society, and thoughts about remunerated work in particular?

These issues lead us into the post-war years, where the socio-economic conditions of the time are investigated. Again there is evidence of diversity in the tightness of the labour market and I shall explore the evidence and reasons for that. The socio-economic context shall further be related to what was occurring on an ideological-cultural level. The timing and character of ideological shifts will be discussed, and cross-national variations will be highlighted.

War-time upheavals

The Second World War can be viewed as an occurrence with the potential to radically upset, and change in the long-run, existing social relations; whether they are production relations (involving employers, employees and the state) or whether they are gender relations (involving relations both in the household, in employment or elsewhere). In order to examine the link between war experiences and changes in the character and extent of female labour force activity, it is first of all necessary to examine in what way social relations in the two countries were affected.

From the discussion in chapter 2 it is possible to speculate which social relations were challenged in the two countries. In Britain, the stress of the war was strongly felt in the production apparatus of the country, the corollary of which was that prevailing gender relations in the employment sphere and in the household came under stress. In the Netherlands, war-time experience put stress on Dutch society in a different way. Being occupied meant that the production possibilities of the country were of little use. The stress of the war lay more in surviving whilst the country was occupied, and working towards a release from occupation. So in first instance there is reason to suggest that the different war experiences in the two societies are likely to have had a different effect on subsequent changes in the gender composition of employment. In Britain, the war had a direct and significant effect on labour distribution, resulting in the much commented on *shock increase* in British women's employment participation; an increase which was presumably absent in the Netherlands. In this section I will start by elaborating on the short-term impact of the war, and discuss 'facts' and figures on women's remunerated work where these are available.

The dispute about the gender implications of World War II centres around the issue whether the short-term impact of the war had long-term consequences. An investigation of the long-term consequences is therefore important in establishing whether the actual *shock increase* in British women's economic activity, and the absence of such a shock in the Netherlands, is related to a sustained higher level of activity after the war. I suggest here that an important indication of lasting change forms the question whether significant changes in attitudes towards women's employment were brought about during the actual war years. This enquiry, then, involves us in examining how the expansion in British women's employment was brought about. Did it involve a change in the prevailing pre-war perceptions of women's role in society? If so, was there radical change or reluctant change and how can these changes be recognized in terms of real changes in employment patterns, such as the use of part-time work and/or a change in the attitude towards the employment of married women, or women with children? Similarly, though the Second World War may not have been the cause of an expansion in the employment of Dutch women, is there evidence that the war caused a change in gender values, which in turn may have had a long-term impact on subsequent changes in the labour market?

Labour consequences of the war effort. British Census figures reveal that from 1931 to 1951, there was a one percentage point increase in the female ratio of the labour force; this rate increased from 29.7 per cent to 30.8 per cent. What happened between 1931 and 1951 with this rate is interesting indeed, but no Census material is available for this period. Nevertheless, an interesting and comprehensive analysis of changing trends in the gender composition of the British work force over the period between 1931 and 1951 can be found in the work of Leser (1952), who uses Ministry of Labour statistics,[1] and which come in a three-fold periodization; 1923-1939, 1939-1948 and 1948-1950.[2] Leser indicates that the greatest change in the gender composition of the United Kingdom work force occurred in the second period; that between 1939 and 1948. The expansion in women's employment reached its peak at the height of the war in 1943. An estimated 22,285,000 people were recorded as being in paid employment in that year, as opposed to an estimated 19,750,000 in 1939. For women, the increase was estimated to be over 1 million; a change from 6,265,000 in 1939 to 7,500,000 in 1943 (Summerfield, 1984, p.29). This means that the female ratio of the British work force increased from 31.7 per cent in 1939 to 33.7 per cent in 1943.

The expansion in women's employment was not the same over all sectors of work. It was especially large in those industries where before the war the ratio of women had been particularly low, like the heavy engineering (shipbuilding, vehicle building and government ordnance factories), chemical and metal industries, and public services industries (Summerfield, 1984, p.29 and Leser, 1952, p.331). In those industries, where traditionally many women had been employed, there was a general decline in the number of workers, mainly because these industries were not considered 'essential' to the war effort. Another area where a considerable number of women were drawn into work was national and local government. Marwick points to the substantial increase in civil service staff during the war, which nearly doubled between 1939 and 1944 (Marwick, 1968, p.292). By October 1944, 48 per cent of civil service employees were women.

As expected, though the first war years saw a significant increase in the female ratio of the work force, the late war years and direct post-war years were characterized by a decline. Leser indicates that the employment disruption stabilized around 1948. What remained in that year of the *shock increase* in women's employment participation? The first point to be made is that there was a net increase in the female proportion of the work force (Summerfield, 1984, p.187, Walby, 1986, p.188, and Leser, 1952, p.327). Four further significant long-term implications may be indicated. The first refers to the expansion in national and local government employment, which did not decline after the war (partly as a result of an expansion of the 'new' welfare state). Though the ratio of women amongst national and local government staff had declined in the inter-war period, the war and post-war period saw a lasting increase in female employees in this sector. By 1948, 37.5 per cent of national and local government employment consisted of women (this had been 17.4 per cent in 1939) (Leser, 1952, p.331).

The second long-term change concerns the continuing decline in those industries where women had traditionally been well represented. The continuing decline in the clothing, textiles and some other 'older' industries meant a decline in the opportunities for women to find employment in this sector. Overall, this would have entailed a decline in the number of women employed, if it was not that increasing opportunities in heavy industries and in services more than counteracted that trend (Leser, p.332). Leser estimates that if the gender ratio in each industrial grouping had remained the same over the war, the decline in traditional industries would have entailed a total decline of 400 thousand jobs for women. Instead there was a 350 thousand increase which is attributable more or less entirely to women's increased presence in service sector work (Leser, 1952, p.335, Bradley, 1989, p.47).

Apart from changes in the structure of employment which affected the work opportunities of women, there were also changes in the patterns of women's employment. A third lasting aspect of the *shock increase* in British women's economic activity during the war concerns the employment of married women. Between 1931 and 1951, the ratio of employed married women increased from 1 to 2 in every 10 married women. To what extend this change may be attributed to the actual war years is difficult to establish. An alternative set of figures, which express the ratio of married working women on all working women (and therefore has the implication of measuring changes in marriage rates amongst women as well),[3] states that in 1943, married women constituted 43 per cent of working women, as opposed to 16 per cent in 1931 and 43 per cent in 1951. A third of the married working women in 1943 had (a) child(ren) under the age of 14 (Summerfield, 1984, p.62, and 1988, p.100).

Part-time working was another working pattern which took on great proportions during the war, and which continued in significance after the war. By 1944, there were a total of 900 thousand part-timers in the British work force, of which presumably the majority were women. After the war, part-time employment did not decline, but increased as an employment arrangement in which mainly older married women were occupied. Summerfield indicates that in 1947, an estimated quarter of the female employed population worked on a part-time basis. That the popularity of part-time employment continued in the post-war period is evident in the fact that by 1965, part-time employment was more common amongst married women than full-time employment (Summerfield, 1988, p.105).

Indications of ideological change. During the first war years, pre-war gender values hampered the participation of married women - with or without children - in war production. Conscription was directed foremost to single women of a particular age-group. Older women, married women, and women with children remained exempt. But by 1943, when the labour supply situation became more pressing, decisions had to be taken about which other women could be called upon. During 1941, when women had first been called upon to volunteer their services, the government had been criticized for not having thought about the practicalities involved. The consequence of this was a complete lack of any provision to facilitate married women and women with children to volunteer their services. From 1943 onwards, certain measures were taken to facilitate the employment of those groups of women, but the nature of these measures, and the timing and extent of their introduction suggest that:

> The government's intentions were to obtain as many women workers as possible without upsetting the conventional patterns of domestic work and childrearing, in other words without disturbing the traditional division of labour in the home. (Summerfield, 1988, p.102)

By 1943, for example, housewives were drawn into war employment by the establishment of part-time work arrangements which were actively encouraged by the government. The idea to organize hours of work to suit the employee must have been rather alien to most British employers. The evidence suggests that where this became a matter of urgency, employers' attitudes did change. Maybe the use of part-time work arrangements during the war facilitated its post-war usage. I would argue, though, that the continued use of part-time employees after the war was also dependent on post-war conditions in the economy, and I will come back to this below. Though it must be emphasized that women themselves had called for part-time work arrangements in 1941, active encouragement of this work pattern must be seen as an important 'indicator of the government's commitment to mobilizing women without upsetting conventional home life ...' (Summerfield, 1988, p.104). The same counts for efforts to communalize time-consuming domestic work; like shopping, laundering, childcare and cooking. By September 1944, 71,806 nursery places existed, though at the height of the war in 1943, only 25 per cent of the under-five year old children of women workers were looked after in nurseries. The government did induce local authorities to provide cheap meals in so-called British Restaurants, whilst large employers were required to provide canteens for their staff. Laundering was changed to an 'essential' service, in order to provide a service to the working population. But overall, according to Summerfield (1988, p.106), none of these efforts constituted a comprehensive substitution for the work women privately did in the home.

What about women's own attitudes towards waged work? Summerfield argues that women's attitudes towards employment had changed, though some women intended to continue work after the war, whereas others did not.[4] Young women in particular had no intention of continuing employment after the war on the basis that they wanted 'to get married', or because 'they had enough to do at home' anyway (Summerfield, 1988, p.108). In contrast, amongst married women in the age-group of over 35s there existed a strong preference in favour of continued employment after the war. In a way this contrasting attitude is not surprising. The attraction for young women, of a home and husband to devote all one's time to had not been changed or challenged by the event of the war. The same, however, can not be said of older married women and married women with children. For many of them war-time employment would have presented a new and acceptable opportunity to earn an income - presumably better than that earned when doing 'hidden' homework (Lewis, 1986, Taylor, 1977 and Wilson, 1980, p.42) - which was achievable in combination with household responsibilities.

And what happened to marriage bars during the war? Marwick and Walby have both argued that the decline of marriage bars in employment was a consequence of war-time changes. Marwick (1968, 1974) explains the long term increased employment opportunities of married women mainly by reference to the changed attitude of employers. Walby ties this in with the marriage bar, by arguing that 'the dropping of the marriage bar during the war was the single most important effect of the war on gender relations' (Walby, 1986, pp.147-8), effectively causing the 'permanent restructuring of women's access to paid employment' (Walby, 1986, p.188).

As has already been indicated in the preceding chapter, there is some contention as to the empirical accuracy of the statement that the marriage bar was dropped in Britain during the war. Indeed the bar was officially, but temporarily, suspended in many industries as well as in the 'better' jobs; like teaching, the Civil Service, and in banking employment (see chapter 5). Only in teaching, where the bar was in first instance suspended, was the bar abolished during war years (i.e. 1944). Abolitions of the bar in other sectors of work took place, strictly speaking, in the post-war years.

And opinions amongst British employers had not changed uniformly in favour of married women's employment. As the results of the employer survey reported in the National Whitley Council Report (1946) on the bar in the Civil Service suggest, these opinions were instead rather divided after the war. Of the five large industrial employers (who had not employed married women before the war), three intended to return to their pre-war practice of operating a marriage bar; one had not yet decided and one was going to abolish it altogether. Of the six county councils (which had all carried a marriage bar,

80

with few exceptions, prior to the war) involved in this small survey, two expressed the likelihood of going back to their pre-war policy stance; three had not yet decided, whilst only the London County Council was positive in abolishing it. So the experience of employing married women during the war by many firms, was not decisive in changing their pre-war views. More importantly, the great deal of wavering amongst employers in the Report suggest decisions could swing either way and depended no doubt to a considerable degree on post-war labour market conditions.

Ultimately, the abolition of the bar in the Civil Service in 1946 indicates that the new Labour government intended to influence the swing in private industry in favour of married women's employment. Given that they urged 'industry to retain married women in employment, it would seem inconsistent that they should announce new rules reaffirming the marriage bar ...' in state employment.[5] The abolition of the marriage bar in the Civil Service seems more related to post-war government policy, than to war-time emergency.

The evidence on the marriage bar suggests two things. Firstly, though the war did see an increased employment of married women, which was accompanied by an often temporary abolition of the marriage bar, the war can not conclusively be regarded as the period in which such bars were dropped. Secondly, more marriage bars seem to have been dropped in the post-war period than in the actual war years. Though this may be regarded as a long-term consequence of the war-time experience of employing married women, I would say that the actual conditions in the labour market in the post-war period were of equal, if not more, importance to the decline of such bars in employment.

The Dutch war-time economy

When the war started in 1939, the Netherlands still suffered from extensive unemployment. The 1930s depression entailed for the Netherlands a lengthy period in which unemployment was high. Table 4.1 shows that it had started to increase by 1930, only to reach a height in 1936 when 349,600 men and 18,800 women were registered as unemployed. By 1939, unemployment had dropped, but 223,700 men and 11,900 women were still out of work. In contrast, unemployment in Britain had reached a height in 1933 (1931 for women); when approximately 23 per cent of the insured work force was out of work. And although unemployment had not dropped to below 1930s levels, it had gone down significantly by the start of the war (Annual Abstract of statistics, 80, pp.134-5), only to rise again amongst women in the first years of the war due to the decline in 'non-essential' industries.

Occupation, the Arbeidseinsatz, and women's remunerated work. In this
context, Dutch mobilization started in September 1939, but was short-lived.
By May 1940, the Netherlands was occupied by the German army, and the
Dutch army was disbanded. Dutch soldiers went back to the positions in the
Dutch work force which they had left before the war (if they had been in
employment). As the war continued, the German occupiers attempted to make
use of the Dutch work force and some of its production possibilities. At least
some Dutch industries were kept busy during the war. Instances include the
shipbuilding industry in Rotterdam; the Dutch weapons industry and the
clothing industries in Dutch cities (Posthumus-van der Groot, 1977, p.313).
Other sectors of work experienced a gradual decline as the war continued. This
was the case in Dutch banks (see next chapter).

Less is known about the extent and characteristics of Dutch women's
employment than is the case for Britain. No employment figures are available
at all for the war years.[6] There is only an indication as to the number of married
women who were employed, since these required an employment permit
(*arbeidskaart*). It may be that Wiener & Verwey-Jonker have used this
information in their argument that there may have been a decline in the number
of employed women in the Netherlands, since over the years of the war, there
was a slight decline in the number of employment permits which were handed
out to married women. In 1939, this was 13,707 whilst in 1943, 10,958 were
handed out. How reliable these figures are as an indication of married women's

Table 4.1
Registered unemployment in the Netherlands (x 1000)

Year	Men	Women
1930	69,1	4,5
1932	260,0	10,6
1934	269,3	10,6
1936	349,6	18,8
1938	288,3	15,1
1939	223,7	11,9
1940-1946	no figures available	no figures available
1947	28,7	3,1
1948	26,0	3,9
1950	53,8	5,0

Source: CBS (1970), Zeventig Jaren Statistiek in Tijdreeksen: 1899-1969,
Den Haag: Staatsdrukkerij (also reproduced in Blok, 1989, p.135).

employment is another matter, but if this evidence is taken as given, there was no breakthrough in the employment of married women in the Netherlands during the war. There certainly does not exist any information which suggests that the employment of married women (with children) was facilitated, and this should not come as a surprise. The only indication that women took on 'men's work' during the war is given by de Bruijn, who mentions that women were tram drivers in Amsterdam (de Bruijn, 1989, p.174). This one example does not support the idea that the employment of women in 'men's work' was widespread. Equally, though household tasks became more laborious and difficult to perform, there are no indications that there was a breakthrough in the sexual division of labour in household work (Blok, 1989, p.33).

The *Arbeidseinsatz*; the demand for Dutch workers to take up work in the German war effort, started soon after the occupation. In the light of the aims of researching the Second World War period, it is both interesting and necessary to investigate the *Arbeidseinsatz* further. How extensive was it? Did it include women and well as men, and if so, what kind of women were called up? In short, are British conscription and the *Einsatz* comparable?

Dutch men were the first to be called up for the *Einsatz*. According to my interviewees, the *Arbeidseinsatz* entailed that every Dutch business was required to supply a percentage of its male work force for this purpose. The result of the call up for men was that gaps formed in the work forces of firms and other establishments, the corollary of which was that the Dutch Civil Service suspended its marriage bar on female employees in June 1942. As in Britain, these women were offered temporary contracts so that they could be sacked again easily when the men came back from Germany.

The call-up of Dutch women came after that of men. Fascist gender ideology endorsed domesticity for women (Blok, 1989, Graaff & Marcus, 1980, Couvee & Boswijk, 1962, Plantenga, 1993) in the same manner as was evident in Britain. Consequently, one important similarity in the call-up of Dutch women and the conscription of British women was that different groups were targeted. The first plans for the conscription of Dutch women for employment in Germany were only made in 1942, but with the exception of women in the Dutch border region, these never materialized. In the meantime, certain groups of women; like young women students, were targeted for work in German munitions factories (Blok, 1989, p.7). On 15 July 1943, compulsory conscription was introduced, but again only for certain groups of women. These included 16-21 year old women (married or not), who were to be put to work in 'vital' war industries, though only on the basis that they should be able to commute between home and work without being away for more than 12 hours. Women of 21 and above (only unmarried), could be put to work anywhere, whilst married women with young children who were not already engaged in employment, were exempt (Posthumus-van der Groot, 1977, p.313, Blok, 1989, p.37).

The major difference between British conscription and the German call-up of Dutch citizens was, of course, that the latter mostly resisted co-operation. Wiener & Verwey-Jonker have pointed to the contradiction which taking a man's place in employment meant for women. Whilst in Britain, employment substitution was seen in a positive light, the reverse was the case in the Netherlands. Here it was felt to be 'treason' to the country's plight (1952, p.17) and the possible emancipatory effects this work entailed was not relevant. It would appear that the call-up of Dutch people was not very efficient, but no figures are available to indicate how many people were involved.

Women in the Dutch resistance movement. Apart from taking up work in Germany, Dutch women have also worked in the resistance movement, though this did not constitute remunerated work. Again, a number of questions may be asked. What resistance work did Dutch women do and what was the extent of it? Did this involve a challenge to pre-war gender relations? And was women's involvement in the Dutch resistance of lasting significance to their position in society in general, and their position in the Dutch labour market in specific?

Let us consider the evidence before us. What did resistance work entail and what tasks were performed by Dutch women? The first point to be made here is that, as was the case in Britain (Smith, 1988), Dutch women were involved in caring for people who had been displaced by the war; a task which did not divert them much from their usual household responsibilities. More so than in Britain though, caring for people in hiding involved risk, since people who were absconding from the *Arbeidseinsatz*, Jews or surviving pilots, were all sought by the Germans. Later on in the war, 'safe houses' also functioned as safe-havens for resistance workers who needed to hide for a while. These houses were often run by older women; called 'aunties'. In the accounts of their role, the nurturing, motherly care and support these women provided for resistance workers is emphasized (Holt-Taselaar, 1954, p.826, Couvée & Boswijk, 1964, p.285)

But assistance for those in hiding involved other tasks as well. Such as finding new and reliable addresses for people in hiding, taking fugitives to different parts of the country and taking food to people in hiding (Graaff & Marcus, 1980, pp.66-67). Women were involved in this work, but also in (i) the falsification of documents, identity cards etc., and the transport of these and food coupons; (ii) the provision of escape routes for pilots, and accompanying pilots to neutral countries, like Switzerland; (iii) working in the illegal press, and the distribution of this material over the country; (iv) working as couriers for the resistance movement. This included being a contact between illegal organizations, the illegal press and the printers, or working for Dutch intelligence. Lastly, women were also involved in violent resistance. Here their tasks included shadowing people who might be the target of a liquidation; providing the administrative and caring support for the so-called *knokploegen* (assault groups); transporting weapons to and from a place of action; and occasionally women were involved in the actual action. Some women have also been involved in the organizational and managing side of the resistance movement.[7]

Having indicated the type of work involved in the Dutch resistance, and what tasks were performed by women, one wonders how widespread active resistance was amongst men and women. Graaf & Marcus estimate that, without the inclusion of resistance which took place solely within the confines of the home (i.e. keeping people in hiding etc.), approximately 25,000 Dutch people were involved; of whom about 3,000 (or 12 per cent) were women (1980, p.45). From their survey amongst resistance workers they found that 50 per cent of resistance work done by women concerned couriers' work; whilst 30 per cent had been involved in helping people in hiding. 25 per cent said they had worked in the illegal press (these tasks are not mutually exclusive). They furthermore conclude that more women had been involved in the illegal press than men, though more men had been involved in espionage and violent resistance work (Graaff & Marcus, 1980, p.59). So in absolute terms, active resistance was not widespread amongst Dutch people, and men were more involved than women. Nor did this resistance work challenge established notions of proper gender roles. Women were mostly involved in a serving or supporting role, and their presence in resistance work was often regarded as valuable exactly because it contradicted prevailing images of femininity.

Graaff & Marcus have further noted the background details of the women who were resistance workers. They were likely to be women who participated in employment, were members of a political party, or who formed part of a friendship circle associated with either of these (1980, p.37). Again, it was mainly young and unmarried women, or older women who were active in resistance work; married women with young children were least likely to do resistance work. All this suggests that it is unlikely that Dutch war-time activities challenged ideological notions on the position of women in society.

Taking stock

In this section, I have reviewed some of the research on the implications of the Second World War on the position of women. The area covered by this research has been extensive, and I have here chosen to limit my review to relate closely to the question what, if any, lasting employment features resulted from the war, which affected Dutch and British women, and married women in specific. In Britain, the aim of the organizers of the war; the British government, was to utilize the country's human resources in the best possible way, without radically upsetting established cultural values. Hence, when women with significant domestic responsibilities were finally called up to help in the war effort, no radical solutions were put into place to make their work easier. Indeed, some public nurseries and communal canteens did exist, but these were not numerous, and did not outlast the war years long.

One employment pattern which did not challenge established gender relations; part-time working, did become a popular employment form during and after the war. But it could be argued, as I do below, that part-time working improved the income earning potential for women with substantial domestic responsibilities, and it is possible that without its utilization during the war-time, this employment form would not have taken off so quickly as it did in Britain. Existing restrictions on married women's employment were temporarily suspended, but war-time experiences of employing married women do not appear to have been decisive in changing the attitudes underlying marriage bars permanently. The particular circumstances of the post-war years are equally important to such an explanation. The same, I would argue, applies to the expansion in opportunities in service sector work. In British commentaries on the effects of the war on British women, I believe that this has not been sufficiently taken into account.

Although this does not sound very positive, long-term changes in the position of women in employment are more substantial and tangible in Britain than in the Netherlands. Here, there was no exploration of part-time working methods, and the marriage bar in state employment returned in the post-war years. The only tangible change Schwegman can distinguish relates to the views of confessional political women. Many of these women had been involved in the Dutch resistance, and after the war they were ready to fight for their equality within their parties and in political life more generally (Blok, 1989, p.39). These confessional women (those from a Protestant background first) joined the *Committee 'with-the-long-name'* (see note 13, chapter 3) - which resumed its activity to fight against the marriage bar in state employment after the war. This move signalled the start of a lengthy and slow period of change in confessional thinking about the place of women in society (and hence in the sphere of employment).

The socio-economic context of the post-war period

Here, a socio-economic history will be sketched which is to serve as a background to an exploration of changes in women's waged work in Britain and the Netherlands between 1945 and 1965. This, then, is by no means a comprehensive economic historical account, but rather serves as a sociological history which is directed towards such features which are considered of importance to the research question at hand. It may be recalled from chapter 2 that Dutch socio-economic explanations of the later integration of Dutch women in formal employment relations have concentrated on late industrialization (de Bruijn, 1989), and the relatively high Dutch productivity rate over time (Plantenga, 1993). Here, I will look in a more detailed manner at the relative state of the labour markets in the two societies. What is interesting here is that there are a number of indicators that labour market tension was an issue in Britain throughout the war and post-war years, whilst in the Netherlands this was not the case until about the mid 1950s.

The list of indicators which supports this hypothesis includes firstly the legacy of the war and pre-war years. As discussed above, the Netherlands entered the war-period with a significant level of unemployment. But whilst unemployment had not disappeared in Britain, the level of activity during the war meant full use of available labour resources there. Secondly, it can be no surprise that the two societies entered the post-war years starting from a different level of activity. Post-war reconstruction will be discussed in this context and will involve looking at the intermediation of the state and its post-war policies in the economies of both societies. Thirdly, there is the social and economic background to the labour supply side. In addition to agricultural rationalization, of central importance here is a comparison of population growth. These indicators will be brought together, in evaluating the implications for the relative state of the labour market in both countries at the time, and quantitative changes in women's waged work.

Reconstruction and post-war policy

The post-war period between 1945 and 1965 may be characterized as one of unprecedented economic growth in both societies. In fact, when one looks more closely at the economies of Britain and the Netherlands, a somewhat more varied picture is evident. The rate and character of growth is not the same over time and between both societies. Generally, the 1960s were years of greater growth than the 1950s. Equally - as will be discussed in more detail here - the period between 1945 and 1950 was one of reconstruction in the Netherlands, and can not be considered as years of growth. In Britain, on the other hand, the level of economic activity experienced during the war did not decline significantly. It seems clear then, that the two societies started the post-war years from a different economic position, and a different aggregate labour market situation.

Taking the experience of World War II as the starting point, it seems that whilst both societies were fundamentally affected by the Second World War, they were affected in different ways. As must be clear from the above discussion, Britain's economy was directed towards fighting the war, whilst the Dutch economy was subject to German occupation. Here, economic life became deregulated as the Germans attempted to steer Dutch resources into their own war economy and started a process of plundering. Therefore, when the war was over, in 1945, the Dutch faced considerable damage in a number of respects. In summing these up, Messing points to the physical and psychological costs which the Dutch population had to pay; the damage done to the infrastructure, industry and agricultural stocks; and the financial chaos which resulted (Messing, 1981, p.43). In Britain the legacy of the war was, though visually less clear, not less damaging. Here, the costs of the war had left the country without assets, leaving it in a perpetual cycle of balance of payments problems.

> In the course of the war, Britain lost the equivalent of a quarter of its national wealth. Its overseas assets had been sold off to pay for the war. In 1914 they had equalled total domestic wealth. Income from these assets had enabled Britain to run a large deficit on the balance of trade. The wartime sale of overseas assets ended all that. (MacInnes, 1987, p.19)

The loss of income from foreign assets was perpetuated by the fact that Britain's export industry had been geared towards war-time production, so that it had no resources to pay for essential imports of food and raw materials.

So whilst both societies experienced destruction; of housing, infrastructure and industry, the scale of this destruction was, relatively speaking, much larger in the Netherlands than in Britain. The difference, then, lies therein that during the direct post-war years, that is between 1945 and 1955, the Netherlands had to undergo a wider and relatively more costly reconstruction, before the economy could return to normal. Dutch reconstruction demanded extensive financial resources, but these were very scarce for a number of reasons, including the financial debt which had accumulated over the war years; the allocation of resources to fight an imperial war in Indonesia; and the Dutch contribution to the Korean war. As a consequence, the Dutch economy was rather slow in the first 5 years. Indeed, in 1947, economic production was still only 76 per cent of the pre-war level (Blok, 1989, p.19). Dutch reconstruction did provide employment opportunities. In 1945, the *Dienst Uitvoering Werken* (Service for Works Realization) provided work for the unemployed in the reconstruction program, in which in 1950 still 20-30,000 people were employed (Messing, 1981, p.51). Also an estimated 140,000 new jobs were created between 1948 and 1951 (de Bruijn, 1989, p.163), but the creation of new jobs through the recovery of industry must have been limited in these first years, exactly because of the slow overall recovery.

In both societies, recovery was facilitated by Marshall aid. Britain received the largest chunk of it, because of its balance of trade problems. These problems, however, did not significantly slow down the economy after the war. This did not mean that the country returned to pre-war normality quickly. Instead, all the indications are that the government consciously influenced a slower winding down of the war effort than had been the case after the First World War. Consequently, the conscription of women continued for some years after the war (Walby, 1986, p.205). Reconstruction and a quick start with building the new welfare state also indicate that the economy must have been steady in the sense that the first 5 years after the war saw significant labour shortages.

Another indication of the cross-national variation in labour market tightness during these years is government post-war policy itself. When considering how post-war reconstruction was organized in both societies, one can again see similar themes. Both societies saw the presence of an interventionist government apparatus (as opposed to the *laissez faire* style of government of the pre-war years), steering the economy into certain directions. An ideology of co-operation - working towards the common good - which had characterized Britain during the war, was actively propagandized after the war in both societies. Equally, for the first time in parliamentary history, both societies saw a labour presence in the first post-war governments. But apart from these similarities, there were distinct differences as well.

The social and economic chaos which existed in the Netherlands just after the war was the source for a distinct form of co-operation in what is known as the *Harmonymodel* (conflict avoiding model). After the election in 1946, a *rooms-rode* (Roman Catholic and Socialist) coalition was formed, and this new government produced an interventionist economic policy package which was to counter the losses brought about by the war, and which was designed to develop the Netherlands industrially. In order to get the economy off the ground and restore the damage of the war, the government actively sought and gained the co-operation of employers and employees under the slogan of the common good. The first 10 years of recovery, therefore, were politically organized by a combination of a strict economic policy package; supported by the state, employers and employees alike, and Marshall aid (Messing, 1981, p.46).[8] With the creation of work high on the political agenda, it may be assumed that there were significant labour supplies present (or expected) in the future.

The sacrifice which Dutch workers had to make was present in the form of a strict wage policy; wages were not allowed to increase above the cost of living. The unions shared in the aims of the politicians to create more employment and agreed as to how this was to be accomplished.[9] The years after the war see the institutionalization of labour relations in the Netherlands. This not only signalled a wider acceptance of the existence of unions in the Netherlands, but was also part of a wider formation of institutions which supported the interventionist role of successive Dutch governments in the future.[10] A negative consequence for the unions was that they, in effect, relinquished influence on a firm level, for influence at state level.

The 1950s signalled the first decade of significant economic growth; the gross national product increased by 4.9 per cent (Messing, 1981, p.57) in that decade. Because of the strict wage-policy, a situation had been created where the wage-level in the Netherlands lay below that of surrounding countries. The economic aims set out after the war seemed to be producing the required effects in the sense that the 1950s saw a growing tension on the labour market. This was evident in the rising inflationary pressure on wages. 1954 saw the first real increase in the wage-level since the war, and at the end of the 1950s, there was agreement that wage-changes should be set at the level of changes in productivity. The end of the 1950s was characterized therefore by the end of the *rooms-rode* coalition (1958), and the break-down of the *Harmonymodel*. The various themes of Dutch post-war policy; the job creation policy; the success with which the Dutch government institutionalized labour relations; the way in which it was able to keep to its strict wage policy; and the timing of the breakdown of the *Harmonymodel*, all support the idea that the Dutch labour market was not tight in first instance.

In Britain, the post-war Labour government under Attlee made a determined attempt to continue the national spirit of co-operation for the common good - which had been the hallmark of Britain's successful war endeavours. The expectation had been that the post-war years might bring the return of unemployment. In the short term because of demobilization, and in the long term, because it was expected that - as had happened after World War I - an inflationary boom might lead to deflationary policies, and hence unemployment. The Attlee government assumed an interventionist role in these years under a policy package known as the *Post-War Settlement*, the main aims of which were:

> Government intervention in the economy to promote full employment, a Welfare State of equal rights to health care, education, a job or subsistence. (MacInnes, 1987, p.18)

With full employment as a main aim, demobilization was consciously arranged to take place slowly, over a number of years. The dreaded unemployment never materialized. Indeed, the main labour related problems during the 1940s and 1950s were the shortage of skilled labour, and wage restraints.

The wage restraints which the British government appealed for seemed in first instance more related to the threat of wage inflation due to full employment, than as a means to make the labour force cheaper. The latter had been the main objective of the Dutch government. In the event, it seems that the British government had more difficulty in putting its wages policies into practice than was the case for the Dutch government. Certainly, the fact that Britain's labour market was tighter over these first post-war years, provides one rationale as to why this might be so. And possibly the fact that many of the government's policies were based on the voluntary co-operation of the unions and employers, played a role too. It would appear that the claim to work together for the common good was not as much a reality in Britain, as was the case in the Netherlands (Blok, 1989, de Bruijn, 1989, and Messing, 1981).

Comparing the post-war policies of the Netherlands and Britain, then, reveals many similarities. But the main differences seem clear too. Whilst for Britain, the post-war years involved the problem of how to keep full employment given its balance of trade problems, for the Netherlands, the problem was how to create full employment. The two societies, then, faced different labour market situations. As I indicated above, there is furthermore a labour supply side theme to this issue, to which I will now turn.

Population growth and immigration

Figures on population change show that the rate of population increase in the post-war years was much greater in the Netherlands than in Britain. As can be read from Table 4.2, between 1950 and 1960, the annual rate of population growth in the United Kingdom was 4.4 per thousand in the population, compared to a rate of 12.6 in the Netherlands.[11] What these figures come down to is that the absolute increase in the Dutch population, between 1945 and 1964, was nearly 3 million; it changed from 9.22 million to 12.04 million. In other words, in 1964, the population was 32.5 per cent above the 1945 level (Messing, 1981, p.64). In Britain, the population increase between 1945 and 1960 was 8,342,000. Or a rise of 19.6 per cent on the 1945 level (Census).

Given these figures, the question is whether the difference in population growth in fact materialized in opposing population concerns in the two societies. Well, in Britain, a concern with the decline in the birthrate was present (see, for example, Wilson, 1981, p.47). In the past, this concern had been accompanied by an ideological rejection of the employment of married women. But Wilson points out that under the circumstances of the post-war years, it would have been unthinkable to demand women's return to the home. Compulsion, after all, did not stem with the assumed freedom of liberal ideology, which was *en vogue* in post-war life. But the population question

Table 4.2

Annual rates of population growth per thousand in the population

Period	United Kingdom	The Netherlands
1950-1960	4.4	12.6
1960-1970	5.7	12.8
1970-1975	1.9	9.2

Source: United Nations (1979), Labour Supply and Migration in Europe: Demographic dimensions 1950-1975 and prospects (p.5).

was linked to the question of labour supply (as happened in banking, see chapter 5). But the commentary was one of acceptance, certainly not one of 'what can we do to increase the population growth?'.

In the Netherlands, the government and other interested parties had a contrasting concern. This was how to cope with a growing population. In the Queen's speech of 1954, the continuing issue of population growth was presented as a challenge to Dutch resourcefulness.

> Het snelle tempo, waarin onze beroepsbevolking groeit, blijft ons land stellen voor een werkgelegenheidsvraagstuk op lange termijn, voor welke oplossing industrialisatie en exportvergroting, aangevuld door emigratie, nodig zijn. (Blok, 1989, p.24)
>
> (The quick pace with which our working population grows, continues to pose an employment problem in the long term, for which industrialization and export increases, in addition to emigration, are needed.)

But also here, the government's stance towards this increase was not one of control or compulsion. Birth control, especially at a time when the Catholic pillar still had a strong political influence, was unthinkable. In the same way in which a compulsory stimulation of child birth was unthinkable in the British liberal climate of the 1950s.

Another indication of the relative state of the labour market is to look at the moment when employers and the governments of the two respective societies started to look for alternative labour supply sources. In commentary on the labour demand implications of post-war capitalist accumulation, latent agricultural workers, women and migrant workers have been named as alternative labour supply sources (Miles, 1987, Braverman, 1974). With the absence of a latent agricultural labour force, it can not strike as surprising that the British Nationality Act of 1948 and the Economic Survey of 1947 appeared on the policy scene in the same year. The British Nationality Act 1948 gave people from British colonies and Commonwealth countries the right to settle and work in Britain (Jenkins, 1988, p.312). When this right ended in 1962 with the Commonwealth Immigration Act, half a million people had made use of the opportunity which was offered by it. The Economic Survey for 1947, at the same time, encouraged the greater employment of women.

In the Netherlands, there was, as pointed out by de Bruijn (1989), a latent agricultural work force, which required re-employment as rationalization in agriculture made them redundant. A culmination of debates on the employment of married women, and the first mention of recruiting migrant workers became audible in the 1950s. It is during the 1950s that the search for labour reserves generated a debate amongst members of various pillars, about the idea of engaging married women in the waged economy (this will be further discussed below), and though the tide of public opinion was changing, it is clear that this did not take place overnight. Here too, there was a small amount of migration from the Dutch colonies; Surinam and the Dutch Antilles (Miles, 1987, p.147), but it was during the 1950s that the first migrant workers from the Mediterranean area were recruited.[12] However, the real breakthrough in the increased employment of both migrant workers and married women, for the Netherlands, came during the 1960s. A total of about 34,000 labour licences were handed out to migrant workers in 1960 (of whom three quarters were male). In 1965, this had increased to 63,000 (with a male ratio of 90 per cent) and in 1968, the number of licences handed out was 80,000 (male ratio 87 per cent) (CBS, 1963-64, p.103). Still, with a total labouring population of just over 4 million, the ratio of migrants amongst them remained below 2 per cent in this decade.

The ideological context of the post-war years

The distinction between socio-economic and ideological considerations which I make in this chapter, is artificial. In reality, the two articulate with each other in intricate ways, as was clear when rationales behind marriage bars were explored in chapter 3. But also in this chapter, there is a need to consider the manner in which ideological concerns combine with changes on a socio-economic level in the forging of social change. Having investigated the war years, and looked at the social and economic conditions of the post-war period in relation to the relative state of the respective labour markets, in this section the ideological contentions of post-war life will be explored.

Interestingly, the debates on the characterization of these ideological contentions in both societies argue for a clear link between such ideology, and their message about the role of women in society. Two themes are evident. On the one hand, both societies see a return to a morally more regulated society, which, it has been argued, may be considered a response to a loosening of such ties during the war time. At the same time, modernizing ideological trends become more evident. As suggested by Crompton and Sanderson (1990) in a British context, liberal/equality ideologies take on an enhanced meaning; an aspect which may be recognized in the establishment of the welfare state. Equally, Plantenga (1992, 1993) and others have pointed to the slow but increasing significance of modernizing ideas in Dutch post-war society, which also contained elements of equality thinking.

Het kantelende tij (the tilting tide)

In a nutshell, the Dutch ideological climate of the period 1945-1965 can be characterized as one of change, but not in the first instance. The direct post-war years feature a return to the pre-war pillarized society, but the antagonisms between the different pillars is replaced by the perceived importance that co-operation is the only way forward for a destroyed nation. The *Harmonymodel* integrates Dutch society under an ideology of consensus, though recently, it has been argued that underlying this consensus, a movement of de-pillarization was underway (Stuurman, 1984). It is this movement which, during the 1960s, gives rise to renewal thinking, in which Dutch youth play a significant role. Ideological concerns about women's role in society (and hence notions on women's employment), it is argued, closely relate to these overall changes (Plantenga, 1992, p.140).

De Bruijn, amongst others, argues that whilst the pillorized social order returns to Dutch society in the post-war years, the dire situation facilitates the presence of both traditional and modernizing forces. The need for reconstruction demands the co-operation of all - taking prominence over the antagonisms felt between the pillars prior to the war.[13] The *Harmonymodel* is, in fact, a policy-mix of these traditional and modernizing forces. On the one hand, greater industrialization is seen as the answer to many of the economic problems the Netherlands faces (including the question how to provide work for the future generation). On the other hand, there is a continuing moral concern - with the unruly youth, unmarried mothers and increasing divorce rates of the war years (and which later returns in arguments about the implications of industrialization) - which signifies the continuity in traditionalist thinking, especially amongst the Confessionals. The policy answer, de Bruijn suggests, is found in a solidification of the family as the fundamental building block of Dutch society (de Bruijn, 1989, p.169).

It is obvious what role women get allotted here. Post-war family policy portray woman as wife and mother and this does not merge easily with the notion of a working married wife or mother. De Bruijn is eager to point out, though, that the acceptance of the family as the building block of Dutch society has a different meaning for the Labour Party in the coalition, than it has for the Confessionals. To the latter, modernization means a threat to the family, whilst for the former this is not the case. It is not surprising to find that, when the Netherlands is confronted with increasing labour shortages, Confessional family thinking becomes regarded as an inhibiting force on the continuing process of industrialization (de Bruijn, 1989, p.172). The debate on married women's employment, then, is both focused on, and is most lively within Confessional circles.

The antagonism between confessional ideology, and labour supply shortages, certainly does not lead to an overnight attitude change towards married women's employment: not in government policy, nor in general. According to Morée, the 1950s and the 1960s need to be regarded as a period of:

> Schoorvoetende acceptatie van gehuwde vrouwen met kinderen als werkneemsters ten gevolge van een toenemend tekort aan arbeidskrachten ... (Morée, 1992, p.78).
> (reluctant acceptance of married women with children as employees, as the consequence of an increasing shortage in labour supply ...).

The 1950s is mainly a decade of debate, whilst the 1960s is the decade of change. Let us look at the 1950s debates on married women's employment in more detail, for there exists, in fact, a body of documents and reports specifically on the issue. The origin of these documents varies, from the government, to the Catholic and Christian pillars, and the Socialist and Liberal Parties. Since these debates have been well documented (see for example Blok, 1989, de Bruijn, 1989, Morée, 1992, and Plantenga, 1992, 1993), I shall suffice here by giving a short interpretation of these accounts.

As may be remembered from chapter 3, the Dutch state operated an official marriage bar on its own employees from 1924 onwards, though the degree with which the bar was implemented varied - as the Dutch Labour Party (*Partij van de Arbeid* or *PVDA*) MP Mrs Tendeloo kept emphasizing in the post-war period - with the state of the labour market. So the Second World War years, and indeed the direct post-war years had seen the non-implementation of the official marriage bar in state employment. However, discussions on the marriage bar issue within the state carried as theme the temporary nature of this situation and the bar was implemented again in 1947. Tendeloo's call to have the bar removed was ignored, though she did succeed in getting the bar investigated by the committee-Ubink in 1949. When its Report *Het vraagstuk van de gehuwde ambtenares* appeared in 1952, it did not suggest the bar ought to be abolished. A parliamentary motion by Tendeloo in 1955 finally achieved the objective; she managed to get a small majority for the suggestion that the government should revise its stance on the marriage bar (Blok, 1989, p.124). In the event, the government only honoured this motion in 1957.

As the government was a coalition between the Labour Party, and the Catholic People's Party (the *KVP* or *Katholieke Volks Partij*), Catholic thinking very much influenced the line of government policies in those years. In actual fact, the timing of the change in government policy concerning the marriage bar, very much reflects a change in Catholic thinking on the matter. But the latter was rather slow to develop, and did not involve all Catholics at the same time. Hence in two reports (1951 and 1953) by the Catholic *Centrum voor Staatskundige Vorming* on the subject, the traditional Catholic stance of the role of married women in society is still very much in evidence. But in a publication by the *Nederlands Gesprekcentrum*[14] in 1956, a partial change is evident. This publication embodied the views of Dutch academics, and it forms proof that a change was evident in the standpoint of some confessionals; namely academics, on the matter of married women's employment. Elsewhere, Catholics took longer to change their views. Plantenga, who discusses as example the predominantly Catholic town *Tilburg*, argues that the lack of a mass media, and the continued influence of Catholic thinking in this town, must be regarded as the explanation for this delay (Plantenga, 1992, p.161).

Given the strength and length with which married women's participation in work outside the family home had been opposed, it can come as no surprise that ideological conditions were attached to the change. When there finally was a more general agreement that the state had no part to play in what was increasingly considered to be a decision of private concern (following the rise in liberal/individualist views, which was also very much part of British post-war political ideology), the dominant ideological perception which remained agreed that, yes, there could be no objection to the employment of married women, but only if this employment did not stand in the way of women's primary duties; that is, her role at home, especially when this involved the care of children. So the change in ideological thinking about married women's employment during the 1950s, which can be traced through the then contemporary reports and discussion papers, did not include an attitude change on the employment of mothers with children. It was only in the 1960s, Morée argues, that there was a turn around in this respect, but only where it involved older children. The employment of mothers with young children remained a social taboo, however, even amongst women's groups of the time (Morée, 1992, p.80).

Only halfway to paradise

In *Only Halfway to Paradise*, Elizabeth Wilson (1980) guides us through the post-war changes in general ideological perceptions, and how these related to ideological perceptions on the role of British women. The ideological climate in Britain directly after the war shows many similarities to that, discussed above, in the Netherlands. As was the case in the Netherlands, a determined attempt was made to continue the war-time ideology of 'one nation'. Here, too, post-war policy (incorporating distinct moral messages) called out the importance of the family. Wilson captures these similarities by arguing that in the direct post-war years:

> A complex act of reconciliation between the classes was being attempted ... It was hoped to preserve the sense of one nation that war had created, by building a new and democratic community, of which Commonwealth was the expression overseas and the welfare state at home. If full employment was to end the class war, the other side of this coin was to be the community in which family life would find its full expression. (Wilson, 1980, p.17)

But whilst in Britain, the unifying feat was to be accomplished between the different classes of society, in the Netherlands, the divergent interests between different pillars was at stake.

If family life was to be the unifying factor in these post-war efforts, there was a need to make it more appealing in the eyes of post-war women. Attlee and Beveridge (and Bevin during the war) were very aware of the drudgery of working class women's domestic life. So for a brief period after the war, the belief was present that an interventionist strategy, like the one formulated for the wider society, should be applied to domestic work as well. Homemaking could become perceived as a rewarding career, if the drudgery was taken out of it. So it was suggested that 'washing all clothes, cooking every meal, being in charge of every child for every moment when it is not in school - can be done communally outside the home' (Beveridge, 1948, p.264). These ideas never materialized however, and in the end, there was little the government did offer women to support them in their housekeeping role.

At the same time, the direct post-war messages which the government gave to British women were contradictory (Wilson, 1981, Crompton & Sanderson, 1989).

> From the beginning, the Attlee government was attempting a juggling feat, trying to promote ideals of family life while simultaneously desperately in need of labour for the work of peacetime reconstruction. (Wilson, 1981, p.43)

Wilson, then, supports the point which I argued above; that there was tension on the British labour market directly after the war. The government's contradictory stance was directly related to this, in the fact that it, through the Economic Survey of 1947 (Cmd. 7047), called women up to join the work force. However, 'the terms of this appeal really set the limits within which the employment of women was perceived and understood at this time, and for many years afterwards' in that the government:

> Was not asking women to do jobs usually done by men, as had been the case during the war. Second, the labour shortage was temporary, and women were being asked to take a job only for whatever length of time they could spare, whether full time or part time. Third, (they) were not appealing to women with very young children ... (Wilson, 1981, p.44)

So in their efforts to enthuse more women to join in the country's work force, the British government certainly did not want to challenge the sexual division of labour in employment, nor the existing sexual division of labour in the household. Its post-war position on what could be requested from women was the same as during the war years.

During the 1950s, the idea (which had circulated in the first years after the war) of any government intervention in the private sphere of the home, became - linked as it was to the communism of Eastern Europe - more distasteful than ever. Welfare support, in the form of provisions like childcare facilities, were never discussed, if this was, in any case, wanted by British women. And soon a distinctive British pattern developed, described by Myrdal & Klein (1956) as women's dual role, in which British women would participate in the sphere of employment, but only when and for the time that it suited their household responsibilities.

All the same, the government did, in those first post-war years, try to convince British business that a marriage bar was no longer acceptable. For once, the government influenced Civil Service employment policy by facilitating the abolition of the bar in the Civil Service, and in the 1947 Economic Survey, they argued in favour of married women's employment. But these measures did not find all-round support. Indeed, discussions implicating marriage bars continued into the 1950s, particularly in those sectors of private employment, which were still looked upon as middle class occupations; banking employment included. Nevertheless, the ratio of economically active married women continued to increase. If the ratio of married women in work changed from 10 per cent in 1931 to 21 per cent in 1951, in 1961 32 per cent of married women were economically active and the ratio in 1971 was 47 per cent.[15]

One last - and important - issue needs to be addressed here. Two related, though differently formulated, arguments exist which construct post-war change in the extent of British women's economic activity, as limited. The first is present in Hakim's recently formulated argument that British women's increased employment in the post-war period is a myth. Hakim argues that the change is one of statistical recording; prior to the war the often 'occasional, casual and part-time' work that - especially working class - women did was systematically ignored in Census recordings, after the war this was no longer the case. The second argument, that of Wilson, suggests that for working class women nothing much changed between their pre-war and post-war conditions of life. Working-class women, 'had always been exploited workers' (Wilson, 1981, p.53), and the post-war fuss about married women's employment, according to her, was mainly about middle-class women.

The problem with these accounts, I think, is that they underestimate the significance of the different employment relations working women faced in these respective periods. Whilst the hidden and casual types of homework of the pre-war years were very much hidden from view, part-time work of the post-war years was performed under formal employment relations; taking place in factories, and later offices, for set wages and often on a permanent basis. Though it is well known that the conditions of part-time working are most likely to be worse than those of full-time working, the difference between hidden employment and part-time employment is that whereas the former prevents any legislative intervention, the latter does not. In this respect, trends in the respective countries were similar in that women found themselves increasingly in modern and formal employment relations, as opposed to traditional and hidden ones.

Exclusionary ideology and social construction in Dutch post-war employment figures

I have, on various occasions, made reference to the problems involved in comparing Census data over the various years of this study, and between the Netherlands and Britain.[16] An important aspect of these problems concerns the social construction of labour force figures. If official figures reflect the social definition of what counts as employment or not at any specific time, it follows that in a social environment where the economic activity of women (or certain groups of women) is considered as socially undesirable, labour force statistics are likely to underestimate the employment of that group of workers. As such, employment figures are in themselves evidence of ideological contentions on the employment of certain groups of workers. With these points in mind we will return to the employment figures of the post-war years, starting with the Dutch figures, and well with the question in what way the *volkstellingen* of 1947 and 1960 are related to the ideological climate on women's employment of the time. The curious feature (evident in table 1.1) of these two counting years is that there is both a relative and an absolute decline in Dutch women's economic activity. The absolute decline of 15,000 women, needs to be seen in the context of a 302,000 absolute increase in the total labour force.

This decline has been explained in a number of ways. Firstly, by tracing the structural changes in the Dutch labour population. De Bruijn and Plantenga agree that women's recorded employment figures have seen a decline in traditional work relations; including the categories of *medewerkende gezinsleden* (co-working family members) and domestic service, and a rise in formal wage relations in the service sector and in manufacturing (de Bruijn, 1989, p.175, Plantenga, 1987, p.9). The point is that the decline in the traditional forms of employment over this period was greater than the rise of work in the 'new' service sector occupations and manufacturing. In relation to the relative figures, the CBS (*Centraal Bureau voor de Statistiek* or Central Statistical Office) itself comments on the denominator factor; that is the rise in the total population of youngsters (reflected in the population increase) and older people, who are not part of the work force (CBS, 1960, p.13, de Bruijn, 1989, p.229).

The interesting point is that the Census figures support our discussion above, that the 1950s are not a breakthrough in terms of married women's employment. In their discussion, the CBS point out that amongst married women not many work outside the family home, and that the number who do so have even declined in the period; from 10 per cent of the female work force in 1947 to 7 per cent in 1960 (by 1971, this had increased to 15 per cent). Given this, the 1950s trend of marrying at a younger age must be regarded as a further factor contributing to the average decline in the aggregate rates (CBS, 1960, p.14). This point mirrors a similar trend in Britain (discussed earlier on in this chapter). The structural changes just discussed also apply to married women. Married women constitute a major part of the decline in the category of co-working family members.[17] As co-working family members, married women are specifically found in agriculture and trade, as wives of farmers and small private businessmen. The decline of married women in those sectors is (at 88,000) significant, and indeed greater than the rise of working married women in the service and manufacturing sectors (which is 61,000) (CBS, 1960, p.39).

The decline in the ratio of married women included in the figures of co-working family members seems sound in the context of the - already discussed - reduction in agricultural workers as a result of agricultural rationalization. But, according to Plantenga, this decline is at least partially a result of a changing notion of what constitutes work. Counting farmers' wives and the wives of small business men into the employment statistics partly depends on the significance these women (and for that matter census interviewers) attribute to the household part and the business part of their work. It is therefore likely that, in an ideological climate where women's household tasks carry higher social esteem than the business part of their work, the latter is underrated, leading to an underestimation in the census figures (Plantenga, 1987, p.10). So it may be argued that the decline in women's employment over the period 1947-1960 was at least partly a result of underestimation.

However, some questions remain. It must be clear that the ideological climate against the remunerated work outside the domestic home of married women had a lengthy history. Why was it exactly when this ideological climate was questioned that the Dutch Census should display a noticeable degree of underestimation in married women's economic activity? Some speculative - and contributive - factors may be brought forward. Firstly, in the light of post-war efforts to consolidate family life, the worth of women's domestic work was made more public, and consequently gained in social esteem. Secondly, 88,000 married women disappeared in the agricultural and trade sector. The argument that confessional ideology was particularly strong amongst the agricultural population has some justification, and this section of the working population would not have been at the vanguard of confessional ideological change on the stance towards working married women. One might particularly expect to find women who give voice to the worth of their domestic work amongst these confessional women.

Turning to the 1960s, census evidence seems to support Morée's argument that the 1960s are characterized by an overall increase in married women's employment. Between 1960 and 1971, the absolute increase in the number of women who form part of the labour population amounts to nearly 300,000 (*Volkstelling* of 1960 and 1971). De Bruijn estimates that on average, each year around 31,000 more women participate in work outside the domestic sphere (de Bruijn, 1989, p.243). This increase is primarily due to an increased participation of married women which is 294,000 (including widowed and divorced women). The increase in women who are not married is 31,000. The small increase in this group, despite the relatively high natural increase in the population may be attributed to the increased participation in education which de Bruijn estimates to be 5,000 per year. The percentage-wise increase over this period is higher for the female labour force than for the male labour force; 54 per cent and 46 per cent respectively.

Conclusion

In this chapter, two interlinking and articulating sources of social change related to the position of women in remunerated work, gender ideology and labour market tightness, have been investigated in an effort to illuminate the different 'moments' at which the recorded economic activity ratios of women in the two societies increased. Consequently, the investigation was restricted to

101

the years between 1940 and 1965, and special attention was given to the war years (1940-1945) and the direct post-war years (1945-1960). The findings do illuminate the cross-national differences found in work force recordings, and indicate some interesting cross-national differences in the cultural composition of sociality.

The first point I want to make is that researching the war years using the comparative method has been useful. The contrasting war-time experiences were described in some detail, and on that basis some firmer statements could be made about the long-term consequences of that period in history on women's position in the sphere of remunerated work. In Britain, the war years provided the opportunity to experiment with part-time working, and to experience the employment of married women. In the post-war years, these patterns of employment were consolidated because of continuing labour market tightness. The latter was partly a result of government efforts to avoid a recurrence of the post World War I situation. In the Netherlands there was no experimenting with part-time working, and marriage bars resumed their prevalence in post-war society. My discussion of post-war indicators of relative labour market tightness suggest that the socio-economic conditions in the first 10 years after the war did not push for a shift in ideological thinking.

Secondly, the disappearance of the marriage bar in British state employment in 1946, and subsequently in many other types of employment was also a culmination of the growing influence of liberal ideologies and the demands of a tight labour market. I have argued that the part-time working methods may also be linked to liberal/egalitarian ideology. Whilst this form of work did not challenge the domestic gender order, it did provide the opportunity for women (and in particular working class women) to earn an income in formalized employment relations, and as such signalled a change in the conditions of women's paid work from the pre-war period. A liberal/egalitarian ideological climate did not take shape in the Netherlands until the end of the 1950s. Why this should be so is related to the peculiar cultural formations of sociality.

The pillarized cultural order was restored in the Netherlands after the war, though politically the Socialist and Catholic pillar had to manage a successful restoration together. Egalitarian thinking was never part of Confessional ideology, and it was not until the latter became increasingly regarded as standing in the way of progress that shifts in the ideological position on women's remunerated work came about. Significant evidence that practice followed ideology is found only in the 1960s. The Socialist attitude towards working married women differed from that of the Confessionals all along, but with the exception of a few (like the female Labour MP Mrs Tendeloo), this issue did not rank highly on the list of political priorities. Change in the ideological contention on married women's employment in the Netherlands was staggered; the variations depended on one's membership of a specific

102

pillar, and within the confessional pillars on one's education background (Plantenga, 1992). Having said that, it would appear that ideological change was staggered in Britain as well. Indeed, in considering the evidence presented here, a change in attitudes towards married women's employment appears to vary on the basis of class in Britain. And a sensitivity of that difference is necessary if one is to understand the staggered decline in marriage bars here.

Notes

1   Some of the other sources of employment statistics drawn on in the secondary literature include H.M.D. Parker (1957), *Manpower: A Study of Wartime Policy and Administration*, London: HMSO, G.M. Beck (1951), *Survey of British Employment and Unemployment 1927-1945*, Oxford: Oxford University Institute of Statistics.

2   Each of these periods corresponds to a statistics collection period in which the Ministry used the same definition of employment and unemployment. Between these periods, the definition was changed so that the three periods are not strictly comparable (Leser, 1952, pp.326-7).

3   Women were marrying at an earlier age over this same period; Smith even talks about 'a revolution in the marital status of young women' (1986, p.221). So whilst in 1931, 42 per cent of all women in the age-group 25-29 were single, in 1951 only 22 per cent of women in the age-group were.

4   Summerfield relies for her information on two social surveys carried out in 1944 and 1948 by Geoffrey Thomas. See Summerfield, 1984, p.204 for references.

5   Cabinet minutes cited by Smith (1988, pp.219-20). Reference is *Cabinet minutes, 9 September 1946, Cabinet 80 (46) 6, PRO, Cab. 128/6.*

6   Blok has tried to find these, without success, by approaching the CBS, the Ministerie van Sociale Zaken, Ministerie van Ekonomische Zaken, Arbeidsinspectie, Ekonomische Voorlichtingsdienst en the Rijksinstituut voor Oorlogsdokumentatie (Blok, 1989, p.135, note 36).

7   Gesina van der Molen, a Dutch confessional politician, who wrote a thesis against the employment of married women prior to the war (see bibliography), is an often mentioned example (Holt-Taselaar, 1954, p.819, Graaff & Marcus, 1980, p.66).

8   Messing sums the three important features in this policy package up as follows. Firstly, a strict wage and price policy was introduced, the aim of which was to improve the competitiveness of Dutch industry (which,

in turn, was to improve the collapsed export market). This was related to the second aspect; the job-creation policy, which was to be accomplished through industrialization. Apart from the creation of a cheap labour force, other facets of this policy were aimed at inducing firms to invest and to establish themselves in the Netherlands. To make the Netherlands economically interesting, investment and tax facilities were provided, the state participated in some firms, whilst it actively supported research and technology. It also formed the so-called *Herstelbank* (recovery bank), which was to provide short and long-term loans to firms where the investment risks were high.

9   An interesting question is, why the Dutch trade union federations agreed with these government measures. Blok suggests that the explanation for this is two-fold. On the one hand, she argues, this attitude is explained by the success of the government's claim to working together. On the other hand, the Dutch labour movement (and labouring classes) shared with politicians the memory of the 1930s depression and its vast unemployment. The fear for a return of unemployment, she argues, 'heeft tot ver in de jaren vijftig een verlammende invloed uitgeoefend op de aktiebereidheid van de vakbeweging' (has had a paralyzing influence on the action willingness of the labour movement, reaching far into the 1950s) (Blok, 1989, p.20). There were also warnings about the post-war population expansion. It is therefore not surprising to find that there was ample support for a choice by the unions for more employment to the detriment of individual employee's wage-demands in the direct post-war period.

10   The following laws, established in the first 7 years after the war, are examples of this: the law *Buitengewoon Besluit Arbeidsverhoudingen (BBA)* of 1945, which entailed that employers and employee organizations were legally bound to the setting up of institutionalized forms of labour relations; the law of *Publiekrechtelijke Bedrijfsorganisatie (PBO)* of 1950; the law of the *Ondernemingsraden (WOR)* (works councils) of 1950; and the formation of the *Sociaal Economische Raad (SER)* in 1952. The *SER* was established to advise the government on its social and economic policies, and consisted of an equal number of employer representatives, employee representatives, and members chosen by the Crown.

11   It has to be borne in mind that these figures include changes in the birthrate, death rate and migration.

12   Blok (1989, p.26) mentions the positive stance of the *Nederlands Verbond van Vakverenigingen (NVV)* (Netherlands Union of Trade Unions) in 1955, towards the employment of Italian migrant workers.

13   The post-war coalition between Labour and the Confessionals is a striking example of this effort to put disagreements on one side. Such a coalition would have been very unlikely prior to the war.

14   The *Netherlands Gesprek Centrum* was an association, the main aim of which was to bring together various interests groups, in an effort to facilitate the understanding of the various opinions and standpoints held by them (Plantenga, 1992, p.147).

15   It should be noted that these figures vary as to whom is quoted. The figures here follow Westergaard & Resler (1975, p.98), also quoted in Wilson (1981, p.41). The figures provided by Hakim (1979) are slightly higher, p.1931 - 11 per cent; 1951 - 26 per cent; 1961 - 35 per cent; 1971 - 49 per cent. This variation (which can also be found when calculating the Dutch figures) arises through the choice of denominator, as a result of the various population groups used. Some of these variations include: (1) the total female population, (2) those above 14 years of age, or (3) only those between 15 and 64). Figures may further vary according to whether divorced and widowed women are incorporated; and in relation to Britain, whether figures are solely for England and Wales (as Hakim, 1979 does), for Britain (including Scotland), or for the United Kingdom (also including Northern Ireland).

16   I am not the only one to have commented on this. Others have also commented on the problems involved in using census material. In Britain, for example, Joshi & Owen (1987) have argued that there is a need to adjust census data to make them comparable over time, because 'the way in which economic activity was defined altered from census to census' (1987, p.55).

17   At 152,000, co-working married female family members form the greater part (e.g. 16 per cent) of the 21 per cent of women working in this category in 1947. Equally, the decline in this category between 1947 and 1960 is mainly due to the decline in married women in this category, which in absolute terms changes from 152,000 to 64,000. (CBS, 1960, p.39).

5 Feminization in banking employment

The central theme in this chapter is to trace the feminization of banking work forces in the period 1940-1965. This is narrowed down to the feminization of clerical bank work - the major component of work found in banks - following Crompton's argument that a distinction is required between three occupations found in banking work; that of clerk, secretary and typist. The latter two differ from clerical work, in that these occupations were already filled by women throughout this century, whereas the opposite is true for clerical bank work.[1] It is here that one can find a change in the gender ratio during this century. Moreover, unlike clerical bank work, typing and secretarial work did not feature a career hierarchy; once a woman was employed in these occupations, there were few opportunities to 'move up' (1988, p.123).

The increase in the number of women banks employed on their clerical staff has been a long drawn-out process, which started before the Second World War. In particular with respect to British banking, evidence supports the point that the 'introduction' of women into clerical work did not occur at the same time in all banks. Women were taken on as clerical workers during W.W.I,[2] but as is clear from the discussion below, these women were replaced after the war by permanent male staff. There exists conclusive evidence that two British banks employed female clerical employees between the wars. Savage (1993) has traced the introduction of female clerical staff in Lloyds Bank, and argues that it started to take on female clerks from the late 1920s onwards, but he does not provide figures supporting the point that significant change actually occurred in the gender ratio of Lloyds Bank's clerical staff. Similarly, evidence which I collected from the Bank of England's archive indicates that this bank already had a large ratio of female staff before the Second World War. In contrast, many of my Dutch and British interviewees have stressed the point that there were few, if any, female bank clerks in their banks before World War II. Some of that evidence will be brought up here. But the figures provided in table 5.1 support the point that at least in British banks, clerical feminization had not progressed far before W.W.II.

The investigation in this chapter again concentrates on the socio-economic and ideological conditions of the time, in this case, however, those which operate at this sector level, allowing for a comparison of the banking sector with the national level accounts of the previous two chapters. Before this task can advance, there is first of all a need to expand on the characteristic employment organization in banks, and to indicate some further features of male and female bank employment.

Table 5.1
The female ratio of British bank staff: 1931-1961

British Census		Other[1]		Bank of England[2]	
Year	F/M%	Year	F/M%	Year	F/M%
1931	20.0			1934	40
		1939	22.4	1940	50
		1942	42		
1951	36.9	1950	34	1948	56
1961	44.5				
1971	53.2				

Sources and notes:

1. *The Kennett Committee Report for 1939 and 1942 (1942, p.4); Leser for 1950 (1952, p.327).*
2. *The Bank of England archives.*

Banks have often been described as having an employment organization closely related to the essence of their activities. Before the move towards retail banking, which started during the 1960s, banks were mainly service providers for the business community and the well-to-do (owners of money and wealth), and they needed to ensure their customers' trust. This, then, 'encourages an air of caution, sobriety and conservatism' (MacInnes, 1988, p.131). Such conservatism or traditionalism was evident in the work practices of banks (e.g. in the rules which guide credit decisions), but it also permeated employer/ employee relations. The traditional employment organization in banks was thus characterized by a number of specific features.

It has been argued that employment relations in banks have not remained static over the years (Crompton, 1989, MacInnes, 1988, Cressey & Scott, 1992). In describing the features of traditional employment relations in banks, apart from registering gender, there is a need to be sensitive to changes in these relations over the time period of the research, as well as differences in these relations between the two societies. In order to allow for changes over time, a distinction has been made here between the periods 1940-1965 and 1965-1990. History, however, does not happen in decades (Wilson, 1980, p.7); social change is rather and often a gradual process. This periodization should therefore be taken as an indication of when change was occurring. In the first period, certain identifiable features have characterized banking employment, and these will be outlined below. Some of these features are still characteristic of banking employment today, but several important changes have taken place from the 1960s onwards. These changes will get attention in chapter 7.

Employment organization in banks: 1940-1965

Traditionally, the employment structure of banks in both societies has been a hierarchical one, where the relations between the different grades of staff was patriarchal and traditional. The employment hierarchy consisted of a relatively small management at the top which branched out to encompass those who fulfil the other tasks in the bank; ranging from head office and branch managers, through to the larger number of routine clerical staff. In those years, the size of the head office of individual banks would not have been very large. And though there did not exist an official grading structure in banks in both societies, a hierarchy was clearly evident. In the establishment books of Britbank from the 1950s, there is a clear employment structure and hierarchy amongst those who staff the bank's branches. From the top downwards, this hierarchy consisted of a branch manager, who was aided by the accountant. In the larger branches, there might also be a teller. These were followed by clerks and clerkesses. Branches might further have a messenger (for non-clerical work) and apprentice clerks. The typical branch of Dutchbank, during the 1950s, had a similar employment set-up.[3]

In Dutch banks during this time, the distinction made between *beambten* (subordinate officials) on the one hand and *procuratiehouders* (managing clerks; those who are able to sign their name as guarantee of the bank's financial support) on the other, carried much importance. Being appointed *procuratiehouder* carried both financial and status benefits. The latter was evident in the patriarchal attitude of one Dutch bank, which had separate elevators for *procuratiehouders* and its other staff (interview with Mrs K.). Nowadays, *procuratiehouders* still exist, though the appointment does not carry the same status and meaning as it used to do (Tijdens, 1989, p.228).

The relationship between bank employees on the different rungs of the hierarchical ladder used to be one which was based on patriarchal authority.

The manner in which meaning was given to the authority relations within banks varied from accepted ways in which subordinates and their superiors addressed one another, to rules and regulations concerning dress. Even during the 1970s, in some Dutch banks, superiors allowed themselves to address their subordinates by their first names, whilst the latter were expected to address their superiors with 'sir' (Wierema, 1979, p.123). During the 1960s, it was still accepted practice that male employees did not grow a beard or moustache in one Dutch bank (Tijdens, 1989, p.228), whilst women were not allowed to wear trousers during the 1950s in the *Twentsche Bank* (interview Mrs J.). Variety between banks in the meaning given to authority relations furthermore suggest that work cultures differed too. Some interviewees even spoke of a status hierarchy between different banks in this period.

Banks operated internal labour markets during this period. Important indicators of the existence of internal labour markets are the characteristic means by which recruitment, promotion and training were organized. Young people were recruited straight from school to fill the bottom of the hierarchical work structure and recruitment of older people was very rare. Most banks only recruited youngsters with some form of secondary education, and hence ensured that they recruited from the middle classes. General appearance, family background and in some cases, religious background, were further important factors in recruitment. Traditionally, bank employment has meant a job for life. Bank managers were interested in youngsters with ability, whom they could train and form into general bankers over time, so that the various posts in the bank could be filled from within. The internal labour market meant that when posts became available in the hierarchy, someone from a lower level would be moved up into it. This labour market in theory provided the possibility for bank employees to start at the bottom and to move, with experience and seniority, into higher positions in the bank. During the 1940s, 1950s and 1960s, one could expect that management themselves had all run through the lengthy career ladder of the bank after starting at the bottom.

The severity with which banks in the two societies have adhered to the principles of operating a strict internal labour market appears to have varied. Overall, it seems the case that British banks have been more strict in this respect. There are a number of indications for this. Firstly, British banks have an agreement with each other that they will not take on employees from other banks and individual banks strictly adhere to this rule. They did so in the past, and still do so today. One can think of several reasons why such an agreement is in their mutual interest, but one of them certainly is that, by operating as monopoly employers, British banks effectively made it impossible for their employees to gain a better deal in another bank. Dutch banks may not have recruited employees from other banks very often, but this certainly happened. Some of my interviewees had worked in more than one Dutch bank, or had moved into banking after working in another job before that. A second indication that Dutch banks have not always adhered to the principles of an internal labour market is their recruitment of a certain number of 'experts'. Amongst those were often university graduates. Though the recruitment of university graduates into banking did not take off until the 1960s in either society, Dutch banks had university graduates amongst its personnel at a time when British banks were still weighing up the pros and cons of recruiting graduates.

One important implication of promotion in an internal labour market is that not everyone can be at the top of the career structure at the same time. And because there were/are only a limited number of posts at the top of the career ladder, it was/is likely that not everyone who desired this could make it to the top either. Consequently, between employees who endeavour to 'move up' there has always been a level of competition. It is understandable that when a lot of bank staff see their work in career terms, staff management brings with it certain problems. Matters concerning recruitment, training and promotion need to be well thought through. But even then, problems may be encountered along the way. I will argue below that such problems were directly related to feminization in British banks in the post-war years.

The various aspects of banking as an occupation were learned by bank employees over the years of their employment. At the same time, there was also the opportunity to study for the bankers' exams. In Britain, the significance which has been given to studying for these exams as a means of getting on, varies between the different banks. In Britbank, young male recruits in the post-war years were required to sit the exams if they wanted to get on (interviews with Mr B. and Mr G.). In other banks, this was not always necessary. In the Netherlands, the equivalent of the British Bankers' exams, the *NIBE* training programs, only got off the ground in the post-war years and it is fair to say that Dutch banks never regarded these exams in quite the same manner as some British banks did.

Locating gender in this employment set-up

These features of banking employment; the work hierarchy, the patriarchal relations between employees and their superiors, the internal labour market with its specific recruitment and promotion patterns, together formed what may be called the gender blind employment structure in British and Dutch banks. The organization of employment was, however, 'explicitly gendered' (Crompton, 1989, p.143). The process of clerical feminization was accompanied by several gender differentiated employment features.

One crucial feature was the age profile of employees; clerical feminization amongst finance sector staff in the period under consideration was a

110

feminization of young women. In commentaries on the characteristics of female bank employment in the 1960s, this feature stands out clearly (Heritage, 1983, p.134, Wierema, 1979, p.104). The Census supports the idea that this feature was established as clerical feminization progressed in extent, since over the war period (Census periods 1930/31 and 1947/51), there is a change in the female/male ratio of finance sector staff in the under 24 age-group from a female minority to a female majority in both societies. By 1960, both societies have a female ratio in this age-group of around 2/3. In the older age-groups, however, there is little change in the gender ratios. Here the male ratio remains well over 60 per cent over these same years.

Apart from the youth of female bank employees during this period, a number of other features may be elicited. The first of these is a relative absence of married women amongst female bank employees in the earlier period under consideration.[4] In Britain, the presence of married women has increased in absolute terms, and as a ratio of finance staff as such, between the 1951 and 1981 Census. Whilst in 1951, 7.9 per cent of finance staff were married women, in 1981, 26.7 per cent were. However, the ratio of married women to unmarried women has, in the finance sector, remained well below that of British industries on average, indicating how significant the presence of young and unmarried female staff was in the finance sector at this time. For Dutch banks no numerical evidence exists. But the accounts of my informants speak for themselves. The employment of married female bank staff was, certainly in the first two decades after the war, unheard off.

The recruitment of young (and hence unmarried) staff into banks is not gender specific. It corresponds well with the internal labour market which banks operate. It may be argued, though, that in the direct post-war years, there is a distinct preference in banks for young and unmarried women. There are obviously two sides to the employment of women in the banking sector. On the one hand, Heritage (1983) and others have commented that most of the young women who were recruited into banking during that time did not expect to follow a career in banking, in the way the men did. In this respect, banks were dependent on existing ideologies around women's employment at the time. On the other hand, women were not expected by their bank to follow a career either. This is evident from a number of employment policies which banks operated during that time. Looking at these involves us, as Witz and Savage have pointed out, in indicating 'the gendered processes internal to the bureaucratic processes' (in this case) of banks (Witz and Savage, 1992, p.6). Or, by operating certain employment policies, bank employers may have used existing gender ideologies, but by doing so reinforced and institutionalized these. In this way, they must be regarded as active contributors to the maintenance of particular forms of gender relations.

One such employment policy was the marriage bar. In both societies, a marriage bar existed in banks before the Second World War, during the war and thereafter (though it was relaxed during the war in Britain and in some Dutch banks just after the war). In many British banks this policy continued to affect marrying female employees until the end of the 1950s. Here, such a bar was often accompanied by a marriage dowry. Marrying female staff received a sum of money, in lieu of their pension rights. In Dutch banks, the marriage bar lasted until into the 1960s, though here marriage dowries were not as common. Britbank operated a marriage bar on its female employees until 1960, and it had a marriage dowry until much later. Dutchbank also had a marriage bar, but until the mid-1960s; known to its employees as the *Ooievaarsregel* (stork rule).

A second employment policy in which banks gave voice to their ideas concerning female members of staff involved salaries. Salary scales differed between men and women in both societies into the 1960s. Often, the salaries would be the same for the first number of years, after which female employees would get paid increasingly less as their years of service increased. Since the bank *CAO* (collective bargaining agreement) in the Netherlands contained different salary scales for men and women until the mid-sixties as well, Dutchbank would have paid its female employees less than its male employees. Britbank also operated divergent salary scales for its female and male employees, starting after the probationary period of three years had been served. Equality of pay was introduced in the mid-sixties.

A third feature of the gender-divided character of banking employment, which is harder to pin down as an explicit employment policy, refers to the areas in the occupational hierarchy were women could be found. Women could not be found in the higher regions of the occupational hierarchy of banks. Given that a marriage bar was enforced on women and that decisions about career moves were based on seniority and length of service, it is not surprising that there were relatively few women in the higher regions of the occupational hierarchy. However, that gender played an important part in the promotion decisions of both British and Dutch banks is evident in the fact that even amongst the older and unmarried women in the bank, promotion in the way male employees enjoyed it, was uncommon (if not unheard of). Young women employees were recruited into a job, whilst male bank employees were recruited to follow a career (Blackburn, 1967, Heritage, 1983 and Crompton, 1989).

Given these indicators, there can be no doubt that the employment organization in banks in both societies was 'explicitly gendered'. My argument, then, is that in relation to clerical feminization, banks in both societies went through three stages, and each of these stages reflects a particular stage in the character of patriarchal relations in banks. The first stage was the time when women were formally excluded from the clerical staff of banks. The second stage is the period in which women were recruited into clerical work, but because marriage bars were in operation, their inclusion was only partial. The third and last stage is the period when marriage bars, and other formal modes of exclusion no longer exist; women are formally included into clerical work, but this does not mean that informal means of exclusion have disappeared. This chapter centres on the shift from formal exclusion to formal/partial inclusion of women in clerical bank work.

Summary of contrasts and similarities

In the light of the above discussed features of the gendered nature of employment in banks in the period under consideration, two kinds of comparison may now be made. Firstly, the cross-national differences and similarities in the gendered patterning of banking employment - taking into account our previous elucidation of developments in the gender composition of bank staff - can now be summarized as follows:

1. Banks in both societies were characterized by an increase in the ratio of women amongst their staff in the period 1940-1970.
2. The increase in female bank employees was not as significant in Dutch banks compared to their British counterparts.
3. Feminization of clerical bank staff in both societies has been accompanied by similar gendered features; female clerical workers were first and foremost young and unmarried women, working in the lowest regions of the employment hierarchy.

In terms of the broader objective of this chapter, it is further necessary to contrast developments in the banking sector with aggregate labour developments. Again, several distinctive features may be summarized:

1. Whilst the increase in British women's bank employment mirrors the increased presence of women in employment on an aggregate level, in the Netherlands this is not the case. Here, the increased female ratio amongst bank employees stands in contrast to the relative stability in women's economic activity on an aggregate level. This feature, though interesting, shall not be addressed here.
2. The increased presence of women in banking employment was mainly an increase of young and single women. This contrasts with the British aggregate trend of the rise in married women's remunerated work. In the Netherlands, where there is no quantitative increase in married women's employment patterns during the period between 1945 and 1960, this banking pattern is hardly surprising.

With this preliminary discussion on the characteristics of banking employment in the background, we will now move onto a discussion of the socio-economic and ideological trends in banking employment in the period between 1940 and 1965.

Employment disruption during the war

Employment in British banks was certainly affected by the advent of World War II. The questions addressed here are how banks managed their employment affairs during the war, and whether the war gave rise to long-term changes in the gender ratio amongst bank employees, and in the conditions of bank employment. This will be contrasted with the situation in Dutch banking during the war years.

Employment matters in British banks

From the beginning of hostilities, a steady flow of young male bank employees left their banks to join the armed forces. The speed and extent with which staff were withdrawn from banks is evident in that by the time the war was at its height, British banks had together released 55 per cent of their pre-war male staff (Checkland, 1975, p.596, *The Bank Officer*, 1942, June, p.2, The Kennett Committee Report, 1942, p.4). This reduction in staffing levels entailed that banks had to find alternative sources of labour supply in a short time. This was found in women, older men, and men who were declared unfit for the army.

There is little disagreement that the expansion in female bank employment over the war years was significant. But few concrete figures are available. In the Bank of England, the number of female employees increased from 1,687 in 1939 to 2,673 in 1942; a rise of 58 per cent (BoE archive E31.1). Table 5.1 shows that in 1942, women formed 42 per cent of bank staff, whilst in 1939, women had only constituted 22.4 per cent of total staff in the Clearing banks and the Scottish banks together (The Kennett Committee Report, 1942, p.4).

The empty places were mainly filled by young women[5] but married women were also employed. Married bank women had either worked in a bank before they married, were spouses of male bank employees who had departed, or were staff who got married during the war. The Bank of England kept a count of the number of their female staff who married and continued their employment with the bank. In 1943, 72 female staff married, and 50 of them stayed on. Between 1943 and 1947, a total of 533 women staff married in the Bank of England, 262 of whom stayed on and moved onto the Acting Ranks.[6]

The Kennett Committee looked at the possibility for the increased use of part-time employment in British banks. In the Report it was acknowledged that part-time work had not been used much by 1942, but that there were opportunities for doing so 'especially for homogeneous blocks of simple clerical work in large centres' (The Kennett Committee Report, 1942, p.2). Little evidence is available about the extent to which banks followed these guidelines, but if the Bank of England is taken as a guide - 13 of its 2,594 female staff worked part-time in 1943 - it would appear that almost no use was made of this form of employment.

Measures taken by British banks to facilitate the war-time emergency. In the first years of the war, then, banks experienced a radical overthrow of their pre-war employment practices, and these changes were accompanied by a number of employment decisions. Together, these signal how banks managed the war years in terms of their employment.

The first decision made was that all male employees who had left were promised a place in the bank after the war was over. In its wake followed the decision that all staff taken on during the war were employed on a temporary basis. That bank managers did not want to recruit anyone permanently was supported on the grounds of uncertainty about post-war conditions and consequently a concern with being faced with too many permanent staff after the war.

As suggested above, another policy step taken in response to the war-time emergency was to suspend the operation of the marriage bar. The Bank of England announced its decision officially in 1939 (BoE archive: E31.4). During the summer of 1939, the Committee of London Clearing Bankers took the same decision (*The Bank Officer*, 1940, February, p.14). That this policy was indeed seen as a temporary measure was clear by the fact that marrying female staff were, without exception, automatically transferred to the temporary staff. Another implication of the large exit of male employees was that women were moved onto more responsible work, often without much extra training. In the Bank of England, for example, it was recorded that in the accountance department:

> After four years of war, permanent women clerks are to be found doing work in every office of the department which, prior to 1939, was undertaken only by the permanent male staff. (BoE Archive E31.1: December, 1943)

But it seems clear that the extent to which women 'moved up' into the higher regions of the banking hierarchy should not be exaggerated. The management of British banks remained firmly in the hands of its male managers.[7]

Possibly related to this is another specific feature about women's employment during the war; this is that many women bank employees studied for their banker's exams. This behaviour stands in stark contrast to that of their peace-time colleagues. So over the war years, the number of women who sat their exams first rose, and than declined. In 1940, 98 women sat their exams; this reached a height in 1942, when 598 women sat the exams; and declined over the following years again to a low of 75 in 1948. At the same time, the number of men sitting the exams plummeted. Between 1940 and 1945, the number of men who sat the exams in those years declined from 763 to 69. There is no doubt that female bank employees were stimulated to study for the banker's exams. Bank management had a distinct interest in a 'better' trained female staff, since most banks had lost a large percentage of their experienced male employees in a short time. This meant that new female recruits:

> ... had to all of a sudden learn the game pretty quickly, cause the customers were still coming in. So there was a very quick learning process. (interview Mr T.)

The likelihood of post-war continuity in war-time employment policies. So the war forced British banks to introduce several changes in the way they managed their employment affairs. But how likely was it that these changes would be used to model bank employment in the post-war years? It seems to me that the very nature of most policy decisions made that likelihood very slim. Many of the policy changes carried a 'temporary' tag, as is clear in the fact that no new war-time recruits or married women had security of tenure. Moreover, the war-time situation did not entail the complete run-down of gender distinctions characteristic of banking employment prior to the war. Apart from the fact that women had made only limited advances up the employment hierarchy, a further much commented on issue is the continuity of inequality of pay during the war.

A perusal of relevant source material reveals a diversity of discourses on the direction post-war staffing ought to take.[8] Yet, it seems to me that the voices that mattered - found in journals like *The Banker* and *The Bankers' Magazine*, and which represented the views of bank management - were quite clearly against the reduction of gender distinctions in banking employment. Indeed, these discourses were full of explicit discriminatory talk, which belittled the importance of women's contribution in bank work during the war, and came up for the rights of permanent - and other - male staff.

As early as August 1943, *The Banker* carried an article on *Post-war Personnel Problems,* in which it was pointed out that the major future personnel problem facing banks was the return of permanent staff - read: permanent male staff - from the forces (*The Banker*, August, 1943, p.77).[9] This concern may be interpreted to mean several things, one of which is that the 'suitable' return of permanent male staff should get priority over and above the interests of all other staff. So with respect to married women, the correspondent pointed out that 'it has not been the practice of banks to employ married women', implying that the decision about what to do with married and marrying female staff should not pose a problem. More tricky was the case of single women. Some of them had taken on 'senior duties normally taken on by men' and had done this job well. It was suggested that though these women would not find it easy to return to routine work, they must have realized that this 'promotion has been of a temporary nature, and this fact is emphasized by the grant of temporary financial recognition'. The financial increments those women had enjoyed doing this work was to be regarded as their reward, but their war-time contribution was no reason for permanent change. Indeed, it was argued that any permanent changes in the position of bank women ought to depend entirely on the desires and needs of men returning from the forces.

> The men when they return will not wish to remain for long in the positions they occupied prior to joining the services; (...) they will hope to be given the opportunity of proving their ability in the higher posts. Whether women are to be given opportunities to undertake more senior positions is a matter of long-run policy *for consideration afterwards*. (*The Banker*, August, 1943, p.77. italics my emphasis)

On the other hand, the concerns about the young men were more charitable than that. Hence it was lamented that:

> Many demobilized young men find that there is no place for them in the offices where they served their brief apprenticeships. ... That none of them have a legal claim is not the beginning and the end of the matter. They are precious national assets and must not be allowed to waste; they are youngsters whom a war not of their own making has robbed of a start in life ... the banking community has some sort of duty to see that its doors shall be flung as widely open as possible to those whose only fault has been that of belonging to a particular age-group. (*The Banker*, December, 1943, p.106)

Brief though the arguments in *The Banker* and *The Bankers' Magazine* may have been, they denoted their male favouritism with clarity. The argument was not, however, that women should be expelled completely from banking employment. Far from it. They had a place in British banks, but what kind of place that was, was actively constructed in the post-war years, in the light of further employment problems.

Decline and deterioration in Dutch banking

Employment conditions and developments in Dutch banking closely resemble the aggregate developments discussed in chapter 4. Unemployment was spoken off as a major social problem before as well as during the war, by all the Dutch interviewees who worked in a bank during the war (4 in total). Mr S. started work in the *Nederlandse Handel Maatschappij* (*NHM*) in 1939, when he was 16 and he had finished his *MULO* education.[10] He agrees that it was very difficult to get work at the time, including clerical work, and he remembers his parents' reaction when he was offered work in the bank:

> ... en ik hoor mijn ouders nog zeggen, je boft! Ja, je boft. (interview Mr S.)
> (... I can still hear my parents say, you're lucky! Yes, you're lucky.)

This was on the eve of the war, but the beginning of the war did not entail an immediate improvement in the labour market. At least this is the impression I get from Mr F., who started work with the *Rotterdamse Bank* in December 1941. To the question why he wanted to work in a bank came the answer that he did not particularly want to work in a bank, but after looking for a job for 5 months since gaining his *MULO* diploma, this was the first job offered to him and he could not refuse it (interview Mr F.). He and his wife Mrs F., who worked in the Dutch bank *Mees en Zoonen* during the war, agree that at the beginning of the war, it was still rather difficult to get work.

All four interviewees experienced some form of interruption in their bank employment during the war. Mr A. remembers that the banks:

> ... hebben wel mensen af moeten staan die in Duitsland te werk werden gesteld. Dat was bij ons bij de bank ook. Degene die niet gehuwd waren, of gehuwd waren en geen kinderen hadden, die zijn ehh die hebben bij een bank in Duitsland gewerkt. (interview Mr A.)
> (had to supply people who were put to work in Germany. That was also the case in our bank. Those who were not married, or who were married but had no children, they are ehh they have worked in a bank in Germany.)

The extent to which banks 'lost' staff due to call-up is clear from the employment figures of the *Twentsche Bank*. In their head office in Amsterdam, 627 staff were employed in January 1945. Of those 627 staff, 73 were absent at the time, whilst in January, one year later, 15 of those staff still had not returned (TB archive: nb. 772). So though there was displacement in Dutch banks too, this did not reach the same level as in British banks. The call-up to Germany, then, was one possible reason why substitution might have occurred amongst bank staff, so that those who had left for Germany (or who had gone into hiding) were replaced with other staff (for example, women). Was this indeed what happened?

The answer would appear to be no. Many bank employees indeed left their work during the war, and those who went were guaranteed that they had a job with the bank on return, but these places were not filled with new staff. So why was there no substitution of departed employees? Two reasons may be put forward. On the one hand, the extent to which staff was displaced by the war, as just indicated, does not appear to have been of the extent to which this happened in Britain. At the same time, as the war continued, the work load of individual banks reduced significantly, and there is even some indication that Dutch banks were overstaffed during the war. De Vries has characterized the situation in the banking sector during the war as one of 'achteruitgang en verwording' (decline and deterioration) (de Vries, 1992, p.44). Through the drain on Dutch resources, a balance of payment deficit and a deregulation of the money supply were the result. The banks faced a decline in their normal business practice, their supply of loans went down, whilst their receipt of credit increased. My interviewees also remember the decline in the amount of work. Mr A., for example, returned after mobilization in 1940, to find that the work in the foreign trade department he had worked in, had all but stopped. So he asked for a transfer, and moved to the accounts department. Here he worked for 2 years and says:

> Maar vanaf dus ... 10 Mei 1940 tot aan 42, heb ik elke dag 2½ uur in de koffiekamer gezeten. Der was niks te doen. Daar heb ik bridgen geleerd. (interview Mr A.)
>
> (But from 10 May 1940 till 42, I have spent 2½ hours every day in the canteen. There was nothing to do. This is where I learned to play bridge.)

So in his case it would appear that his bank was overstaffed during the war, though he claims that no-one was sacked because of it in his bank. According to Mr F., the *Rotterdamse Bank* did not sack any of its staff either, whilst Mrs F. remembers that because of the decline in business at the end of the war, her bank was only open three mornings a week (interview Mr and Mrs F.). Nevertheless, no staff were made redundant.

The underlying trend in clerical feminization

The Second World War meant a net-increase in women's employment in British banks in quantitative terms, as is clear from the figures presented in table 5.1. This change needs to be seen in the context of other - long-term - changes in banking employment. One of these, the increased use of machinery in banks, was also associated with the increased recruitment of women clerks (Savage, 1993). Book-keeping machines, like the *Burrough* machine, had been in use to some extent before the war. Their usage during and after the war became more widespread, though it may be argued that war-time labour requirements contributed to the introduction of mechanical aids - the Kennett Committee Report, for instance, put pressure on banks to introduce labour saving methods.

Mechanized book-keeping methods, which were being introduced in banks in both societies, may be regarded as one of a number of reasons why female clerical work was on the increase in banks. The suggestion that there was a further reason which favoured the use of female employees in banks is further supported by Dutch evidence. As just discussed, there was no substitution of male by female staff in Dutch banks. Even so, an increasing number of women found employment in Dutch banks. That this was by no means a homogenous process; i.e. occurring in all banks and their various departments at the same time, seems clear from the evidence of Mr A. and Mr S., who both worked in the *NHM*. According to Mr A., there was not really an increased presence of women in the head office of this bank until the expansion of the 1960s. But Mr S., who worked in a provincial branch of the same bank, clearly remembered that there was a change. When he had started with the bank in 1939, he had no female colleagues at all. But his branch got a new manager during the war, and the gender composition of the branch changed quickly. By 1950, 5 of the 9 staff of the branch were women.[11] Mr S. did agree that it was very unusual to find a branch with so many female staff at the time, and he attributes this peculiarity to the preferences of the bank manager. It is not hard to imagine that in a time-period when more women entered a variety of white-collar work, there will have been diversity between individual managers in the degree to which they associated with the exclusionary ideology which had characterized banking employment for so long. This might suggest that the liberalism, which has been associated with changed attitudes towards women's remunerated work, were also evident in the recruitment practices of some bank managers.

Socio-economic conditions and banking feminization in the post-war years

In the years immediately following the war, the employment in banks in both societies was subject to considerable unrest. British banks had to deal with the consequences of the war on their staffing. Dutch banks were busy establishments in the first years after the war as a result of the country's efforts to regain control over the money supply. In both societies, banks indicated the existence of staffing problems. But how persistent this was, and what the characteristics of this were, differed.

120

For British banks, it soon became clear that staffing the banks brought up different issues and problems than had been the case before the war. One of the important reasons was that the economic climate before and after the war was completely different. What seems clear is that British banks experienced a continuous and lengthy period of staff shortages, which was narrowed down to a concern about the shortage of specifically male employees. The latter was, however, also related to internal staffing problems. In the Netherlands, banks also experienced a labour shortage, especially in the first 5 years after the war. But the indications are that this did not last, nor generated the sort of long-term problems which were discussed in Britain. In what follows, I will look in more detail at these staffing issues in the respective countries.

Staffing British banks after the war

British banks encountered a variety of problems in the reorganization of their male staffing. On the one hand, the return of bank staff from the forces did not proceed overnight, as demobilization was spread out over 3 years. Moreover, the introduction of compulsory military service entailed that the banks' apprenticeships were disrupted, without the banks having any guarantee that these youngsters would return to them. On the other hand, not as many male staff returned as had left.[12] For as it turned out, the direct post-war period generated rather larger staffing problems than were anticipated during the war. Moreover, these problems were mostly not associated with the war. The anticipation of these problems was signalled by a series of articles on staffing issues and problems, started in *The Banker* of 1948.

> Among senior executives and other thoughtful people in the banks, long-range questions of staff policy and organization are causing more concern than perhaps at any other time since the banking system assumed its modern shape. Social changes arising partly from the war, but also from the fundamental trend of population, have radically altered the problem of clerical staffing as understood in the past. (*The Banker*, April, 1948, p.19)

The crux of the problem was that clerical work was quickly declining as a popular career option for men. This was undermining the 'proper' operation of the internal labour market, in the sense that it had become difficult to recruit and retain the type of young men who would fill future management posts.

Possibly the most salient reason for this trend was the lasting tightness in the British labour market. Throughout the post-war years, complaints were voiced about the difficulties of recruiting male staff. The Bank of England complained throughout the 1950s about its difficulty in recruiting both male and female staff, and labour shortage problems were not just concentrated in the South of England. Following *The Banker's* discussion papers in 1948, the *Scottish Bankers' Magazine* argued in 1952 that the:

> Shortage of suitable recruits has been the constant lament of most staff managers ever since recruiting recommenced after the war. (1952, p.200)

Between 1958 and 1964, the Scottish Bank Employer's Federation commissioned 4 reports, the objective of which was to investigate the tight labour supply of men, and what could be done about it.[13]

The labour supply problem experienced by British bank employers was a symptom of Britain's general full-employment economy. On the one hand this meant that there was stronger competition from other employers for the kind of youngsters the banks sought. On the other hand it meant that work expectations changed in a way which did not favour the sort of career banks offered youngsters. So whilst job security definitely was a desirable attribute of bank employment during the recessions of the twenties and thirties, in the post-war period, with its full employment, employment security became less salient compared to other features of employment.

One of these was income. Banks, with their offer of life-long employment, had a salary structure which was attuned to this. This meant that the salary level during the first years of service was very low, significantly increasing only in later years of service. At the beginning of the 1950s, the yearly income of an apprentice would be in the region of £110. Buying a suit alone would cost you £10 in those days, Mr G. pointed out. So in comparison to other types of employment, the pay which a young bank employee received was rather low and this did not impress those who sought immediate financial reward.

These negative features were further exacerbated by the fact that the other 'reward' for men working in a bank; the prospect of a career, did not look rosy either. Traditionally, male bank staff have had to be content with years of doing simple clerical work before they could expect to get work of a more responsible nature in the bank. Savage has indicated that the number of years which Lloyds' male staff had to 'wait' before they attained a managerial position, increased over the inter-war years. Interestingly, this reached a peak in the post-war years, when 62 per cent of the male staff who had been recruited between 1914 and 1925, had to wait for over 28 years to attain a managerial position (Savage, 1993, p.203). The large number of 40 to 50 year old male bank employees, 'waiting' for the expected promotion, became known as the 'age-bulge' problem. And the point is that all British banks suffered from this problem after the war.

The 'age-bulge' was, in fact, a maldistribution in the age-structure amongst bank employees, which was a result of the over recruitment of male employees in the years after the First World War (when British banks retracted from their war-time recruitment of women). The post World War II years further exacerbated the maldistribution in the age-structure, by causing an underrepresentation in the younger age-groups. The latter was due to low male recruitment during the war, and the limited return of pre-war male staff.

So youngsters could clearly see that the career path of bankmen was a slow affair. Indeed, in view of the post-war situation, there was no guarantee that one would eventually become - what many aspired to - the manager of a branch. British banks recognized that the popularity of clerical work had declined as a career option for many young men precisely because of this reason. 'Bright' youngsters, in search of a future career:

> ... will judge the prospects by the men they know, though they may ultimately attain a good position, have to wait until they are on the threshold of fifty, or even older than that. (*The Banker*, 1948, p.25)

So what solutions were suggested to this problem?

In the discussion papers in which the staffing difficulties were outlined, there was no overall agreement about how these problems could best be tackled. Several suggestions were put forward. One type of suggestion involved a general tiering of bank employees. One way of achieving this involved the introduction of a new grading system, in which employees of different ability could make different rates of progress. The other suggestion involved recruitment. As it was indicated, in the various discussions, that the 'bright' boys the banks needed were now likely to go to university, it was suggested to consciously target this group and to make a career in banking more interesting for them. In *The Banker*, then, a two-tier system of recruitment was suggested in which university graduates were recruited into a first division of employees with its own pay-scale and accelerated career structure.

The other suggested solution involved the recruitment of women. Why an increased recruitment of women was to provide an answer to the problems is an issue which has already been addressed by others (see for instance Crompton, 1986, Crompton & Jones (1984, p.3), Cohn (1985a) - in relation to the British Civil Service, and Savage, 1993). The increased presence of women facilitated male career prospects simply by the fact that the number of competing males was reduced, whilst the recruited women did not - and were not allowed to - compete for the 'better' jobs. This same point is echoed in the banking debate.

> It is true that a large proportion of the girls and young women who enter the banks have no wish or intention to make their work a career. A large number, probably up to as much as 80 to 90 per cent., will leave the

123

banks before they reach 30 years of age, the bulk going at about 24 to 28 on account of marriage. *On the face this looks like an unsatisfactory state of affairs, but is this really so?* Outweighing some of the disadvantages of this continued intake and exit is the fact that it does enable a great deal of the humdrum junior routine work, as well as machine accounting, to be carried out by young (and, on the whole, enthusiastic) *staff who are not obsessed with the idea of gaining experience on other work with the idea of promotion.* Furthermore, *the turn-over operates against the building up of a large middle-aged staff of men,* or, for that matter, women, on salaries and with pension rights, etc., much in excess of the value of the work they do. (*The Banker,* 1948, p.28, italics my emp.)

In the event, more prominence was given to the increased recruitment of women than to a recruitment policy which included university graduates.[14] The question which remains is why preference was given to feminization? This question will be addressed below.

Staffing Dutch banks after the war

In the first instance, it would seem that Dutch banks suffered from similar staffing problems as British banks; the former also experienced problems in holding onto their junior staff. Dutch bank employers also complained about high competition levels by other employers, and the low starting wage was also discussed. Several major differences are however evident. Firstly, the staffing problems in Dutch banks were of a temporary nature. Recordings of the problem can be found in publications dated between 1945 and 1950; thereafter, no further relevant discussions are present.

The origins of the Dutch staffing problems were different too. In fact, they appear to be directly related to two aspects of the interventionist new government's post-war policies. In the first place, following the new law *Buitengewoon Besluit Arbeidsverhoudingen* (established in 1945), Dutch banks were required to set up an employers' federation, with the aim to collectivize wage agreements. In the event, it was 1948 before the *Nederlandse Bankiersvereeniging* (the Dutch Bankers' Federation) started this task. But by 1950, the first *CAO* was agreed. Between 1945 and 1948, employee matters, especially where it concerned wages, were discussed in meetings which included government representatives, the *Stichting van de Arbeid* (the Joint Industrial Labour Council) and the trade unions which represented bank employees, working under the collective name of *Bedrijfsunie*.

Secondly, a phenomenal amount of work was generated in the Dutch banking sector, because the government instructed Dutch banks to help with the *geldzuivering* (monetary reform), the *effectenregistratie* (stocks and shares registration) and the *vermogensregistratie* (capital registration) (de Vries, 1992, p.46). During the monetary reform, every Dutch inhabitant was required to hand in their paper money for registration. Mr F., who worked in the *Rotterdamse Bank* still remembered the mountains of 100 guilder notes which were piled up in the corner of his branch. For a whole year, he said, he worked overtime every evening of the working week (interview Mr F.). Equally, in the minutes of the directors' meetings of the *Twentsche Bank*, reference was made to the rise in work levels. It would appear that by February 1946, this had reached crisis levels.

> Voor de spreker is het geen vraag meer of wij zullen vastlopen, maar wanneer dat zal gebeuren (Archive Twentsche Bank)
> (For the speaker the issue is no longer whether work will get stuck, but when this will happen.)

Work pressure continued into 1948, when departmental heads complained that they needed extra help immediately, and that staff members were becoming overworked. Only in 1949 were there signs that work pressure was reducing in this bank.

The amount of overtime - which was very often not paid for - in combination with low starting wages, and an evaluation as to what could be earned elsewhere, drove many new bank employees into other work soon after starting. This connection is made by Mr B., who answered to my question whether it was difficult in 1945 to get work in a bank that:

> Om bij een bank werk te krijgen was niet zo moeilijk, maar om het daar vol te houden, dat was vrij moeilijk. Omdat de meeste ... die zagen andere baantjes die wat makkelijker lagen, en die in feite ook meer revenue opleverde. (interview Mr B.)
> (To get work in a bank was not difficult, but to remain there was quite difficult. Most of the employees saw that there were other jobs which were easier (in terms of workload, my emp.), and which, in fact, also earned you more money.)

That there were plenty of opportunities may sound surprising, especially in the context of the argument in chapter 4 that the first post-war years were characterized by a slack labour market in the Netherlands. But one needs to bear in mind that we are here talking about a select group of youngsters; namely those who had a secondary education. Like British banks, Dutch banks only recruited youngsters with a secondary education. For some banks, the four year *MULO* was sufficient as an entry qualification. Other banks, like the

Twentsche Bank, required *HBS* as entry level. Now whilst in Britain, secondary education became free with the 1944 education reforms, in the Netherlands secondary education had to be paid for by parents until the 1960s. In the often parochial climate of the period, youngsters with secondary education remained a scarce resource.

Now, it was accepted knowledge in those years, that banks did not pay their youngsters well. But it was exactly when the labour market for youngsters with secondary education became tight in the first post-war years, that the government curbed wage increases. And Dutch banks found themselves in a position from which it was difficult to escape; of having to pay their young staff less than their competitors. In the wage negotiations of 1947, the conflict in interests between the government wages policy, and the banks' needs to increase wages, were evident. Bank employers argued that there needed to be a minimum wage rise of 30 per cent for the employees in the 18-21 year old age-group, and that any offer below that level:

> ... zou het bankbedrijf voor onoverkomelijke moeilijkheden stellen. Het is immers voldoende bekend, dat door talloze grote en kleine werkgevers (...) aan jonge menschen salarissen plegen te worden betaald welke de voorgestelde maxima ver overschreiden. (archive Werkgeversvereeniging voor het Bankbedrijf: document dated 19/2/1947)
> (... would pose insurmountable difficulties for the banks. It is, after all, well known, that countless large and small employers pay young people salaries which far exceed the here suggested maximum.)

The insurmountable difficulties were the high turn-over of staff, which in turn was affecting the age-profile of staff. Turnover was so bad, that Mr B. compared the bank to a *duiventil* (Waterloo Station), which indeed is the impression you get when considering that in the *Twentsche Bank*, where 117 new employees were recruited between January 1945 and April 1946, a staggering total of 114 employees left in the same period.

Under these circumstance, some exceptions were made to the otherwise stringent recruitment rules. In 1946, for instance, the *Twentsche Bank* recruited a 32 year old unmarried woman, with the argument that the circumstances allowed them to divert from their normal regulations. In 1949, there are reports that some married women (3 in all) had continued work in that same bank, one of whom worked for half days. The bank's directors pointed out, however, that this was a temporary ruling. At the end of 1949, when overtime work had declined, these women were asked to leave. But there is no indication that the staffing problems prompted an increased recruitment of female staff.[15] Indeed, no connection was made in the discourses about these staffing problems and female labour (as was the case in British banks). In 1950, the work generated by the monetary reform and registration of shares and capital finished, a *CAO* had been arranged, and complaints about the turnover of staff ceased. During the 1950s, no other important employment matters were recorded. The absolute number of female staff did increase in this sector, but compared to the increase in British banks this was not as significant.

Class and gender culture in banks

In an economic environment of full employment, and in the context of a number of self-defined internal employment problems, British banks chose as immediate solution an extensive feminization of their clerical staff. Feminization in Dutch banks also continued into the post-war years, but not to the same extent as in the British banking sector. In what has preceded, I have argued that at least one important explanation for this is the absence of a full employment aggregate labour market in the Netherlands, in addition to an absence of a self-defined internal labour problem.

But this still leaves a number of questions unanswered. Given the above discussed staffing problems in British banks, why was feminization - in the particular form this occurred - given priority over the other suggested solutions? And why was it that marriage bars lasted as long as they did, given the fact that these restrictions to married women's employment had disappeared in most other types of work? In order to understand these issues more fully, we have to explore the culture peculiar to the banking sector in the two societies further.

Gender relations in banking employment need to be termed patriarchal in the sense that historically, the deployment of female clerical staff can be argued to have entailed distinct benefits for banks themselves, but also for their male employees. In order to understand how the interests of male employees and their employers coincided firstly in women's exclusion from clerical work, and secondly in their partial inclusion, it is necessary to see how 'gender and class intersect in the construction of identity' (Witz, 1992, p.26). The concurrence of interests between the male bank employee and his superior worked within the sphere of employment, but also in the domestic sphere. Feminization in conjunction with a marriage bar favoured bank men not just in facilitating their banking career, it also supported their claim to the leadership of a middle-class family. Bank men could potentially gain as men as well as in class terms with the introduction of women to clerical work. I will argue below that it may further be argued that by accepting this gendered culture, women could also gain in class terms.

It is further necessary to recognize that employee-employer relations in banks were patriarchal in a different, though related sense. As argued at the beginning of this chapter, bank employers exerted a patriarchal authority over their employees (including their male employees), and this authority was extended from the sphere of employment to the more private and domestic aspects of employees' lives. Because of the authoritative relationships within banks, bank employers played a significant role in the construction of a middle-class gender identity amongst the banks' employees.

I want to argue here that there are three related reasons why British clerical feminization in the post-war years occurred in combination with a marriage bar. In the first place, marriage bars, as discussed in chapter 3, served as a symbolic indicator of 'proper' middle class family relations. As such, they fitted in well with the general construction of middle-class culture in banks, to which employers contributed significantly. Secondly, then, the patriarchal ideology discussed above remained significant in British banks, and in the face of the rising significance of liberal/egalitarian ideology, which had by that time influenced state policies. Why this should be so is, I believe, related to the very character of patriarchal relations in banking employment; these did not generate sufficient voices of disagreement from amongst the rank and file. And, last but not least, in British banking marriage bars served a symbolic function in the boosting of the male career.

But how did British banks compare with Dutch banks in this respect? Well, the first two themes also operated in Dutch banks. But the cross-national difference in the trend of marriage bars meant that Dutch banks operated bars within the context of an ideological climate in which marriage bars were the rule rather than the exception.

The shift to formal-partial inclusion and middle-class identity formation

In British banks, it was and still is very common for bank employees to play golf. The practical values of playing golf are evident in that later on in their career, bankers would play with their business associates, a point brought forward by some of my informants (both Dutch and British). The importance of the relationship between business and the social life of the local community is evident in the account of others, who acknowledged to taking up directorships or committee positions for that reason. Certainly in the direct post-war years, bank managers enjoyed a degree of respect in their local communities on a par with the local doctors and teachers, and involvement in the social life of those communities was as important in maintaining and gaining business, as was direct customer contact during official business hours. As most of the banks' clients were well-to-do; middle and upper class customers, bank managers certainly had to fit into that kind of social environment. This is one reason why it is important to recognize that bankers at the top of the hierarchy, and those at the bottom had their 'fortunes ... tied up through the significance of career mobility' (Savage, 1993, p.197). The youngsters, who would follow their superiors in managing the bank in due course, had to espouse to the middle-class culture of the superiors and their future clients. Bank managers, therefore, had a vested interest in nurturing such a culture in their youngsters.

And this is what they did, but not just in their male youngsters, but in all their staff, by the presence of rules of behaviour and such things as staff societies, through which middle-class values were communicated. My Dutch interviewees gave some telling examples of how middle-class culture was stimulated through their bank's leisure activities. *Mees en Zoonen*, for one, had an actively organized work culture. Mrs T. and Mrs H., who both worked in this bank, reminisced about the good collegiality which existed amongst the bank's staff. According to Mrs T. there was a pleasant atmosphere, and she clearly indicates the middle-class connotations of the leisure time activities which the society stimulated.

> Der was ook een hele bloeiende personeelsvereeniging. Ik heb daar ook nog een beetje classieke musiek leren waarderen, en zo, en daar werd heel erg veel aandacht aan besteed. (interview Mrs T.)
> (There was also a flourishing employee society. I have also learned to appreciate classical music there a little, etcetera, and a tremendous amount of attention was given to this.)

In the same line of thought, Mrs H. remembered trips to the opera on her boss's birthday (interview Mrs H.).

Another, equally important, way in which middle-class identity was constructed was through a middle-class understanding of family life. If an informal agreement of bank employment was the offer of a career for men, than the flip-side of the coin was that such a career could support a 'proper' family, *and* was supported by a 'proper' family. Bank employers in both societies did not take a backseat approach in relation to this issue; in the pre-war years, banks in both societies operated a marriage bar on their male employees to ensure that their employees were able to support a family before they started one. In their employment contracts, male employees signed a ruling which stated that they were not allowed to marry until they had reached a particular annual salary. Marrying before that salary was reached resulted in dismissal. This effectively meant that you were not allowed to marry, as a man, before you had reached the age of 26 in Britbank (Interview Mr T.). These bars disappeared before the advent of W.W.II.

The linking of success at work with a 'successful' family life, is an idea which, even recently, has been expressed by bankers.[16] This is one area in which a class dynamic interrelated with a gender dynamic. The bank, as workplace,

129

served as one spatial setting where heterosexual relationships developed, but were also encouraged. Banks did not segregate the genders into spatially different workplaces; a strategy of segregation followed in the history of some other white-collar occupations (Cohn, 1985a). Quite a number of my interviewees, then, remembered or were/are so-called bank couples. So bank employees of different genders not only worked together, but started romances and married each other.[17] In Britbank's employee newsletter, marriages amongst the staff were reported and often accompanied by photographs of the wedding couple. The same newsletter served as an advertising place for wedding rings.

Though there is little written evidence which would support my claim that heterosexual and 'proper' relationships were actively encouraged by the bank, in some of my interviews employer interference in their employees' private lives is quite clear. Mrs T., for instance, reminisced about a lesbian relationship between two of her colleagues. Homosexuality, she said, was of course a taboo, and when their relationship became public, she remembers scenes between the parents and the boss, which resulted in the sacking of both girls (interview Mrs T.). Adultery was not accepted behaviour either. Again Mrs T. remembered how a married male *procuratiehouder* in Amsterdam, who started a relationship with a female colleague, was (in Mrs T.'s words) banished to Rotterdam by the bank, and placed on a lower graded post. He was punished for his deviant behaviour. So 'normal' heterosexual identification was stimulated in banks, and 'abnormal' behaviour was punished. These notions of what was 'proper' sexual behaviour, I would argue, can not be seen loose from the construction of middle-class identities in the banks. What is clear, however, especially in these last examples, is that banks did not shy away from an active interference in the private lives of their employees.

The shift to formal-partial inclusion and employer authority

Crompton & Sanderson (1990) have linked the post-war decline of marriage bars in British employment to the rise of an egalitarian/liberal ideology. This ideology questioned the interference of employers - and other institutions - in matters which were regarded as the concern of the individual. As I argued above, post-war culture in banks remained patriarchal. This was the case for Dutch as well as British banks. Bank management decided on employment policy, and my informants supported the view that this prerogative was accepted by many bank employees. As an employee, it was argued by one interviewee:

You accepted that ... these were the rules and regulations laid down by your employers and eh yours was not to reason why. (Interview with former Britbank employee Mr G.)

But apart from this view that you could not influence employer decision taking, I want to bring up another reason why female bank employees might not necessarily have held strong views against the bar. In the manifold studies on the reactions of working class women towards patriarchal strategies against their access to employment, it has been pointed out that historically, working class women have often chosen in favour of their perceived working class interests, and not their shared interests as women. In relation to banking employment, the same can be argued, but then in terms of middle-class women associating with middle-class ideals. In the post-war period, whilst it would have been very hard (if not impossible) for bank women to gain status and social standing through a career in work, this could be reached by marriage to a husband who had a successful career. The clearest statement of how - given the constraints on their choices - bank women often directed their ambitions in life towards finding a 'good' husband, was given by one of my Dutch interviewees, Mrs V.

Mrs V. forms a telling example of a woman who was very ambitious, already early on in her life. Her aspiration was to break away from her rural and rather poor background. But there never was a role-model which showed her that she could realize her ambitions through work. The highest a woman could reach in the bank at the time was to become a secretary. So she did not direct her ambitions towards her work only, but also to her future life as wife. She said:

Ik werkte wel altijd ergens naar toe, (...) mijn ouders hebben het zo arm en der gebeurt eigenlijk niks, ik hield al heel jong van musea en van ja, goeie dingen zo hè. En ik dacht, goh, ik probeer toch een jongen te vinden die dat heeft. Dus daar zocht ik dan ook echt wel om hè. Probeerde dan toch wel mezelf zo te veranderen; van ja een heel eenvoudig meisje (...) toch dat je je overal kon bewegen, en dat je meer kansen kreeg in dat soort dingen. En dat is ook zo gebeurt. (Interview Mrs V.)

(I always worked towards something, (...) my parents were poor and nothing happened (in the place where she lived), I loved museums and yes, the good things (in life) from when I was young. And I thought, I'll try to find a boy who has these things. So I really searched for that, and tried to change myself from a simple country girl (...) so that you could move around everywhere, and that you increased your chances in that sort of thing. And that is the way it happened.)

It is these aspirations which stimulated her move away from home to Amsterdam, where she continued to work in the same bank, lived in rooms, and became more independent. Amsterdam obviously provided the setting to change herself into a worldly person, and provided the opportunity to meet the sort of man she hoped to marry. In 1960, she married her husband, who was also a bank employee (but who came from a higher social background than she did) and it was his career she stimulated in their married life. He went on to become bank manager, which in turn reflected on her. Mrs V., therefore, reached her ambitions in life, not through a career of her own, but through her marriage with a career man.

The shift towards formal-partial inclusion; cross-national differences

So marriage bars fitted in well with the middle class culture which was actively constructed in banks, not least by bank employers themselves. But the post-war employment problems resulted in extensive feminization and a gender tiered employment organization, rather than an overall tiering of recruitment and grading, for another reason. A two-tiered recruitment policy would have entailed the creation of two streams of male employees, one of which would have constituted a group of men destined for the routine type work of the bank. Savage has pointed out that such a situation is ideal for the ghettoization of employees (Savage, 1993), leading to a greater likelihood of trade union association and organization, to which British banks (and for that matter Dutch banks) have not looked upon in favourable terms.

Introducing women on a 'temporary' basis (i.e. by operating a marriage bar) may also be regarded as a strategy to prevent this from happening. Evidence supports the point that 'temporary' female bank clerks were a difficult group of employees to organize (Blackburn, 1967, Heritage, 1983). The presence of 'temporary' women also reduced the chance of ghettoization amongst male employees because feminization vastly improved the career chances of male employees. Women did not - and were not meant to - join in the competition for career posts. A gender-tiered employment organization, therefore, both ensured and strengthened the continuation of class relations as they had previously existed. Employing women, of course, also solved some of the problems with recruitment overall.

But in the historically specific conditions of the post-war years, one wonders whether growing trade-union activism was perceived as the greatest threat. Indeed, between 1945 and 1950 trade union male membership remained around the 22,000 level, only to increase to 35,000 by the end of the 1950s (Blackburn, 1967, p.277). Given industry-wide employment levels (see table 1.4), trade union membership amongst bank staff increased slightly during the 1950s, from 15 per cent to 18.5 per cent. This suggests that some male bank

132

employees may have given voice to their discontent by joining unions. But it is likely that the difficulty of recruiting men in the first place, and their subsequent high turn-over rates was more important, because it resulted in managerial loss of control of the internal labour market. Consequently, the primary concern was to make the banking career more appealing to youngsters, and a more appealing picture of that career was actively constructed during the 1950s, partly on the basis of gender difference.

The latter is related to a further relevant issue. In chapter 3, we discussed the debate about the relationship between the presence of marriage bars and married women's employment rates. During W.W.II and after its abolition of the bar in 1949, the Bank of England monitored the employment patterns of their marrying female staff. Whilst many marrying female staff had stayed on during the war years, in the post-war years they were less inclined to do so. In 1952, for instance, only 8 per cent of their marrying female employees were still in the bank's employment after 2 years of marriage. This confirms that marriage bars were not necessary to make female employees effectively 'temporary' employees, because marrying female staff left on their own account; either on marriage or shortly thereafter. So why did many British banks impose such a bar? My suggestion is that if the marriage bar did not have any real affect on the length of women's employment, it was, amongst other things, used as a symbolic means to boost the male career.

It could be argued that the salience attributed to the Institute of Banking (IoB) exams served a similar purpose. In Britbank, male youngsters were reminded of their special position in the bank in a number of ways. Firstly, they were special, and had to show that they were, by following the Institute of Bankers (IoB) exams. It is possible that the contents of the course was not the only important aspect about the course. Following the course, and sitting the exam, also fed into the relationship building between the bank and its male employees, making this at the same time more permanent. In addition, during the late 1940s and 1950s, the banking journals abounded with news about the establishment of training centres in various banks. These centres offered male youngsters training in which they learned about aspects of bank work, other than they were familiar with through their own work. In all, it would appear as though British banks stimulated a greater awareness in their male youngsters that they were following a career in the bank, and that their place in the bank was a permanent one.

Women's work in the bank was constructed in contradistinction to this. The male career was, what women's work was not, and vice versa. Hence, after so many bank women had sat their IoB exams during the Second World War, the ratio of women who sat the exams during the 1950s and 1960s was very low indeed.[18] Women were not invited onto Britbank's internal training courses, either. In those post-war years, male youngsters were offered a picture in which the barriers (in terms of competition) to advancement in the banks, which had been so obviously present for the older members of staff, had all but disappeared. Feminization helped to advance this picture, but it could only do so if women's work was not perceived as a threat to the male career. The marriage bar was a valuable symbolic means in achieving this.

There is no evidence of Dutch banks 'boosting' the male career. In fact, Dutch banks do not appear to have structured their employment set-up along such determined lines as was the case in British banks. Whilst British banks backed away from the creation of a general tiered employment structure during the 1950s, Dutch banks did not. They did recruit male youngsters with different educational qualifications, and these did not all have the same career chances. Evidence of this forms the *Twentsche Bank* where, according to Mrs J., there were definitely two grades of male clerical employees during the 1950s. The male youngsters with a *HBS* education went onto the *NIBE* course, whilst those with *MULO* did not. This created a group of male youngsters who:

> Echt wel zo'n beetje gezien werden als de toekomst van de bank. Dus die hielden daar ook wel aan vast. (interview Mrs J.)
> (were really regarded as the future of the bank. Thus (these youngsters) also held onto that idea.)

So Dutch banks were far more relaxed about their approach to male youngsters than British banks, and this case-study would suggest that Dutch banks could be more relaxed as well.

Conclusion

Two comparative themes have dominated the discussions in this chapter. The first theme was the cross-national diversity in the extent to which clerical work in banks feminized. Following an outline of the gendered character of banking employment at the beginning of this chapter, this theme was translated in a concern with the shift from women's formal exclusion from clerical bank work, to their formal but partial inclusion. The second comparative theme in this chapter was to investigate the relationship between national developments and developments specific to the banking sector in the two societies. In reality, these two themes have become integrated in the discussion.

It is my contention that in addition to an underlying and slow process of clerical feminization in banks in both societies, socio-economic conditions during the war and post-war years were decisive in speeding this process up in

Socio-economic context	
National level	**Banking sector**
Britain	**Britain**
• Continuous labour market tightness.	• Following national trend, continuous labour market tightness.
• Increased female economic activity is linked to married women working part-time.	• Banking specific internal labour problems.
	• Resulting feminization involves young and unmarried women working full-time.
The Netherlands	**The Netherlands**
• Relatively slack labour market.	• Bank specific labour market tightness between 1945 and 1950, thereafter mirrors national trend.
• No average increase in female economic activity, but underlying structural shifts.	• No other bank specific labour problems.
• No shift in married women's employment and no part-time working.	• Smaller increase in female ratio of bank staff, also existing of young and unmarried women.

Figure 5.1   **Cross-national comparison of the socio-economic context at national and banking sector level**

Britain's banks. These conditions, summarized in figure 5.1, sometimes mirrored and at other times contrasted with the socio-economic and cultural conditions identified as operating at a national level. Unlike Dutch banks, British banks suffered from a lengthy and continuous period in which their labour market was tight, a trend which mirrored aggregate labour market conditions. Severe internal (and bank specific) labour problems aggreveted the overall situation, and British banks threatened to lose their grip on their internal labour market. Dutch banks, in contrast, did not suffer from similar internal labour market problems.

The feminization of clerical work which followed contrasted with the aggregate trend, in that female bank staff were young and worked full-time. The reason for this difference needs to be sought in the ideological-cultural context at the national level and at the level of the banking sector in specific

Ideological-cultural context	
National level	**Banking sector**
Britain • Liberal/egalitarian ideology shift. • Class-patriarchal sociality. • Some signs of change in attitudes towards working women (Marriage bar decline and rise in part-time working).	**Britain** • Patriarchal/middle class culture, resulting in above banking specific feminization pattern, which contrasts with national trend.
The Netherlands • Slow shift towards liberal/egalitarian ideology in 1950s. • Pillarized-patriarchal sociality . • Signs of change in attitudes towards working women timed at end of 1950s.	**The Netherlands** • Patriarchal/middle class culture, resulting in above feminization pattern, which mirrors national trend.

Figure 5.2   **Cross-national comparison of ideological-cultural context at national and banking sector level**

(see figure 5.2 for a summary). In Britain, the war and post-war period had seen a shift towards a liberal/egalitarian ideology. This had contributed to the decline in marriage bars and the rise in part-time working amongst older married women specifically (Jephcott et al., 1962). In contrast, there was no shift in the cultural gender/class relations characterizing British banking employment, leading to a phase of formal-partial inclusion of female clerical staff. Feminization in Dutch banks was similar in form (i.e. young women were employed until they married), but this mirrored, rather than contrasted with the aggregate ideological-cultural context.

Notes

1   Though research similar to that of Crompton has not been done in the Netherlands, there were some indications that a similar trend was evident there. See section *The underlying trend in clerical feminization* below.

2   The Bank of England archive states that women were employed

from the 8th of November 1893 onwards, but there is no indication whether these women were employed on the bank's clerical staff (BoE archive E31.4: paper of date 19.11.59). The advent of W.W.I pushed British banks into recruiting women for their clerical work for the first time. This is supported by an article entitled *The Bank Clerkess* in the *Dundee Advertiser* of 17 April 1917, which stated: 'The Scottish Banks are most dignified and conservative institutions, earning handsome dividends, with very little concession to modern business methods. But even they have had to bow before the storm raised by the War Demon. Thus long after every other business office had introduced girl clerks, the Banks, by the summary process of getting their male clerks taken from them, have been compelled to resort to female assistance.' (article present in Britbank's archive).

3   From my interview with Mr R., it would appear that a similar employment structure existed in the branches of Dutchbank. During the 1950s, Mr R. was the 'right hand' of the *directeur* (manager) of a small branch with 6 employees. Next to them, there were: a *kassier* (teller or cashier clerk), a *boekhouder* (clerk) and two women.

4   It is difficult here to turn to the respective Censuses, since details about married women's employment in the Dutch *Volkstellingen* is scarce (this most likely reflects the ideology around married women's employment at the time). More information is present in the British Censuses, from which the figures provided stem.

5   Evidence for this was provided in interviews with former employees. In the medium sized provincial town where Jane C. started work in a Britbank branch in 1941, all the replacement staff were young women. One of Jane's tasks in the bank was cheque-clearing. This involved her in meeting the juniors of the other banks which had branches in this town (about 6 in all), and exchanging the cheques belonging to each specific bank. All these juniors were young women, like Jane, who herself was 16 when she was recruited.

6   The Bank of England used the term 'Acting Ranks' for those members of staff who were engaged on a temporary basis during the war years.

7   When report was made, for example, in *The Bank Officer* (March 1942) concerning the appointment of a woman Assistant Staff Manager in Barclays Bank (who, in addition, came from outside the bank), this was obviously the first time this had occurred. Thereafter, no further reports exist of women filling managerial positions in the organ of the Bank Officer's Guild.

8   The Bank Officers Guild, for instance, drew up a *Women's Seven Point Charter*, the details of which can be found in *The Bank Officer*

of December 1943 (p.5). It includes as first point the removal of the marriage bar. This is followed by a demand for a minimum living wage for all new entrants to the bank, a demand for equal pay scales and equal pension provision, equal opportunities to advancement in the employment hierarchy and some other points. In the Bank of England there was also a war-time debate about whether to abolish the bar permanently (BoE archive, E31.4, May - September 1944), and whether female bank staff should be given the permanent opportunity to work higher up the employment hierarchy. See for a more detailed discussion Martens (1994, chapter 5).

9   An article with a similar patriarchal tone was published in *The Bankers' Magazine* of November 1944. It led to a counter response in *The Bank Officer* early in 1945, since the former magazine's editors refused to publish commentary on the article. I.E. Stearn, in her response on the letters' page (*The Bank Officer*, April, 1945, p.2), remarked that it was not common for this magazine to comment on women's bank employment. In view of the fact that the end of the war was near, the magazine's editors obviously found it relevant and important to state their ideas on how banking employment ought to be organized.

10   The secondary education possibilities in the Netherlands during those years were: (1) *HBS*, which stood for *Hogere Burgerschool*, was a 5 year education with middle-class connotations; (2) *MULO*, which stood for *Meer Uitgebreid Lager Onderwijs*, was a 4 year education which was assumed to be a continuation of primary education, and less costly than its 5-year alternative; in addition, there was the (3) *MMS*, or *Middelbare Meisjes School*, which was specifically for girls (presumably whose parents were concerned that they acquired the right moral preparation for their future life as wife and mother). In 1953, planning started for a new education system, though it was only in 1962 that the so-called *Mammoetwet* (Mammoth Law) was introduced.

11   During our discussion, Mr S. backed his story up with photos of the branch at the time. In one of those, said to have been taken in 1950, the bank manager, Mr S. and another male colleague, are surrounded by another 5 female members of staff.

12   It is impossible to put figures to this. Mr T. asserted that perhaps only 20 to 30 per cent of those staff who had left to the forces eventually returned, but I do not know what those figures are based on. But other sources also support the fact that certainly not all bankmen returned. In an article entitled *Stocktaking*, F.S. Taylor commented 'Another disheartening feature of the recent past has

been the exodus from the banks of a number of men who attained high rank and obtained excellent administrative experience in the Forces during the war.' (*The Scottish Bankers' Magazine*, 1952, p.201)

13   The so-called Dr. Johnston Files were provided to me by Mr Alan Scott, of the Committee of Scottish Clearing Bankers.

14   In Britbank, for instance, the first university graduate was only recruited in 1959 (Britbank archive).

15   Taking the *Twentsche Bank* again as example, we can establish the following gender ratios amongst the youngsters it recruited in the direct post-war years.

Table 5.2
The gender ratio of new recruits in
the *Twentsche Bank*

Period	Total recruitment	Of whom women	Female ratio
Aug-Dec 1945	45	22	48.9
Aug-Dec 1946	71	29	40.9
Aug-Dec 1950	67	31	46.3

Source: Archive Twentsche Bank: file on salarissen en tantiemes.

16   Fairly recently (1984), Dr. A. Batenburg, who is/was a member of the *Raad van Bestuur* (board of directors) from the *ABN*, made the following comment; quoted in Tijdens, 1989, p.229.
'Een van de voorwaarden van het goed functioneren van de man is een goed en stabiel thuisfront en dat wordt hoge mate door de vrouw bepaald.'
('One of the preconditions for the good performance of the man is a good and stable home life, and that is to a large degree influenced by the woman.')

17   Again, this is evident from my interview with Mrs T., who said:
'Och, en de jongeren ja dat ging toch best wel vrij gezellig met elkaar om hoor. Het was niet dat je zegt van der was zo'n relatie van de mannen en de vrouwen apart, nee hoor. En der waren natuurlijk ook diverse <u>normale</u> relaties die daaruit kwamen, die dus met iemand van de bank trouwde.' (Interview Mrs T., ul. my emp.). ('oh, and the young ones related quite well with each other. There wasn't an atmosphere of what you would call, men and women separate, no.

And there were of course a number of <u>normal</u> relations which resulted from that, thus that you married someone from the bank.')

18   The female ratio of those sitting for the bankers' exams reached a height of 82.1 per cent in 1945. In 1960, only 3 per cent of exam candidates were women (Source: Scottish Institute of Bankers' *Annual Reports*).

Part 3
GENDER INCLUSION IN WORK FORCES
1965-1993

6 The rise in part-time working

In terms of the gender composition of their aggregate work forces, both Britain and the Netherlands experience a continuous rising trend in women's employment participation in the contemporary period. Yet, attention must be drawn to an interesting difference; the rate of change in women's employment participation is more significant in the Netherlands than in Britain. If Dutch women's economic activity has historically 'lagged behind' that of British women, the last 25 years have seen Dutch women 'catching up' (see chapter 1). Apart from this difference, it is the similarities in gendered configurations of the British and Dutch work forces which stand out; two significant examples being the high ratio of part-time working, and the relative unavailability of child care facilities in the two societies. Given these features, it is now time to return to the research questions introduced in chapter 1. These were:

1. How can we account for the 'recovering of ground' in Dutch women's economic activity compared to British women, in the contemporary period (1965-1993), and
2. How can we account for the particular form which this expansion took?

The similarities just discussed encourage the view, presented in some theories on women's increased labour force activity, that the work experiences of women in the two societies are rather similar. My argument will be that work experiences of Dutch and British women, now and in the recent past, vary considerably. In support of this argument I will present a detailed analysis of the rise in part-time working amongst women in the two societies, and related to it, developments around child care provisioning. Before this is attempted, I will firstly present a more detailed picture of change and continuity in the gender composition of the Dutch and British work forces.

Trends in gendered employment patterns

Following the employment statistics presented in tables 1.1 and 1.2, it was argued in chapter 1 that the post-war years were not characterized by the increased economic participation of Dutch women. Consequently, employment rates of Dutch women were significantly lower than amongst their British counterparts. In the contemporary period it would appear that Dutch women's economic activity has mostly 'recovered' from this divergence. Given this aggregate trend, what can be said about the character of that change? Given the fact that contemporary commentaries have argued in favour of a clear link between a decline in the quality of women's employment and labour force feminization over the last 25 years (Humphries & Rubery, 1988, and Hagen & Jenson, 1988), it is of considerable interest to investigate the part-time/full-time split of labour force feminization.

That the last decades have seen a continuing rise in part-time employment in Britain is supported by evidence presented in Humphries & Rubery (1988). In an interesting presentation of employment statistics[1] from the *Department of Employment Gazette*, they have shown that between 1971 and 1986, there has been a drop in the level of male employment; not much change in women's full-time employment (with some drops and rises between 1971 and 1986), but a continuous rise in women's part-time employment. In effect, they argue, 'it is the growth in female part-time work which has driven up the aggregate series' (Humphries & Rubery, 1988, p.91). This feature is further supported by MacInnes, who argues that between 1981 and 1986, the aggregate level of part-time employment rose in the British economy by 330,000 (MacInnes, 1988, p.12), whilst full-time employment places dropped by 1 million (see table 6.1).

However, if we consider figures covering the last 5 years of the 1980s, we must admit that full-time employment recovered from its decline in the early 1980s. Between 1985 and 1991, there was an increase of nearly 1.3 million full-time work places. 885 thousand of these full-time places were taken by women, 459 thousand by men. Yet, over the whole period between 1985 and 1993, the difference in full-time places is only 338,000, a difference which is due to a rise in women's full-time employment and a decline in men's full-time employment (see table 6.1). Tables 6.1 and 6.2 provide evidence that the rate of increase in women's full-time employment places in the late 1980s, which Hakim (1993) makes so much off, has stopped in its track in the early 1990s. Considering the overall employment picture, it may be argued that the two recessionary periods (i.e. the early 1980s and the early 1990s) have both resulted in a decline in full-time employment places. And whilst this period has seen a continuous increase in part-time work places, the extent of this increase has not been sufficient to change the ratio of part-time working in the total

Table 6.1

Absolute changes in full and part-time employment places in Britain and the Netherlands (1971-1993)[2]

Year	Britain		The Netherlands	
	part-time	full-time	part-time	full-time
1971-1983[1]	--	--	537,000	477,000
1981-1986[2]	330,000	1,000,000	--	--
1985-1993[3]	858,000	338,000	1,174,000	342,000
1985-1993[3]				
women	547,000	800,000	821,000	86,000
men	311,000	-463,000	353,000	256,000

Sources:
1. CBS (1978/1983/1988), Social Year of the Netherlands (Note that the part-time figures include only those with a working week of less than 25 hours).
2. MacInnes (1988, p.12).
3. Eurostat Labour Force Survey.

work force much. If this ratio increased from 21 per cent to 23 per cent between 1981 and 1986 (following MacInnes, 1988, p.12), between 1987 and 1993 it remained stable (following Eurostat).

I have argued elsewhere that a similar clear statement as that provided by Humphries and Rubery for Britain can not be given for changes in Dutch women's employment participation (Martens, 1994, p.366). Even so, between 1971 and 1983, there was a slight overall increase in male employment; a fair increase in women's full-time employment (full-time including women working 25 hours or more a week), and a significant increase in women's part-time work (part-time including those with a working week of less than 25 hours).

As table 6.2 indicates, in the latter half of the 1980s, the rise in Dutch women's aggregate employment was not different from the preceding years. In 1993, women's full-time employment was up by 10 per cent on the 1985 level, whilst part-time employment was 92 per cent above the 1985 level. In absolute terms, part-time employment amongst the total work force rose by over 1 million places in these years, whilst full-time employment rose by approximately 350,000 places (table 6.1). As a consequence, part-time employment rose significantly as a percentage of the total work force: that is from 22 per cent in 1985 to 35 per cent in 1993. A further point of interest is that amongst part-time employees, the ratio of men has increased over these

Table 6.2
Trends in full-time and part-time employment in the Netherlands and Britain (1984-1993)

The Netherlands

Year	Men	Women	F/M%	Women f/t	Women p/t	Women p/t%
1984/5 (x1000)	3,349	1,660		857	892	
1984	=100	=100	33.1	--	--	--
1985	100.8	105.7	34.1	=100	=100	51.0
1986	104.8	107.7	33.8	--	--	--
1987	112.0	126.7	35.9	105.0	134.8	57.2
1988	111.6	131.0	36.8	107.9	140.0	57.5
1989	113.3	134.6	37.0	104.4	150.1	59.9
1991	118.2	148.4	38.4	115.5	165.1	59.8
1993	119.0	160.0	40.0	110.0	192.0	64.5

Britain

Year	Men	Women	F/M%	Women f/t	Women p/t	Women p/t%
1984 (x1000)	13,929	9,835		5,481	4,354	
1984	=100	=100	41.4	=100	=100	44.3
1985	101.8	102.8	41.6	102.8	102.8	44.3
1986	101.5	104.3	42.0	103.8	104.8	44.3
1987	102.5	107.1	42.4	106.5	107.9	44.5
1988	105.9	111.0	42.5	111.4	110.4	44.1
1989	108.6	116.2	43.0	119.0	112.7	42.9
1991	105.9	116.5	43.7	119.0	113.3	43.1
1993	100.7	116.5	45.0	117.4	115.3	43.8

Source: Eurostat Labour Force Survey.

same years from 22 per cent to 26 per cent. In 1993, 15 per cent of Dutch male employees worked on a part-time basis, whilst in the UK only 6.6 per cent of male employees did so (Fagan et al., 1994:151).

In comparative perspective, the absolute number of part-time jobs increased significantly in both societies over the 1980s. However, taking into account the difference in the size of the work forces in the two societies, there can be no doubt that the rise in part-time working took place on a larger scale in the Netherlands than in Britain. In this respect, the Netherlands also stands out from other OECD countries. Whereas in 1979, the ratio of part-time work amongst working women was higher in 5 other OECD countries (Norway, Sweden, Denmark, the UK and Australia) than in the Netherlands, in 1986 the Netherlands had the highest ratio (Sociaal en Cultureel Planbureau, 1988, p.447). Fagan et al. (1994, p.131) have shown that the United Kingdom and the Netherlands still have the highest levels of female part-time working in Europe, but in 1991 the ratio of part-time working amongst Dutch women was significantly higher than amongst British women (60 per cent as opposed to 43 per cent).

Explaining the 'paradox'

In contrast to the period covered in part 2, the time period of part 3 is one of economic uncertainty and recessions. So whilst in the previous period the aggregate rise in women's formal employment was related to the tightness of the labour market, in the current period this link can no longer be made. Given this, it is understandable that commentaries have voiced their surprise at the fact that, in the context of rising unemployment in OECD countries in general, the aggregate female activity rate has continued to rise (e.g. Jenson, Hagen & Reddy, 1988, Crompton & Sanderson, 1990).

In chapter 2, I reviewed some of the debate relating to this contemporary phenomenon, and I argued there that the explanatory framework for the 'paradox' of continuing feminization in a period of economic uncertainty, put forward by Hagen & Jenson, is open to a number of objections. The main objection is that by concentrating on an explanation of the similarities in the 'course' of feminization in OECD countries, their account ignores cross-national variations in the gender patterning of employment and employment experiences. The corollary of this is that their analysis does not provide the basis for understanding the divergent rates at which women's economic activity has increased cross-nationally, nor does it allow explanation of differences underlying apparent commonalities in the gender patterning of national labour markets. For instance, even though it is now a recognized social fact that the ratio of part-time working in the Netherlands and the United Kingdom is higher than in other European labour markets, recent commentaries have refuted the idea that part-time work experiences are qualitatively similar in these two societies (Fagan et al., 1994, Rubery and Fagan, 1994).

In considering gendered labour markets in the context of contemporary restructuring, Rubery & Fagan acknowledge that whilst distinct cross-national commonalities exist, '... wide variations can still exist between European countries in the ways in which labour markets have been transformed ...' (Rubery & Fagan, 1994, p.145). These variations, so the argument continues, relate to the '... different societal systems of social and economic institutions' found in European nation states (1994, p.144). Rubery & Fagan identify four categories of institutions; - labour market regulation; - the industrial system; - the labour market system; and - social reproduction, which are argued to be relatively autonomous, though interrelated and part of a dynamic process of change. Roughly speaking, the industrial and labour market systems involve the forces which generate labour demand and labour supply respectively. Subsumed under the system of labour market regulation are state regulation as well as - what is called - 'voluntary regulation' which occurs at the middle range and micro level of markets and firms. The system of social reproduction 'includes both familial and state systems of childrearing and support for the unemployed and inactive. ... Social attitudes to labour market participation, particularly women, young and older people also come within this sphere' (1994, p.142).

Although Rubery & Fagan agree that a comprehensive analysis of the subject matter at hand needs to be sensitive 'to the diverse national institutional systems and historical backgrounds' (1994, p.145) of different societies, in this article they do not provide a 'detailed focus on the components of national economic and social systems' (1994, p.144). Instead, they usefully describe cross-national differences underlying a number of gendered labour market patterns. I believe that Rubery & Fagan's framework is helpful for the analysis of contemporary labour force feminization by focusing our attention. At the same time this framework reflects the continuing concern in this book with the socio-economic and ideological-cultural context underlying social change. Showing due sensitivity to 'the diverse national institutional systems and historical backgrounds' (1994, p.145), the main task in the rest of this chapter is to explain the development of part-time working in the two societies. Having said that, little reference will be made to the industrial systems of the two societies. Instead, the focus here will be on labour market regulation and - what Rubery & Fagan call - the system of social reproduction.

Neo-conservatism and the rise in part-time working

The rise in part-time working in the Netherlands has generated 'better quality' jobs than in Britain. Fagan et al. illustrate this point by providing a number of contrasting features. In the United Kingdom, for instance, women are more likely to experience occupational downgrading when 'returning' to the labour market, and in particular where this return involves part-time working. Looking at the occupational distribution, it may further be noted that whilst 28 per cent of Dutch professional employees work on a part-time basis, this ratio is negligible in the UK (1994, p.138). This would suggest that in the Netherlands, part-time working is possible in at least some well paid and 'good' quality jobs (see also chapter 7 to compare banks in this respect). Having said that, 75 per cent of women part-timers in both societies work in services and distribution (the two lowest paying sectors in the two economies).

British women are also argued to be more at risk of being low paid. Fagan et al. relate this to the different wage structures in each society. The Netherlands has industry-wide bargaining systems in conjunction with a national minimum wage, whilst the industry-level bargaining system in the UK is declining, and no minimum wage exists. A comparison of average hourly wages consequently shows that UK female part-time workers get the worst deal. On average they earn 75 per cent of the wages of their full-time counterparts, whilst their earnings are a mere 58 per cent compared to the hourly wages received by full-time men. Importantly, the hourly rates for Dutch female workers is the same regardless of whether they work full-time or part-time (Fagan et al., 1994, p.139).

One reason Fagan et al. bring forward to explain the qualitative differences in part-time work is that it 'has expanded in the Netherlands and the United Kingdom within two quite different policy and regulatory environments' (1994, p.148). In Britain, employers have been able (if they so wished) to introduce increasingly poorer part-time work places - and women have increasingly needed to accept these - because of high levels of unemployment on the one hand, and because consecutive British governments have actively deregulated the British labour market (Walker, 1988, Humphries and Rubery, 1988, Fagan et al., 1994). In the Netherlands, the rise in part-time working has been facilitated by a diverse mix of policy aims. These include the aim to increase labour market flexibility, to deal with unemployment and a concern with furthering women's emancipation (Fagan et al., 1994, pp.131-3).

The shift in labour market regulatory policies in European societies has been conceptualized as a shift from Keynesianism towards neo-conservatism (Hagen & Jenson, 1988). Neo conservatism has had (and still has) a major influence in the political and economic spheres in Britain. In comparison, in the Netherlands new conservatism also influenced(s) state economic policy, but this was never as wide-ranging or as radical as in Britain. On speculating as to why this is so, a number of historical and culturally specific reasons may be brought forward.

The British experience

The explanatory model put forward in Hagen & Jenson is corroborated by commentaries on the consequences of contemporary economic restructuring for British women's employment. Humphries & Rubery, for instance, have argued that contemporary uncertainty and recessions, from which neither manufacturing nor service sector businesses have been exempt, have increasingly meant 'the adoption of cost-effective employment policies dictated by pressures to improve efficiency in highly competitive conditions' (1988, p.96). Under these conditions, they argue, the perceived advantages of part-time employment differ from those present in the full-employment conditions of the 1960s. Part-time work places were on the increase then because recruiting married women (often mothers) was often the only way in which staff shortages could be filled (see chapter 7 for the relevance of this in the banking sector). During the 1960s, therefore, the expansion in part-time work places was to a large degree directed by supply side factors. Humphries and Rubery have argued that in the contemporary context the power-balance has turned. In contrast to the 1960s, the expansion in British part-time employment has been directed mainly through employers' preferences or demand side factors.

There is no doubt that state economic policy has been instructive in bringing about the conditions under which these changes could develop. The relationship between these changes and the quantity and quality of women's employment after the first major recession is described as follows:

> Lacunae in the coverage of protective employment legislation, uneven patterns of demand, favorable fiscal arrangements, and encouraging developments in technology have attached significant economies to the use of part-time work. In practice, therefore, the expansion in the number of females employed has been brought about not only by substituting female for male labour-hours at the aggregate level, but by the sharing out of female labour-hours over an increasing number of women. (Humphries & Rubery, 1988, p.96)

In its unbroken stretch of 14 years (in 1993) in power, the conservative government (first under Thatcher and then under John Major) had an undisturbed chance to develop and implement its new conservative ideas. One well-known facet of this policy, implemented in the early days of this government, was to break down trade union power. It is maybe indicative of Britain's peculiar class relations that in the sprouting up of these 'new' political ideas, trade unions became a major target. As Britain's economic situation appeared to decline, trade unions, throughout the period 1960-1980, became increasingly seen as the crux of the problem. Full employment experienced during the 1960s had heralded a shift in industrial relations from bargaining on a national level towards bargaining at plant level through the intermediation of shop stewards. This resulted in an increased occurrence of strikes, especially in unofficial (and highly newsworthy) 'wild cat' strikes and hence:

> In the popular press and in political debate the shop stewards became a symbol of trade union irresponsibility, and workplace conflict came to be seen as the major problem underlying poor productivity performance and Britain's economic problems. (Eldridge et al., 1991, p.25)

And trade unions continued to be seen as 'problems' during the 1970s, when strikes in the public sector (especially in the 1979 'winter of discontent') stimulated this view.

Eldridge et al. (1991) have argued that 1979 heralded a distinct shift in economic policy, in that the new Thatcher government no longer had the maintenance of full employment on its list of priorities. Indeed, it may be argued that the opposite was true; it saw the previous government's guarantee of full employment leading to inflation. Central to the government's economic thinking was making the supply side more flexible; and to reduce government interference in the economy so that market forces could take over. In effect, the government's 1980s policies were mostly:

> Centred on legal restrictions on the way trade unions could organize, increases in inequality of incomes (to reward 'enterprise') and expanding the role of the private sector. (Eldridge et al., 1991, p.30)

One of the first consequences of this shift in policy was a staggering rise in unemployment, from a level of 1.25 million in 1979 to 3.25 million in 1983 (Eldridge et al., 1991, p.32).

In considering the consequences of this distinct move towards new conservatism on British women, Walker has argued that 'the overriding priority of government policy - to restore the profitability of British capitalism' takes centre stage (Walker, 1988, p.229). In their effort to make 'markets work better', the British government has implemented its policies on itself as well as others. Consequently, it has endeavoured to 'reduce the role of the state and make individuals and families more self-reliant' (Humphries & Rubery, 1988, p.92); making significant government expenditure savings in the process. In justifying these actions the Thatcher government has rhetorically been involved in upgrading the importance of *the* family (i.e., the traditional bourgeois-familial model where the husband is breadwinner and the wife his dependent) in the same way Britain's direct post-war government had done. Many of the social services provided now by the state, so the argument went, really belonged in the private domain of the family, or were services which in any case should be provided by private businesses, so that freedom of choice would make these services more efficient.

Walker argues that this rhetoric contains an indirect discouragement of married women's employment, although it never gave rise to distinct policies. In fact, policies appeared to have had the opposite effect of stimulating the creation of marginal jobs in the economy on the one hand, whilst reductions in government expenditure, especially in the area of social consumption, have increased the need of (especially) women to seek more income on the other. The latter is illustrated by a number of examples, including the lack of social services to keep up with the demands of an increasing elderly population; severe cuts in the provision of school meals; and cuts in the health service (Walker, 1988, pp.234-5). The consequence has been that more time needs to be spend on caring tasks in the home, and whether this work involves making packed lunches, caring for children, ill relatives or the elderly, it falls mostly on the shoulders of women. In addition, more money has to be spend on self-provisioning (e.g. on packed lunches, doctor's prescriptions etc.), increasing the need for women to earn more income. Lastly, there has been increasing pressure to provide social services on a voluntary basis, work which is again mainly done by women.

Cuts in government expenditure have also affected public sector employment. Especially in the social services where the ratio of female employees is high, the government has presented itself as the 'tough' employer, and demanded of local authorities that they follow suit. Job cuts and restructuring have meant 'an erosion of the better paid and more secure full-time jobs, both male and female, and the substitution of relatively casualized and dead-end part-time women's jobs.' (Walker, 1988, p.243). In short:

> State intervention, or lack of it, in the labour market of both the private and public sectors, acts to remove any 'floors' that exist to wages and conditions, to erode the control of organized labour, and to promote the expansion of low-wage, unregulated secondary employment. (Walker, 1988, p.247)

These developments may be contrasted with those in the Netherlands. The closest Dutch governments came to an adoption of neo-liberalism was under the two governments of Lubbers between 1982 and 1989.[3] In the historical build-up to this shift in policy, there were no ideological attacks on the Dutch labour movement. Under full employment conditions, the 1960s also saw a worsening of industrial relations; the wage bargaining system changed from a centralized to a decentralized one (de Bruijn, 1989, p.240), and between 1968 and 1970, there was a wave of strikes. But the difference in relation to Britain was that there was little concern about the 'health' of the Dutch economy. Indeed, economic growth continued until the first oil shock in 1973.

Thereafter people's economic expectations were dampened. There was a realization that the Dutch economy suffered from a number of structural problems (resulting in structural unemployment), and from 1973 onwards, consecutive coalition governments endeavoured to curtail expenditure. Even so, during the 1970s, the loss of employment through the decline in traditional industries, in addition to the growth in the labour force (due to population increases and the increased labour supply of women) was mostly compensated for by a still expanding service sector, which included continued growth of the public sector (de Bruijn, 1989, p.296). Between 1977 and 1981, unemployment rose from 200,000 to 400,000 (de Jong & Sjerps, 1987, p.147).

It seems, then, that the second oil shock resulted in a more determined change in economic policies, and some of the themes present in British economic policy can also be found in Dutch policy. The Lubbers governments, for instance, enforced a strong *'bezuinigings- en privatiseringsbeleid'* ('reduction in government expenditure and privatization policy') (de Bruijn, 1989, p.296), exacerbating the rise in unemployment. Under the slogans of *'zorgzame samenleving'* (caring society); *'maatschappelijke zelfredzaamheid'* (social independence); and *'keuzevrijheid'* (freedom of choice), the Dutch government rationalized the withdrawal of state support of various social services.[4] This reduction of government expenditure was considered an attack on the demands of the women's movement for greater gender equality by many commentaries (e.g. van Arnhem, 1985, de Jong & Sjerps, 1987, Clerks, 1985, Morée, 1989).

They indicate similar implications for Dutch women as Walker has done for British women. On the one hand, it is argued that a reduction of employment in various public sectors affected women's employment in a negative way because women have traditionally been well represented in those sectors. On the other hand, the Dutch women's movement noted with cynicism that the tasks provided in these services were thrown back into the private sphere, where women were held responsible for them.[5] In addition, the economic recession and the 'need' to cut expenditure may be regarded as reasons behind the attempt to backtrack on 'emancipating' developments. So in order to make savings in social security, Dutch politicians reached back to *'het gezinsdenken'* (literally: family-thinking) so characteristic of the past. For instance, instead of making moves to individuate the social security system, they reached back to past images of the family in their attack on women's benefit entitlements (de Jong & Sjerps, 1987, p.147. See next section for the relevance of this for the public child care debates).

But these similarities in the consequences of government expenditure cuts do not mean that the similarities in government policy shifts are more important than the differences. Two themes stand out in particular. Firstly, the ways in which government policies were implemented varied. In Britain, this contained strong conflicting aspects, whilst the approach in the Netherlands seemed more consensual. So whilst the British government relentlessly pushed through a number of policies reducing trade union power, the Dutch government and industry discussed suitable measures to increase labour market mobility with Dutch trade unions (de Bruijn, 1989, p.296). This is not to deny, however, that union power had been reduced by the changed economic circumstances in both societies.

The second contrasting aspect is the concern for unemployment. The British neo-conservative argument was that unemployment would be solved through the market, and did not require government interference. In the Netherlands, government regulation was deemed necessary in addressing unemployment, and the form this regulation took was 'redistribution of available employment'. Under the concept *arbeidsduurverkorting* (work duration shortening), various forms of redistribution - one of which was increasing part-time working - were to achieve the aim.[6] It remains debatable whether these policies worked in practice. In a critical commentary on the effects of this policy, Morée points out that this policy certainly did not lead to the creation of new employment places. Instead:

> De stapsgewijze arbeidstijdverkorting heeft onder het toeziend oog van de vakbeweging in het gunstigste geval tot behoud van bestaande arbeidsplaatsen geleid, ... (Morée, 1989, p.79)
> (The step-by-step labour-time shortening has, under the watchful eye of the labour movement, at best resulted in the maintenance of existing labour places, ...)

Hence, one may wonder whether the hidden agenda of these measures was to provide industry with a means to cut employment costs (i.e. similar to the more explicit move in Britain towards a low-wage economy). Nevertheless, these measures did significantly contribute to the reconstruction of the Dutch labour force into a work force with altered working time attitudes (see also Fagan et al., 1994, p.147).

Cultural specificity: state systems

Thus, for a number of historically specific reasons, the adoption of new conservative politics was more widespread in Britain than in the Netherlands. One additional difference which requires attention is the different state systems in the two societies. As must be clear by now, the Dutch system of government works on the basis of coalition formation, whereas since the war, Britain has had a one-party system of government. There are two reasons why this difference is significant. Firstly, in Britain, the governing party has the sole prerogative to develop and implement policies. In practice, this has meant that when the Conservatives took over government under Margaret Thatcher in 1979, the road was clear for its policies to be implemented. In contrast, Dutch coalition governments have to negotiate a 'middle road' between the views of the parties involved.

Secondly, the Dutch coalition system has meant a greater 'turn-over' of governments. Once in power, it is rare for a British government not to finish its period of office (which can last for 5 years). In the Dutch coalition system, governments may break before elections are due, and this happens regularly. In practice, this has meant that the British Conservative government has had an uninterrupted stretch of 14 years (in 1993) in power since 1979; a period in which its new Conservative policies had time to be developed and put in their place. In the Netherlands, between 1977 and 1989, there were 4 different coalition governments. These included, at different times, all three major political parties.

Debates around the public provision of child care services

In the comparison of the gendered characteristics of European Community labour markets, high levels of part-time working are linked to low levels of child care services. This pattern is corroborated for the Netherlands and the United Kingdom in an EC Childcare Network report of 1990, where these societies, in addition to Ireland, are singled out as having the lowest levels of child care services amongst European Community nation states. Given this similarity, the report points to a trend, starting at the end of the 1980s, which indicates an increasing divergence in child care provisioning in the two societies. In terms of the level of publicly funded child care services, it may be argued that, if anything, such provisioning was more extensive in Britain than in the Netherlands during the 1970s. From the end of the 1980s onwards, publicly funded facilities increase in the Netherlands, whilst in Britain only private facilities increase.

I will here elaborate on public debates - from the 1970s onwards - around the provisioning of child care services in the two societies. Such a discussion is important for various reasons. Not only are the level of part-time working and the existence of child care services related, the investigation of developments around child care services also pushes this analysis into the area of ideological and cultural concerns. It would be no exaggeration to suggest that commentaries on contemporary labour force feminization have concentrated on socio-economic and political change, whereas mere lip-service is paid to the relevance of cultural changes. This gives the impression that women themselves have been relatively insignificant as actors of social change. A consideration of cultural changes necessitates that we ask different questions from the ones covered above. These include questions like 'have British and Dutch women changed their labour supply in the contemporary period?' and if so, 'how have these women conceptualized the *combination of parenthood and employment*?' But also, 'what combination restrictions do women in these two societies face, and what have they done to change these?'

That cultural change pertaining to the gender order has occurred in the contemporary period is supported by the heightened presence of feminist discourses. Investigating the impact of second wave feminisms on developments around child care services is relevant here for at least two reasons. Firstly, the influence of the latter on those powerful institutions of modern life - like the state - that give direction to the opportunities available to the individuals in society, is particularly relevant. My argument will be that the impact of second wave feminisms at state level differed between the two societies, and an examination of the reasons behind that difference brings us back to two themes present in the above discussion; the culturally specific character of neo-conservatism and the respective state systems.

Secondly, the recurrence of feminism in the contemporary period is here also interpreted as the embodiment of a critique, shared by increasing numbers of women, of aspects of the existing gender order in their respective societies. The specific grievances voiced by Dutch women were somewhat different from those expressed by British women, and this suggests that increasing numbers of Dutch women were 'unhappy' about different aspects of the gender order than British women. This pinpoints further cross-national differences which necessitate a return to the specific cultural formations which have historically characterized the two societies - discussed in part 2 - and a consideration of what happened to these formations in the contemporary period.

In part 2 of this book, it was shown that in Britain, a cultural reality has historically strongly identified with class relations and class oppositions. To what extent there has been change or continuity in this reality since the Second World War is debatable, but I indicated above that there are indications of continuity in this respect in the contemporary period. In the Netherlands, the historical configurations of a cultural reality have been rather different. Here, until well into the post-war years, the cultural formation which gave meaning to reality may be characterized as a pillarized social order, in which religion played a significant role. Class divisions were evident in the Netherlands, but these were overshadowed by the social relations determined within the pillars, and between them.

An awareness of the divergent, historically specific, cultural formations in the two societies is important in this discussion because it is related to social attitudes around the remunerated work of (married) women outside the domestic home. In both societies, there were strong tendencies to think of a woman's place as the home, resulting, for instance, in such phenomena as marriage bars. Even so, my research suggests that marriage bars were more common in the Netherlands than in Britain, certainly in the post-war years. The explanation for this difference is that the Dutch pillarized social order facilitated the institutionalization of this bourgeois-familial ideology across larger sections of the population (see chapter 8 for a comparison with Plantenga's thesis).

An analysis sensitive to this diverse historical background must conclude that at the beginning of the 1970s, the labour market experiences of British and Dutch women were rather different. In Britain, there had been a steady increase in the employment of groups of women; like married women and women with children, since the Second World War, even though much of this had been in the form of part-time employment. In contrast, by 1970 there had been little change in the Netherlands in this respect. At the same time, the post-war years entailed 'a process of accelerated modernization' for the Netherlands (Pfau-Effinger, 1995, p.7), which has been accompanied by substantial cultural changes. The pillarized order has declined in significance - a process which is argued to have started during the 1950s (Stuurman, 1981, 1984, Plantenga, 1992) - and this decline has been accompanied by a variety of 'modernizing' discourses against the 'old' and 'traditional' social order.

Following Dutch commentaries of the 1970s - including feminists and scholars - it is clear that a major grievance discourse of those years was that Dutch women 'lagged behind' their foreign counterparts in claiming a position in the labour market. Consequently, 'a woman's right to paid work' - a modernizing discourse explicitly opposed to the 'traditional' bourgeois-familial discourse that a 'women's place was in the home' - became a major demand, voiced amongst others, by second wave Dutch feminists at the start of the 1970s. In contrast, the 'right to work' was not emphasized as a major campaigning issue in the British feminist movement because that 'right' had already been achieved.

The point I am making here is that the increase in Dutch women's labour force participation in the contemporary period is strongly linked to a rise in Dutch women's labour supply. This is corroborated by a perusal of commentaries on Dutch feminization in this period (de Bruijn, 1989, Moree, 1992). De Bruijn's, for instance, has argued that:

> Ondanks de economische crisis, de groeiende werkloosheid en de in de jaren tachtig massaal geworden werkloosheid, blijft het arbeidsaanbod van vrouwen stijgen. (de Bruijn, 1989, p.298)
> (In spite of the economic crisis, growing unemployment and the massive proportions of unemployment in the 1980s, the labour supply of women continues to rise.)

The corollary is that the argument that labour force feminization of the last 20 years has been directed particularly by demand-side influences (Hagen & Jenson, 1988) seems to contradict the Dutch experience. Having said that, the question remains how that supply has been operationalized. In the debates around the public provisioning of child care it is clear that 'traditional' and 'modernizing' discourses on the role of women in Dutch society have culminated in an infrastructure which favours a high ratio of part-time working.

Child care campaigns during the 1970s

During the 1970s, discussions around the provisioning of child care in the Netherlands need to be regarded as 'modernizing' discourses being levelled against 'traditional' discourses, in which the latter still have the upper hand. At the start of the 1970s, the historical notion that women are the primary caretakers for children, particularly where one's own children are concerned, was still wide-spread, including in the women's movement itself (Morée, 1992, p.146). Even so, a drive for change in 'traditional' conceptions about the proper roles of women in Dutch society came from the women's movement during the 1970s, when it developed the demand for a reallocation of work in both the domestic and public spheres. One of the ways in which this reallocation was to be achieved was through the public provision of child care facilities.

As 'traditional' discourses still had considerable influence, it is not surprising to find that the demand for public child care provision did not win much support during the 1970s. De Bruijn and Morée have argued that the influence of the early 1970s recession and the continued influence of the confessional (i.e. religious) lobby in the *CDA* were to blame. But they and others have also pointed out that a change in ideological thinking about gender roles was rather slow to develop in other respects. Hence even the Dutch Labour Party, the trade unions and employers' federations held onto the 'traditional' concept of the division of labour based on the male breadwinner and female housewife (de Bruijn, 1989, p.299, Morée, 1992, p.147, de Jong & Sjerps, 1987, p.147). The government did concede to the right of women to be able to combine parenthood with employment, but only to the extent that it did not involve public child care. And politicians did not stand alone here. Dutch public opinion also reflected significant opposition to the employment of women with children of school-going age, if their employment entailed 'alternative' forms of child care. Hence in 1970, 68 per cent of people who had no objection to the employment of mothers were against this if child care facilities were needed by those mothers. In 1979, at 65 per cent, this had barely changed (Morée, 1992, p.148, Sociaal en Cultureel Rapport, 1988, p.378). In effect, consecutive Dutch governments throughout the 1970s stimulated the creation of part-time jobs, by creating part-time jobs in state employment itself, and by providing subsidies for employers to do the same. The 1970s, therefore, are a period in which Dutch women wanted to do part-time work; they were stimulated to do so through government policy; and this development was generally accepted as a positive one in the women's movement.

The British women's movement did not have to deal with the legacy of a pillarized social order of the kind found in the Netherlands. It, however, operated within a different cultural reality; a class society. The provision of free, 24-hour nurseries was one of the first four demands made by the British Women's Liberation Movement. Lovenduski & Randall (1993) have pointed out that a national campaign for child care was slow to get off the ground during the 1970s for a number of reasons. The first of these reasons link in with the already tightening up of public resources during the 1970s, which meant:

> Many influential bodies officially recognizing the importance of child care but few prepared to prioritize the issue. (Lovenduski, 1986, p.78)

On the other hand, the women's movement itself did not form a collaborative national campaign on the issue because of differences within it. Radical feminism (which had considerable support amongst British feminists) effected a negative climate around motherhood - related to their stance on families and marriage. In effect, efforts around public child care did not come from this section of the women's movement, but from the socialist feminists and women concerned about equality at work. These women's groups worked through such institutionalized bodies as trade unions, the Equal Opportunities Commission and later also local government women's committees (Lovenduski & Randall, 1993, p.285). Even during the 1980s, when the stance of radical feminists in relation to motherhood changed, little energy was directed towards this issue (certainly when compared to some of the other campaigns). Nevertheless, there were quite a number of successful local initiatives in the 1970s, concentrated in London and some other larger British cities. It was these initiatives which formed the backbone for the setting up, in 1980, of the National Childcare Campaign (NCC).

In comparison to the situation in the Netherlands, it may be remarked that the 1970s were not very productive in relation to the demand for publicly funded child care in both societies (though in Britain, at least, some provision existed). But the reasons why this was so are somewhat different. Dutch commentaries give the impression that various institutionalized bodies; including the Dutch Labour Party and the trade unions, still held onto a traditional notion of the family and the sexual division of tasks within it. British accounts do not point to this at all. Here there was a certain breakthrough in getting trade unions and local authorities to recognize the importance of child care. The TUC, for instance, produced a *Charter for the under Five's* in 1978 (Lovenduski, 1986, p.115). Instead, due to internal differences within the women's movement, related to Britain's class society, no national campaign got off the ground until 1980. And even then, it would be wrong to argue that this campaign represented the interests of the whole women's movement.

Child care provisioning from 1980 onwards

In an attempt to indicate why, by the end of the 1980s, public money started to flow into the provisioning of child care services in the Netherlands, but not in Britain, one may indicate three points. These are
1. The institutionalization of feminism at state level in the Netherlands and the absence of this in Britain.
2. The degree and timing of neo-conservatism directing policy in the respective societies.
3. Divisions in interests amongst British feminists who campaigned for publicly funded child care.

The Netherlands. In terms of the provision of public child care facilities, the Dutch women's movement did not appear to make much headway at first. Even so, the 1970s did see the start of the institutionalization of the women's movement on state level. The early 1970s coalition under *PVDA* prime minister den Uyl produced an emancipation policy (1975), and was advised by the

160

Emancipatie Commissie (Emancipation Committee). The next government (*CDA/VVD*) installed its first state secretary for emancipation. At the same time as more government expenditure cuts were being introduced, women came together in various pressure groups (de Jong & Sjerps even talk about an 'explosion of collaborations' (1987, p.150)),[7] which in turn formed the basis for the setting up of the *Breed Platform Vrouwen voor Ekonomische Zelfstandigheid* (Broad Platform Women for Economic Independence) in 1982. The broad base of this platform was evident in that women's groups of all the major political parties were represented in it. It must therefore also be acknowledged that this collaboration had the potential for wielding political influence.[8]

There also is agreement in the commentary that the emancipation proposals put forward by the second secretary of state; D'Ancona, was a breakthrough for the influence of feminism on state level. D'Ancona formulated, during the 8 months of the next coalition's government (1981-1982), an emancipation manifesto in which women's economic independence stood central. This policy established the direction which Dutch emancipation policy took in the 1980s. It is not clear to me whether the public provision of child care was made an explicit aspect of D'Ancona's proposals, but in any case, before the *CDA/VVD* coalition started government in 1982, an action group called *Werkgemeenschap Kindercentra in Nederland* had put forward a proposal in which it called the Dutch government up to make resources available for the public provision of child care. This proposal was accepted by the Dutch House of Commons. The latter duly called upon the government to make a start with this provision.

Yet, when the Lubbers government took over power some months later, it argued that publicly funded child care had to wait because of the government's expenditure cuts. Initially, then, the clock was turned back. In a critical article entitled 'Beter nu de vrouwen geweerd dan straks zelf het huishouden geleerd',[9] van Arnhem has pointed out that in 1983, the Dutch government was opposed to the further independence of women in economic and financial terms (van Arnhem, 1985, p.92). The recession recalled from memory the 1930s confessional opposition to dual income families, but whilst the discourse:

> ... tegen het buitenshuis werken van gehuwde vrouwen en moeders tijdelijk weer meer sociaal aanvaardbaar werden ... (Morée, 1992, pp.151-2)
> (... against the employment outside the home of married women and mothers was socially more acceptable for a while ...),

these did not lead to policy proposals (as they had done during the 1930s). Rather the result was a lack of 'positive' action on the part of the government. This is illustrated by the manner and speed with which they started to provide child care facilities. At first, and in similar vein to the British government, the Lubbers government argued that child care facilities should be provided by private rather than public means (Clerkx, 1985, p.89). Waiting for these facilities continued until, in 1986, it was acknowledged that there was a shortage in child care facilities in the *Conceptnota (Her)intredende Vrouwen*. The government pledged to funnel public money into child care services, though the responsibility of organization was relegated to local authorities. Between 1989 and 1993, public expenditure, directed at increasing child care places, increased from 60 million to 350 million Dutch guilders (EC Childcare Network, 1990). In 1989, the level of provision was still very small, with publicly and privately funded provision providing places for fewer than 5 per cent of the under four year age-group. By 1993, however, full-time places (public and private) existed for 12 per cent of children aged 0-4 (EC Childcare Network, 1996 forthcoming).

In relating this to the changes in Dutch women's employment participation over the last two decades, the following may be noted. The rise in part-time working during the 1980s was not just stimulated by economic and political reasons (e.g. the 'reallocation of available employment' theme). At the same time, it is a reflection of the constraints which operated on women's labour supply decision taking, whilst women increasingly wanted to be involved in some form of employment. These same constraints may also be related to the rise in women's full-time labour supply, in that by the mid 1980s, the Netherlands had the highest ratio of childless couples amongst OECD countries. The *Sociaal en Cultureel Planbureau* argues that remaining childless (and delaying the process of getting children) was another way in which Dutch women reacted to the constraints operating on them (Sociaal en Cultureel Rapport, 1988, p.475).

The availability of more childcare facilities in the 1990s have opened up new possibilities for the combination of parenthood and employment for increasing numbers of Dutch women. However, when the *Stimulative Measure Programme* ends (1995), it is the intention that the costs of childcare will be shared mainly between employers and parents. This has raised the issue that such provisions may not be accessible equally to all in the future. In addition, it has been noted that a peculiar combination pattern is now taking shape, in which part-time working is combined with the use of part-time childcare services (Knijn, 1994, EC Childcare Network, 1996). This seems to indicate that current Dutch conceptions of motherhood do not favour the idea of full-time work combined with the use of full-time childcare, as happens, for instance, predominantly in France.

Childcare campaigns in Britain. During the 1980s, the demand for childcare was pursued through socialist feminists and various childcare campaigns of which the NCC was the first. This, Lovenduski & Randall argue:

> Generated wide-ranging debate amongst feminist activists, though the terms of the debate shifted as the decade wore on. But, given all their efforts, and it must be said that their campaigns never really took off in a dramatic way or captured the public imagination, feminists achieved disappointingly little in concrete terms over this period. (Lovenduski & Randall, 1993, p.285)

In examining why this should be so, they indicate a number of contributing reasons.

One of these contributing factors is the way in which the women's movement itself organized around the issue. The setting up of the NCC was a collaborative initiative (much in the same way in which collaborative networks were established around this time in the Netherlands), the 'unity' of which lasted till 1985, when a split resulted in which half the founding members left to form the London Childcare Network (1985-1988). Another body, the Day Care Trust, split off to assume a mainly advisory role on existing childcare facilities. In the same year, the Workplace Nurseries Campaign (WNC) was formed in response to a change in taxation policy in 1984 which entailed that employers' subsidies to workplace nurseries would become taxable. Lastly, and unconnected to the NCC, was the setting up of the Working Mothers' Association (WMA), perceived by other bodies as an elitist organization, catering for the childcare needs of the more advantaged women in British society. A last campaign worth mentioning (maybe because of its inability to gain the active support of the women's movement) is the Childcare Now! campaign started in 1989 by Jenny Williams.[10]

With the setting up of these new campaigning bodies, the aims pursued shifted. Whilst the NCC in 1980 had demanded free publicly funded and community based facilities, the WNC and the WMA agreed with a 'mixed economy of childcare'. This shift in emphasis needs to be related to Britain's new conservatism. It must be recognized as another, very important, contributing factor in the failure by the British women's movement to gain recognition for publicly funded childcare for the under five's. Lovenduski & Randall make the familiar comment that by the mid-eighties, the climate was:

> Not conducive to campaigning for child care - indeed, for any campaigns of a 'redistributory' nature. (Lovenduski & Randall, 1993, p.293)

On a national level, the British government has repeatedly argued that child care provisions ought to be funded through private means, even when, at the end of the 1980s, the 'demographic time-bomb' argument indicated the need for an increased labour supply by British women. In 1993, this was still the common position. Those public facilities which exist - and these are in decline following EC Childcare Network (1996 forthcoming) - prioritize children 'at risk'. Parents who seek to combine parenthood and paid work, have to look for private facilities. The current situation is such that private facilities have increased to a level of 950,000 places; a rise of 39 per cent on the 1986 level. It is relatively easy to see that these facilities favour those in well paid work, leaving poorer women with little choice.

Cultural specificity: state systems

In the previous section, I commented on the divergent political systems in the two societies. This difference, I believe, is also related to the divergent campaigning tactics in the women's movement of the two countries, further illustrating reasons for the successes and failures. As I have indicated in relation to Dutch second wave feminism, channels opened up during the 1970s (primarily in the form of a state secretary for emancipation issues, and an *Emancipatie Commissie*), through which both inside- and outside-parliamentary groups could wield some influence on a national level. The British political system is very centralized, leaving little room for national influence. The consequence has been that the British women's movement has levelled its campaigns primarily at a local government level. In addition, the British movement has often associated with left-wing politics. Lovenduski and Randall indicate that this has inevitably meant that the success of the movement's demands has been linked to the fortunes of the left. As local government power has declined significantly during the 1980s (and as their resources have been cut), the movement's likelihood of success has declined likewise.

Conclusion

A comparison of the gendered employment features characterizing Dutch and British labour markets generates the impression that the similarities are more prominent than the differences. Quantitatively, the rise in Dutch women's employment participation has been more distinct than that of their British counterparts, but the gender composition of both work forces has seen a shift towards more women, which has been accompanied by a rise in part-time working and a lack of publicly funded childcare facilities in both societies.

In this chapter, I have argued that underlying these similar gendered configurations, there are some distinct differences. Firstly, the rise in part-time working amongst Dutch women has been more extensive than amongst British women, and in contrast to the latter, the quality of that work is higher (Fagan et al., 1994). In addition, whilst the track-record in public resourcing of childcare services in both societies has been abominable, the end of the research period has seen an increase in public resourcing in the Netherlands, whereas in Britain there has been an increase in private resourcing.

Given these gendered patterns of employment, I have here provided an overview of the socio-economic (with specific reference to the political) and ideological-cultural context of social change, showing at the same time sensitivity to 'the diverse national institutional systems and historical backgrounds' (Rubery & Fagan, 1994, p.145) of the societies in question. This overview can at best provide a partial explanation of the patterns found, given that neither a comparison of the industrial systems in the two societies, nor a more comprehensive analysis of influences on women's labour supply, were attempted. Nevertheless, a number of interesting findings may be listed which are linked to the course of events.

I have again considered the constitution of cultural formations in the two societies. The historical legacy in Britain of a class society may be associated with the more distinct shift in British politics towards neo-conservatism. The latter has been instrumental in the generation of Britain's low-waged economy, where part-time work has increasingly become poor quality work. The neo-conservative political climate has also negated the public resourcing of childcare services in Britain. The implication is that only private childcare facilities exist. In addition, it was argued that the class reality has not been conducive for unified feminist struggle in favour of publicly funded childcare at a national political level. In this context, only those in the better paying jobs provided by the labour market have seen improvements in their combination opportunities. However, for the great majority of British women (particularly those with children) it is still extremely difficult to be financially independent. This would suggest that the majority of British women indeed have little to 'cheer about in this achievement of record levels of female participation in the paid labor force' (Hagen & Reddy, 1988, p.11). But does the same apply to Dutch women?

It would seem not. Neo-conservatism never took the same extreme form in the Netherlands as it did in Britain. Government regulation is still deemed necessary to maintain the quality of life. One of the reasons why neo-conservatism did not develop in the same way in the two societies is related to the difference in state systems. The post-pillarization period in the Netherlands is characterized by coalition - and hence collaboration - politics, in stark contrast to Britain, where one party politics has greatly contributed to the ability of Conservatives to implement their ideology on society. Diverse state systems may also be drawn on to explain the different ways in which second wave feminisms became incorporated at a national level, contributing to the different successes the women's movement in both societies have had in getting their governments to fund childcare. Lastly, historically constituted cultural formations were referred to, to point out that Dutch women's employment expansion has been driven to a considerable extent by women's changed labour supply.

Notes

1   I am referring here to table 5.1 (Humphries & Rubery, 1988, p.90), also printed as table 4.1 in Rubery & Tarling (1988, p.101).

2   The Dutch, British and Eurostat figures presented in table 6.1 are not comparable. All three statistical sources have specific ways of calculating total work force figures and part-time figures. This is especially important for the Dutch figures between 1971 and 1983. Those working less than 25 hours a week are counted as part-timers, those working 25 hours or more are counted as full-timers. Consequently, some of the Dutch change in full-time work may actually reflect a change in work where the working week is between 35 and 25 hours. The part-time figures provided by the CBS source *Social Year of the Netherlands* thereafter (1980-1990) are not comparable with the earlier figures as the definition of part-time work has changed to include only those working less than 20 hours per week. Eurostat's calculation of part-time figures is made on the following guidelines: (1) 'the distinction between full-time and part-time work is generally made on the basis of a spontaneous answer given by the interviewee' and (2) in the case of the Netherlands those included in part-time figures are self-employed or family workers if they work less than 35 hours a week; employees if contracted to work less than 31 hours a week or if they work between 31 and 34 hours a week and this is usually considered as less than the hours normally worked for the type of work involved (Eurostat, 1985, p.45). I have brought these figures together in table 6.1 as a means of showing trends only.

3   These governments were both *CDA/VVD* coalitions. The three major parties during the 1980s were the *CDA*, the *VVD*, and the *PVDA*. The *CDA* or *Christen-Democratisch Appel* is the contemporary Dutch party in which the older Confessional parties came together. The *VVD* stands for *Volkspartij voor de Vrijheid en Democratie* (People's Party for Freedom and Democratie) and is the Dutch Liberal Party. The *PVDA* or

Partij van de Arbeid, mentioned further on in this chapter is the Dutch equivalent of the British Labour Party.

4   Included were '*gezinshulp, bejaardenhulp, maatschappelijk werk en onderwijs ...*' *(Morée, 1989, p.80)* ('familycare, care of the elderly, social work and education ...').

5   Van Arnhem provides us with a good example of this attempt by the Lubbers government to transfer certain social care tasks back to 'the family'. In 1983, the government held a meeting in which the ministers could respond to the *Discussienota inzake emancipatiebelied op het terrein van arbeid en inkomen* (Discussion paper on emancipation policy in the terrain of work and income). Van Arnhem interprets from the leaked minutes the words of minister De Ruiter of Defence.
'De vraag nu is: wat ziet de minister dan wel graag? Het antwoord daarop luidt: vrouwen moeten haar oude moeder en vader verzorgen, op school bijspringen en allerlei klusjes in de buurt of wijk doen. Zo zei De Ruiter het natuurlijk niet letterlijk, hij zei het zó: "er (bestaat) ook voldoende niet betaalde zinvolle arbeid. Juist in de huidige economische situatie is dit laatste van belang. Het idee dat betaalde arbeid het hoogste goed zou zijn, moet worden gerelativeerd".' (van Arnhem, 1985, p.92) ('The question is: what does the minister like to see happening? The answer to that is: women have to care for their old mother and father, help at school and do all sorts of jobs in the neighbourhood. Of course, these were not literally the words of the minister, he said it like this: "there is also enough non-paid and useful work. The latter is, particularly in the current economic situation, of importance. The idea that paid work is the ultimate good must be put into perspective".')

6   The various types of 'redistribution of employment' policies were:
1. Labour-time shortening. This was to be achieved by either shortening the working week, or by introducing extra days off. The latter were the so-called *ATV (Arbeids-Tijd-Verkorting* or labour-time-shortening) days.
2. The *VUT (Vervroegd Uittreden* or early retirement) regulation, which offered older employees the possibility of early retirement.
3. Part-time employment was also considered a way in which to redistribute employment.

7   De Jong & Sjerps name several of these groups. In the area of social and economic issues the following groups were set up. (1) *het Comité Waakzame Vrouwen in de Gezinszorg* (the Committee Watchful Women in Familycare); (2) *Aktiecomités Vrouwen in de Bijstand* (Action Committees Women on Social Security). These later formed a national body *Landelijk Steunpunt Vrouwen in de Bijstand*; (3) women whose

income was paid through the laws covering ill health formed the *Landelijk Netwerk Vrouwen in de WAO/AAW*. In politics, (1) *het Kamerbreed Vrouwenoverleg* (1981); (2) *het Politiek Vrouwenoverleg*; (3) *het Samenwerkingsverband De Populier (1982/3)*, were set up (de Jong & Sjerps, 1987, pp.149-150).

8   The *Breed Platform's* activities involved employment policy and incomes policy, with in later years an emphasis on the individualization of the incomes (and tax) policies.

9   This is best translated as: 'Better keep out the women now, or sooner than later you will have to learn to do domestic work yourself.'

10   With this campaign, Jenny Williams wanted to draw attention to (1) the dire childcare provisions in Britain, compared to other OECD countries, described in Bronwen Cohen's report Caring for Children, and (2) the recommendations made in this report, written for the Childcare Network of the EC.

7 Formal inclusion in banking employment

In the discussion on clerical feminization in the post-war years, the question why women were introduced to clerical bank work stood central. In the current period, the investigation centres around the forces which either change the gender composition, or which keep this stable. In short, by concentrating on the socio-economic and cultural-ideological context of recent years, I intend to examine the character of the formal inclusion of women in bank work.

In economic terms, the banking sector in both societies continues to thrive during the 1970s, in contrast to the aggregate picture sketched in the previous chapter. As a consequence, banking work forces continue to increase in numbers. Also the female ratio of banking work forces continues to rise. The rise in the absolute and relative number of female bank employees is, in fact, an example of service sector work expansion which contributes to the continuing rising trend in the aggregate figures of women's employment. In addition, there appears to be very much a continuity in the gendered employment relations in banks from the 1960s into the 1970s. If the 1970s are the decade of increased feminist consciousness, this hardly seems to have impacted on banking employment yet.

In contrast, business levels vary considerably for banks in both societies over the last 13 years of the research period. The 1980s are a decade of uncertainty for banks, in which new technology introduction, and a higher (perceived) level of competition from other financial institutions (both on a national and international level) change the face of banking in some fundamental ways. Banks have lost their apparent immunity from the 'outside world' in more ways than just economic. For also in terms of gender relations, change is evident - amongst other features - in the labour supply pattern of female bank staff. During the 1980s, banks also engage in the development of an equal opportunities stance.

Before I elaborate on these themes further, the first task at hand is to present a more detailed picture of employment changes over time, with specific reference to Britbank and Dutchbank.

Trends in banking employment: 1965-1993

There can be no disagreement about the rising trend in bank employment over the period 1965-1993. And in this respect, Dutch banks have been no different from British banks. This rise is evident in the figures provided in table 7.1. By 1988, Dutch banking employment had increased by nearly 60 per cent compared to the 1973 level, whilst British banks had experienced an increase of 52 per cent on their 1971 staff levels. In that same period, Dutch banks experience a steady rise in the female composition of their staff, whereas in British banks the ratio remained relatively stable.[1] There are also indications that the rise in employee numbers was more significant during the 1970s than in the 1980s. This is not so obvious from the figures presented in table 7.1, but Britbank and Dutchbank's employment statistics show this trend more clearly. Before these detailed figures are presented, I will first discuss developments in the gender composition of Britbank and Dutchbank staff over time.

The difficulty in finding figures for the period covered in Part 2 of this book is clear from table 7.2,[2] and this is the reason why no detailed figures of employment in these two banks were presented in chapter 5. The figures in table 7.2 do reflect the points made by me in that chapter. Before 1970, feminization in Britbank occurs at a faster rate than it does in Dutchbank and clerical feminization in these two banks follow the pattern for the sector as a whole. In the contemporary period, the ratio of female employees in Britbank has remained significantly higher than in Dutchbank. Table 7.2 also indicates that the rise in employee numbers within the sector as a whole is reflected in the employment figures of the two banks researched more closely here. Even so, employee growth was more significant during the 1970s than during the 1980s. Dutchbank's employee numbers increased by 75 per cent between 1970 and 1981. Between 1981 and 1989, however, there was relative stability in the bank's employment. The same counts for Britbank; between 1970 and 1981, Britbank's employee numbers increased by 23 per cent (of which 9 per cent may be attributed to men and 37 per cent to women). During the early eighties, there was not much mutation in Britbank's employment either, though in the latter half of the 1980s, Britbank's employee numbers increased again .

As the 1980s indicate a break from the rising trend in the employee figures of the two banks, it is interesting to look at these years more closely. A more detailed picture of employment mutations is provided for Dutchbank in table 7.3. What seems clear from these figures is that the total employment

Table 7.1
Employment trends in the Dutch and British banking sector
(1970-1990)

The Netherlands				
Year	Total	Male	Female	F/M%
1973	78,512	46,159	32,353	41.2
1978	106,420	62,406	44,014	41.4
1983	116,058	65,237	50,821	43.8
1988	124,200	66,100	58,200	46.8
% change 1973-1988	60%	43%	80%	

Britain				
Year	Total	Male	Female	F/M%
1971	281,500	130,500	150,900	53.6
1975	322,300	145,300	177,000	54.9
1978	333,400	148,000	185,400	55.6
1983	363,000	154,800	208,200	57.4
1988	427,300	200,800	226,500	53.0
% change 1971-1988	52%	54%	50%	

Sources:
Netherlands: CBS, *Statistiek Werkzame Personen 1973-1987, (industrial class 81)*. *Britain:* Employment Gazette 1971-1988 *(figures are for banking and bill discounting and come from various issues. All figures are for June, except 1975, 1978 which are figures for September).*

series has remained relatively stable, reflecting a stability in both male and female (total) employment levels. Dutchbank is, in this respect, not peculiar. Tijdens has indicated that three of the four large Dutch banks also have stable employee numbers over the 1980s (Tijdens, 1991, p.23). Underlying the stability in women's employment levels in Dutchbank, there has been a distinct decline in full-time female employment, whilst there has been a significant increase in part-time female employment. Tijdens reflects that this same feature

Table 7.2
The gender composition of staff in Britbank and Dutchbank

	Britbank			Dutchbank	
Year	Total	F/M%	Year	Total	F/M%
1955[1]	1,691	30.2	1956	1,600	--
1958[2]	1,778	32.2			
			1965	2,741	25.9
1970[3]	7,277	51.0	1970	5,734	32.9
1975	7,976	58.2	1975	7,477	34.0
1980	9,057	58.0	1980	9,903	37.0
1985	8,826	56.1	1985	9,649	36.7
1990[4]	20,860	59.2	1990	21,038	41.2

Sources:
Britbank: (1) *Figures taken from Sidney Checkland (1975), Scottish Banking A History, 1695-1973; (2) Figures from the Scottish Bank Employer's Federation; (3) Quarterly figures gathered for the Scottish Bank Employer's Federation; (4) Figures from Britbank. Does not include non-clerical and overseas and off-shore staff.*
Dutchbank: Sociaal Jaarverslag of Dutchbank between 1965 and 1990.

is evident in the Dutch banking sector during the eighties. In the whole sector, part-time employment places increase dramatically, specifically in the period between 1979 and 1985. Thereafter, it levels off. In 1983 alone, 1,476 full-time places become part-time places (Tijdens, 1989, p.238). I will come back to this issue in my discussion below. Part-time working has been on the increase in Dutchbank since its first introduction in the mid 1960s. In 1970, only 3.2 per cent of its staff work on this basis. In 1989, however, 14.2 per cent do so. The ratio of women working on a part-time basis in Dutchbank increases from 23 per cent in 1980, to a height in 1986-1987 of 35.5 per cent. In the early 1980s, however, the extent of part-time working remains level (see table 7.3).[3]

Because Britbank's employment statistics presented in table 7.4 below start from the year 1985 only, these figures do not provide a strictly comparable series to table 7.3. It is furthermore a pity that these figures do not include the early 1980s recession years. There are, however, some useful figures provided in MacInnes (1986), which support the point made by a Britbank manager that there was no rise in its employee numbers in the first half of the 1980s. Between 1980 and 1984, then, Britbank's employee numbers remained stable at around 9,500. But underlying this stability was a shift in women's full-time to part-time working (MacInnes, 1986, p.25). Much the same pattern, in fact, as for Dutchbank in this period. In contrast to Dutchbank, however, Britbank's employee numbers are rising again in the latter half of the 1980s. This increase is spread out. Both the male and female series show a rise, though the increase in female employees is more significant. Underlying the increase in female staff is a somewhat more significant increase in part-time working compared to full-time working. Indeed, the ratio of part-time working amongst Britbank's female staff has also increased significantly since 1980. Then, 8.1 per cent of Britbank's female staff worked on this basis (see note 3). Thereafter, there was a steep increase in female part-time working in the first half of the 1980s, leading to the significantly higher rate of 18.6 per cent in 1984 (for the bank's clerical staff only). In the banking and bill-discounting industry in general, a similar pattern is obvious (Department of Employment Gazette, Cressey & Scott, 1992). After the fusion in Britbank, the part-time ratio remains stable at around 14-15 per cent. In comparison, it is maybe surprising to find that whilst commentaries on part-time working in both societies have stressed the rise in part-time working in banks during the 1980s, rather a higher ratio of female Dutchbank staff work on a part-time basis than female Britbank staff (approx. 35 per cent and 18 per cent respectively at its height). Figures for the early 1990s show that the much publicized declining trend in banking employment in those years is also evident for Britbank. Interesting here is that whilst both male and full-time female employment has been reduced, female part-time employment has continued to rise.

Table 7.3
Employment mutations in Dutchbank during the 1980s

Year	Total	Male total	Female total	Female full-time	Female part-time
1980	=100	=100	=100	=100	=100
1981	101.4	102.3	100.1	--	--
1982	101.4	102.9	98.7	100.4	93.1
1983	102.3	104.0	99.5	100.7	95.5
1984	96.5	97.4	94.9	84.9	128.4
1985	97.4	98.0	96.5	82.5	143.3
1986	100.6	99.6	103.0	85.7	157.0
1987	97.7	97.7	98.5	82.6	151.3
1988	97.4	96.0	99.9	85.6	147.3
1989	99.1	99.1	103.4	88.8	152.0

Source: Dutchbank's Sociale Jaarverslagen: 1980-1989.

I have here traced the employment mutations in Britbank and Dutchbank in the contemporary period, with specific reference to gender and the distinction between full-time and part-time work. These employment figures give a premonition that the contemporary period was a period of tremendous change for banks as financial institutions. Indeed, pressures started to built up during the 1960s. General growth in the economy had a knock-on effect on banks, and the expansion in their business was accompanied by some radical changes; including the growth in retail banking and concentration. The next section is therefore concerned with an examination of these changes and their employment implications - including the consequences for the post-war patriarchal strategy of formal-partial inclusion of women in clerical work.

Table 7.4
Employment mutations in Britbank during the 1980s

Year	Total	Male total	Female total	Female full-time	Female part-time
1985	= 100	= 100	= 100	= 100	= 100
1986	103.0	102.1	103.7	103.8	103.4
1987	108.2	106.9	109.2	109.7	106.2
1988	115.4	112.7	117.5	118.2	113.6
1989	123.2	117.2	128.0	128.5	125.5
1990	129.1	119.5	136.5	135.5	142.5
1991	122.8	109.9	133.0	129.9	150.9
1992	118.6	107.1	127.6	123.5	151.6

Source: Britbank.

But the 1960s were only the start of the changing socio-economic conditions facing banks, and these conditions, though different in kind, continued to influence decision taking concerning the way in which the banks organized their operations during the 1970s and the 1980s. Below, I shall present an account of these changes based on existing interpretations in both Dutch and British commentaries, followed by a more detailed examination of how Dutchbank and Britbank have reacted to these changes in terms of their employment policy development. This is then related to the above shifts in the gender composition of bank staff.

The advance of retail banking

The 1960s were without doubt years of expansion in banks in both societies. One consequence of this expansion was concentration. In the Dutch banking sector, there were three mergers between major banks during the 1960s. Out of the 358 independent institutions operating in the banking sector in 1963, only 145 are left in 1975 (Wierema, 1979, p.37). In the British banking sector there were several mergers between Scottish banks, and one merger between two English banks (Winton, 1982, p.196, Checkland, 1975, p.640). During the 1980s, some further significant mergers occurred, the corollary of which is that the Dutch banking sector is now dominated by three large banks; the ING, the ABN/AMRO and the Rabobank.

The precursor of retail banking in both societies was a development called *branchevervaging* (the fading of the division in markets between the different banks) by Dutch commentaries. *Branchevervaging* occurred in the Netherlands at the end of the 1950s, when the *algemene banken* (general banks) got into liquidity problems due to the demand for loans by the expanding Dutch business community (Kulsdom & Westeringh, 1983). In their search for liquidity, these banks started to tap the market of the *particulier* (the small private individual), and by doing so encroached into the markets of other banks. A similar process has been identified by Checkland in relation to the British banking sector, where an expanding market entailed increased competitive pressure (Checkland, 1975, p.658). The consequence was the breakdown of 'the classic division of functions between financial institutions built up in the nineteenth century ...' (Checkland, 1975, p.660), whilst increased competition led joint-stock banks to:

> Invade new fields by the use of subsidiaries and affiliates, and they extended their own range of services to the public, particularly in the retail banking sector. (Checkland, 1975, p.664)

Retail banking basically constituted the development of a financial services market for the small private individual. This market had various facets. In addition to attracting the savings of the private individual, banks introduced special wage accounts. Initially, the reasoning behind this was that by managing their small customers' incomes, banks attracted private individuals to invest their saving with them. On the other hand, they benefited the banks' liquidity position by reducing the money in circulation. A third facet of retail banking was lending money to the *particulier* for consumer goods and mortgages.

The establishment of the retail market in banking had a number of operational consequences which in turn generated a number of staffing implications.

Firstly, in order to reach the small client, the banks needed to expand their branch network. Britbank's branch network expanded from 241 branches in 1959 to 635 in 1970.[4] The general view in those years was that in order to be known, you had to be seen, and the corresponding motto was to have a branch on every main street corner. Secondly, the retail market meant a tremendous expansion in financial traffic. Kulsdom & Westeringh argue that this encouraged change towards larger scale operations. Hence, in addition to concentration, large administration centres were specifically set up to deal with the increased administrative work. Through the mergers, banks were fewer in number, but the banks which were left became larger bureaucratic networks than before. The culmination of these factors resulted in the growth of head-offices, and regional structures were set up to support head-office functions.

Lastly, *branchevervaging* and retail banking also increased the sense of competition between banks, because their markets had grown more alike. On the other hand, retail banking was relatively expensive. Apart from the increase in the branch network and administrative offices, staff requirements increased overall costs too, and in Dutch banks the costs-benefits ratio decreased from 63 per cent to 35 per cent between 1960 and 1988 (de Vries, 1992, p.47). These two factors are important reasons why Dutch and British banks fell into a spiralling pattern of trying to save on costs. New technological devices and a continuously changing labour process were from the 1960s onwards the hallmarks of banking employment.

The employment implications of retail banking

One clear implication of the expansion in work within banks in the two societies is the increase in the absolute number of staff employed. The latter is directly linked to the various operational changes discussed above. Dutchbank was going through a period of expansion, and it started new branches in quite a number of Dutch towns; all of which had to be staffed. Two of my Dutchbank respondents; Mr I. and Mr L., had been involved in the setting up of new branches in the 1960s. As Dutchbank's branch-network expanded, Mr R. was involved in the organization of two regional centres. At the end of the 1960s, all the administrative work of the branches in South Netherlands was brought together and done with book-keeping machines by 30 part-time staff in the regional office in *Den Bosch*. Britbank employees also commented about the increased scale of their bank's operations. Mr T., for instance, worked in the bank's personnel department from 1957 till his retirement in 1985. When he started in personnel, he remembers having to work through the particulars of the two hundred odd employees working in head-office. By 1970, Britbank's head-office staff had increased to nearly 1,700 (the Committee of Scottish Clearing Bankers' *Quarterly Labour Statistics*).

176

The above discussed changes also had qualitative employment implications. Whilst the expansion in staff really entailed an expansion over the whole range of employment in the banks, quantitatively the expansion was, of course, greater in the lower regions of the employment hierarchy. The expansion of work in the higher regions of the banks' employment ladder was caused, for example, by the increase in branches. More branches meant a need for more branch managers. On the other hand, the increasing sophistication of operations in head-office, and the development of a regional structure also lead to more higher graded jobs. Connected with the latter was the active search by banks for new and more sophisticated forms of office automation, and this demanded experts.

There can be no doubt that retail banking itself created a vast expansion in the lower regions of clerical work, because of the acceleration in small transactions. Mr T., who worked in Britbank's personnel department, compared the processing work involved in these transactions with factory processing jobs. The gender implications of this were also communicated. These jobs, so Mr T. argued, were really only acceptable to very young, mainly female staff, who had just come from school. For any other employee, this work would have been too boring, whilst the bank benefited by not having to pay these youngsters much.

Where administrative work was brought together into larger offices, banks further discovered the potential benefits of flexible working. The cheque clearing department in Britbank's head-office, for instance, started to operate for 12 hours a day, which was organized in three part-time shifts of 4 hours. An added advantage was that in the prevailing tight labour market, there was a ready supply of, mainly married women (with children) - some of whom had worked in the bank before - who were seeking part-time work to fit in with their other responsibilities. These posts were the first part-time posts in Britbank. Mr R. made this same connection for Dutchbank's larger offices. Utilizing part-timers into these jobs was further seen as a means to avoid subjecting full-time staff to a full working week of boring work, whilst part-timers were also relatively more productive for the time they worked.

A last quantitative implication of the changes which were heralded during the 1960s was that with the reorganization of work, some posts which had traditionally carried high esteem in the bank - a good 1960s example is the job of cashier clerk - lost this status. The loss of importance of the cashier task was accompanied by its feminization, a feature well remembered by the staff of both banks.[5]

The 1960s signalled a definite departure from the patriarchal employment relations characteristic of the previous decades in the sense that the explicit forms of gender discrimination disappeared. Wage-discrimination between male and female employees was abolished during these years, and marriage bars and marriage dowries also made their exit. Furthermore, banks started to experiment with part-time working, and for British banks in particular this meant following a pattern which had become increasingly common in the British labour market since World War II.

At the end of the 1960s, banks in both societies actively started to recruit married women, or attempted to hold onto their marrying female staff. This change in practices signalled a turn-around in attitudes towards married women's employment, a development which ran parallel with tight labour market conditions and changes in operations. Voices which outlined the potential benefits of married women's employment, gained the upper hand for the first time in banking history. As discussed in chapter 5, the presence of the bar in banks had been 'rationalized' on a number of grounds. During the period of the bar's disappearance, the negative implications of the bar came to the fore. The main negative implication communicated through interviews was that the bar caused the loss of well qualified and experienced female staff to the bank. These various themes are summarized by Britbank's Mr Z., who argued:

> ... and if you had a good girl, and she was getting married, I think why did she have to go just because she changed her marital status, and I think gradually it was perceived they could stay. But I don't know if (...) all this would have happened some time in the 1950s or thereabouts, I would think gradually, and certainly in the 1960s the banks needed the girls, whether they were married or not married. And I think there was a period at the time when they actually went out and actively sought married women who had banking experience to come back. And later on, I am probably thinking now in the 1970s, late 1960s or 1970s, they were happy to take them in on a part-time basis or on an on-call basis to fill the gaps at peak times and things like that. (interview Mr Z.)

However, the abolition of marriage bars did not always directly precede the positive recruitment of married women. In the Netherlands, for instance, the bar was no longer included in the banking CAO of 1962/3, and according to Dutchbank interviewees, the *ooievaarsclausule* was rescinded in that same year. Yet, it was a number of years thereafter that Dutchbank actively tried to recruit married women (interview Mr R.). Evidence from other Dutch banks suggest that the CAO stipulation of 1962/3 was ignored, and that the disappearance of the bar closely preceded labour requirements. In one Dutch bank, for instance, a bar was still implemented in 1965, but by 1968 this bank had changed its practices by employing 485 married women on a part-time basis in *Amsterdam* (Wierema, 1979, p.133).

Economic pressures and technological change

The active recruitment of married women into bank work diverted from the traditional recruitment pattern. Unlike the youngsters who were recruited into the internal clerical labour market, these women were recruited into specific posts and often on a part-time basis. These new practices were two early aspects of more wide-ranging changes which modified the employment organization - so characteristic in banks in the post-war years - from the 1960s onwards. Below, the main facets of change in employment organization will precede the discussion of the socio-economic conditions facing banks in recent years, and their response to these conditions.

Contemporary changes in the organization of employment

The active recruitment of married women at the end of the 1960s is related to a shift from the traditional/patriarchal character of relations and decision taking in the post-war years, towards a more formal/rational mode of action (Crompton, 1989, Tijdens, 1989). This shift may be recognized in the abolition of the explicit policies of gender discrimination just discussed. It may also be recognized in the formalization of the employment grading structure in banks in both societies. During the 1960s and the 1970s, British banks formalized their grading structure, and Britbank now uses a system called HAY. Dutchbank uses the sector wide BASYS system, which is coupled to a sector-wide collective wage agreement.

Another aspect of the formalization of relations in the contemporary banking sector is the continuously increasing emphasis on formal qualifications. The standard external qualification of new recruits used to be a secondary education. Nowadays, an increasing number of new staff enter with degrees and, particularly in the Netherlands, a higher professional education. If, in former times, bank clerks used to learn 'on the job', now banks have a vast array of internal training courses. Whilst these aspects signal a process of growing formalization of social relations in banks, at the same time a process signalling the informalization in social relations is evident. Dress codes have relaxed, and staff mostly address each other by their first names.

The second major change in the employment organization concerns the internal labour market. There has been a shift from a strict single-tier internal labour market towards a multi-tiered internal labour market. In the post-war years, banks rarely diverted from the long established pattern of recruiting youngsters of 16-17 years of age. This pattern has gradually changed. Two aspects of multi-tiering are evident. One aspect is the recruitment of specific people to fill specific employment positions. Examples are the part-time recruitment of married women in the 1960s and the recruitment of specialized computer staff during the 1970s and 1980s (MacInnes 1986, 1988). The second aspect of multi-tiering concerns breaking up the lengthy internal labour market into segments. At the time of research, Dutchbank made a distinction between three levels in the employment hierarchy; the *lager kader, middel kader,* and *hoger kader* (lower grade; middle grade; and higher grade personnel). The traditional career path in banks, where new recruits start at the bottom of the occupational hierarchy and progress to the top is now closed. Instead, Dutchbank targets those people it expects to fill its future managerial positions by recruiting people with specific external educational credentials. By the early 1990s, this form of multi-tiering had been taken one step further in Dutchbank than in Britbank. In the latter, the traditional career path was still possible, though Britbank's personnel manager thought that this would soon be a thing of the past.

Recently, British commentaries have indicated a third aspect of change. As just about all British banks have announced job cuts in recent years, Cressey & Scott (1992) have argued that the future of British banking employment will be one without the traditional guarantee of a job for life. Whilst there have also been announcements of job cuts in the Dutch banking sector in recent years, mainly in relation to a scaling down of operations in large processing centres, in Dutchbank there remained an emphasis on holding onto existing staff in the bank's employment policies during the 1980s. These issues will be further explored in more detail below.

Operation expansion and automation

With the development in retail banking during the 1960s, the need to seek cost and time saving solutions for the ever expanding operations in banks increased over time. Technologically, banks experienced a shift from mechanized machines and the first electronic machines used in the post-war years towards the use of computer technology. Commentaries in both societies have indicated various phases of technological innovation in banks. One phase consists in the automation of back-office functions. Part and parcel of this are the large processing centres[6] set up since the early stages of retail banking. Another phase is the introduction of technology in the front-office. Cressey & Eldridge point out that one British example of this, the Automated Teller Machines (ATMs) installed at the branch counter has aided cash payments, and cut down on paper work (1987, p.45). The same authors call the third phase 'Out of Office' Automation. Probably the most notable example of this phase has been the introduction of electronic cash dispensers, which in first instance provided the customer with a 24 hours cash dispense service. Now, various other banking services can be handled by these machines, including: balance statements, account statement, and the sending of cheque books. Apart from this development there has also been the introduction of EFTPOS (or Electronic Fund Transfer at the Point of Sale). EFTPOS is the direct debiting or crediting of one's account when retail purchase is made.

The opportunities which have opened up by the introduction of new technology over the last 2 decades have increased dramatically. It is therefore of considerable interest to consider the implications of technology for the organization of bank work, and hence also on bank staff. Yet, forming a general picture of both qualitative and quantitative implications is fraught with difficulties. Part of the problem relates to the fact that the introduction of new technology into bank work has been very piecemeal, affecting mostly small areas of work and staff at any one time. Furthermore, the type of technology introduced, and speed at which it is introduced varies between banks. Nevertheless, in a number of research projects there have been attempts to evaluate the qualitative implications of new technology in various banks (Crompton & Jones, 1984, MacInnes, 1986, Tijdens, 1989). In contrast, there has been little 'quantification' of the employment implications of new technology introduction in banks by interested scholars. Only in the last 4 years, as job cuts have been announced, has attention shifted towards the issue of quantitative implications.

Quantitative implications are of particular interest to us here, because it relates to the question whether and to what extent the introduction of new technology causes change or continuity in the gender composition of bank staff. One way to get at this question is to look at whether the introduction of technology has disproportionately affected types of work where mainly women are employed as opposed to men. Hence, one can say with some certainty that the centralization of routine administrative tasks during the 1970s was accompanied with the feminization of such work, and hence changed the gender composition of bank staff in favour of women. Yet, during the 1980s, there has been a decline in such centres in the Dutch banking sector, and administrative tasks have been decentralized again. In her discussion of this aspect of change, Tijdens does not comment on the quantitative implications of this for women's employment in Dutch banks (1989, pp.215-6). If, however, we are to follow trade union commentaries, cutting jobs at the lower end of the employment hierarchy is most certainly going to affect women disproportionately.

Lastly, it is difficult to pinpoint new technology as the single cause for gender composition changes in a decade where there have undoubtedly been a number of additional factors at work. Some of these will be discussed below. Having said that, let us now return to Dutchbank and Britbank in outlining how these two banks have reacted towards market related pressures in terms of their employment policies.

Coping with change: Dutchbank and Britbank

Retail banking entailed that the markets of banks in both societies became more alike. In the Netherlands, this led to an increased sense of competition, and Dutch banks adopted cross-selling during the 1970s, as a means to make their operations more profitable (Tijdens, 1993, p.74). British banks did not experience the same level of competition because of protective legislation. Even so, throughout the 1970s, Britbank and Dutchbank continued to experience expansion in their operations. The measures to cope with this were increased staff levels and the further introduction of computerized methods of work. In both banks the point is made that the increasing automation during the 1970s does not stem the increase in employee numbers. In the words of a Britbank manager:[7]

> and ... the rate of growth in transactions, writing cheques, you know whatever it might be, was almost going exponential. And we kept saying, if we didn't automate ehh ... we'd be employing everybody in the country.

During the 1970s, therefore, technology creates the means for Dutchbank and Britbank to cope with an expanding work load, without having to increase staff numbers too much.

As illustrated by the employment figures discussed above, both banks experienced stability in the level of employment in the first 5 years of the 1980s. Yet, the causes underlying this stability were different. Following Dutchbank's arguments in its *Sociale Jaarverslagen*, the early 1980s recession created the need for organizational change. The consequences of the recession are well documented; the national recession is argued to have a strong influence on the bank's own profitability, causing slow growth in the national operations of the bank, and a growth in bad debts. As a consequence, the bank experiences for the first time in many years a reduced profit level.[8] It is the recession, rather than technological developments, which is emphasized by the bank in justifying its subsequent employment policy changes.

Dutchbank was quick to react to the decline in its income by curtailing expenditure on staff; it introduced its so-called *volumebeleid* (volume policy) on employment levels. This meant setting targets on the level of staff numbers, to be achieved by a reduction in recruitment and a reallocation of existing work according to the bank's priority needs. The *volumebeleid* continued as a policy throughout the 1980s, explaining the relative stability in Dutchbank's employee numbers discussed above. It also heralded the start of a number of other employment policy changes during the 1980s. I would argue that these policies support the idea that Dutchbank's aim was to 'hold onto its existing staff'. It introduced, for instance, the *formatiebeleid* (formation policy), which is argued to be a policy for 'getting the right man or women in the right place' (*Sociaal Jaarverslag*, 1983, p.8). One aspect of the *formatiebeleid* was to make an inventory of the 'quality' and 'potential' of all its staff. Moreover, following the decline in turnover rates amongst staff (from an average of 10 per cent each year during the 1970s to a low of 3.5 per cent in 1983), the bank introduced its *circulation* policy in 1988. The idea behind the policy was to prevent employees from stagnating in their posts, by getting them to move into new work at least once every 5 years.

In first instance, it would seem as if Britbank followed Dutchbank's example of curtailing employment numbers. During the early 1980s, pressure from competition seemed to increase as the internal financial market was facing changes in regulation (finally pushed through in 1986). In addition, bad debts contributed to a decline in profits. But when confronted with the question why there had been stability in employment numbers, Britbank manager Mr C.'s first response was that Britbank's constitutive partners had decided to curtail numbers in anticipation of the coming fusion. The recession was not mentioned at all by him. It was expected that the fusion would entail further reductions in staff. However, in the event the opposite was true. After the fusion they recognized a need for more staff, hence in the latter half of the 1980s, staff numbers rose again.

As reports in the media in the last 6 years have indicated, British banks have followed one another in resorting to a policy of staff reductions in the 1990s. From Mr C.'s responses, it seems as if the bank now realizes that a stricter employee 'quantity' policy might have been appropriate during the 1980s, but for several reasons this was not realized at the time. The first of these is that the fusion in 1985 meant that thinking about the future direction of employee policy slowed down for a number of years. In the meantime, employee numbers were rising again. Furthermore, Britbank managers themselves did not conceive of more radical changes at the time, maybe feeling less pressure as the British economy went into its next economic boom period. There was, what could be termed, a delayed response, if we follow the remarks made by Mr C.:

> ... thinking back to the way decisions were taken, the sort of thing people had in their minds eh ... it was really just an assumption of continuing

growth, ehh ... and an assumption of continuing profitability and ehh ... margins being maintained and you know, life was about running the system a bit better, not responding to quite a lot of the underlying change we were protected against right through until the late 1980s, because of the, you know, mid-1980s boom.

As a consequence, limiting staff numbers was not the greatest concern.

... so there wasn't that great need to ... to control the numbers. The control of numbers was always seen as important because staff costs were about 70-65 per cent of total costs, so you were always saying let's control the biggest thing. But there were very limited assumptions really about what was controllable ehh ... and when I think back to discussions that took place in boards and management committees ehh ... during the 70s and 1980s, ehh ... we were only fiddling around the margins of things, rather than saying, look, can we do this completely differently.

Another aspect of 'doing things differently' was evident. Both banks endeavoured to radically change the very understanding of what a bank employee was (see also MacInnes, 1989, Cressey & Scott, 1992). Dutchbank's staff were called upon to become more flexible, and to accept change as a continuous aspect of life, whether this involves moving home, retraining for different work, or in accepting different work. The mentality change which Dutchbank wanted was hammered home in every social report of the 1980s.[9] Dutchbank also called for a wider conception of career, to include horizontal as well as vertical moves (and with respect to older members of staff, even the idea of vertical moves down).

In both banks there was increased market orientation. Expenditure in Dutchbank was directed towards those aspects in the business where the bank made its profits: i.e. the market and the client. Throughout the 1980s, the bank scaled down its support functions, and reallocated staff and resources towards the areas where their services are sold. Britbank employees became salespersons of financial 'goods' instead of financial service staff. Related to these trends is the reorganization of branch-networks. Dutchbank has called on its staff and departments to carry responsibility for their own profitability. Nowadays, the bank's branches are grouped together into *zelfstandige eenheden* (independent units) with a *moederkantoor* (mother branch) and smaller *aangevoegde kantoren* (satellite branches). Each of these units is responsible for their own profit levels. Britbank's branch network has changed in a similar fashion, though this shift has been accompanied by a reduction in the number of branches with its own manager.

In comparison, it is clear that Britbank does not share Dutchbank's aim of holding onto staff in the same manner. Indeed, in describing prospective future staffing guidelines, Britbank's personnel manager indicated that one intention was to break down the traditional internal labour market:

> ... we are changing very significantly, or we will change very significantly from recruiting for like a career, to recruiting very much more for specific jobs. Ehh ... and a very much smaller proportion of the recruitment will be based on the assumption that those people will be staying in the organization for a long time.

Dutchbank, in contrast, appears to have set up the infrastructure to encourage employees to stay in times of radical change. Whether and how this relates to the gender composition of staff in these two banks is a topic which will be addressed later.

The character of formal inclusion

Explicit modes of exclusion have disappeared as a feature of bank employment, so in theory the road is now free for women to change their labour supply patterns. The question is whether gender has indeed ceased to be the pivot for distinguishing between 'temporary' and 'permanent' staff. I am here going to explore aspects around the nature of women's labour supply in Britbank and Dutchbank more closely. My argument is that labour supply decisions are part of an ongoing process in the employee's evaluation of their work experience. This means that employees take certain attitudes and assumptions about their future work with them when they start their bank work, but that these feelings may be modified by subsequent experiences. Consequently, below I will explore employee talk which relates to their labour supply decision taking, as well as evidence on Dutchbank and Britbank's willingness to facilitate a change in the labour supply of their female staff. In the next section this will be further related to contemporary restructuring.

Continuity during the 1970s: Sandra's work history

Sandra (a Britbank employee) and Mies (a Dutchbank employee) had worked in their respective banks from the early 1960s. Even so, their work histories were remarkably different. Mies, who worked as a Dutchbank manager at the time of interview, stands out not because her work history is typical for that of bank women in general, but because it is rather unique. Sandra, who now works as a bank officer on a part-time basis, had a work history which

185

reflected the general experience of bank women more closely. Her account is also an example of the continuity of gendered employment patterns in Dutch and British banks from the 1960s into the 1970s.

Sandra worked in Britbank on a full-time basis between 1963 and 1979, when she left to have her daughter - a rather long stretch of continuous full-time work compared to many other female bank staff. This continuity in her employment might have been a reason for progression in the bank. In fact, she did progress as the years went by, certainly when compared to the other female staff. From junior clerk in 1963, she went on to do the ledger and telling work in another branch in 1967. Here she stayed for 10 years and gradually she became the senior clerkess in the branch. Thereafter, she became supervisor in a suboffice which had no resident manager. So yes, Sandra did progress over the years - reaching grade 4 (which is equivalent to grade 6 now) during the 1970s - but this progress was about '... as much as was considered likely, shall we say, ehmm ... for the expectancy for girls in the bank then ...' (interview Sandra). In 1979, being supervisor was about as high as you could get as a woman. The only posts above that in a branch were those of accountant and branch manager, and she knew of only 2 women at the time who were accountants. In the meantime, her husband (who also worked in Britbank, and had started in the same year as Sandra) had progressed one step further than she had - he was accountant in 1979. But then, he had studied for his bank exams, whereas she had not. In her explanation why she had not done them, the dual working of expectancy and ambition comes to the fore. In those years:

> ... there was no real expectancy for girls to do bank exams, whereas now it's much more considered that if you want to attain a reasonable position in the bank, to do the exams would certainly be ... helpful. (interview Sandra)

Mies' working life started in a similar fashion to that of Sandra, but subsequently developed differently. Having started in Dutchbank at the age of 16, Mies learned all the office tasks in her first branch in 6 years. By the mid 1960s, she was the youngest *procuratiehouder* in the bank, and became *adjunctdirecteur* (accountant) in the early 1970s. Mies made it clear that she had always been committed to her work, and her account shows that she worked quite consciously towards her goal, always taking her own initiative in everything. Both women agreed that if a woman wanted to progress like a man in those years, she had to stand out from the rest (men and women). Mies said that she had put three times more effort into her work than others did. Against the advice of her first manager, she did various training courses, and paid for them herself. She had also always been busy networking, which was necessary, she said, in order to achieve. And achieving was necessary in order to get noticed in the bank.

For women like Sandra and Mies, the options in a woman's life were rather clear. You either chose for a career, which was risky because there was no certainty of success, or you chose for a husband and family. Mies chose the former, and never married; Sandra chose for the latter, and did not look upon her working life as a career. Again the link between attitude, ambition and opportunity is most evident in Sandra's account. Sandra did not think of her work as a career, but then again, the women in her age-group did not expect a lot and were quite happy with the work they did. She agrees, though, that if her attitude had been different, or if she had been a single girl looking for opportunities, she would have been very frustrated, for she knew that:

> Over the time that I worked in the bank, women were still ... sort of lesser mortals, shall we say, than men. The bank had been for such a long time a man's job really ... There was this accepted fact, shall we say, that ehhmm men would probably progress better than women. That was kind of ... just seemed to be the norm. (interview Sandra)

The reason why Sandra had stayed on in her job for so long was that she and her husband had decided to wait with getting children. Even so, there had been no doubt that when children arrived, she would stay at home and look after them, just like other women around her did:

> ... then it was quite acceptable for women to go out to work, and then, when they decided to start a family, to stay at home and look after the family. (interview Sandra)

Like Noreen (in Crompton, 1989), Sandra did not stay at home for long, returning on a part-time basis in 1982. However, when Noreen returned to her bank work in 1960, this can not have been very common for British bank women, and certainly was unheard of in the Netherlands. By the 1970s, it became more common for female bank staff who had left, to return to the bank.[10] However, unlike Noreen, most returners in the 1970s and 1980s did not progress in the job hierarchy. It was more likely that they followed in the footsteps of Sandra and her colleagues by returning to lower graded work and less income. When Sandra left her work in 1979, her grade was the equivalent of the current grade 6; at the time of interview, her work was graded 4. In the meantime, Mies continued her work in Dutchbank without a break, and with continued progress up the employment hierarchy.

Many banks (British and Dutch) currently have an equal opportunities (EO) stance, and in some banks, like Britbank and Dutchbank, this stance has resulted in a number of policies. There is, of course, much to be said about the various themes addressed in the two banks under the auspices of EO, but I will limit my account here to the description of those aspects which relate to labour supply decision taking. The creation of part-time working opportunities, career breaks and childcare facilities all fall under this heading. The linkage between progression opportunities and labour supply decision taking shall be addressed indirectly later.

It would seem that in Dutchbank, the extension of part-time working opportunities has been more associated with equal opportunities than is the case for Britbank. This is, for instance, clear from a statement in Duchbank's current EO policy declaration:

> Deeltijdarbeid heeft tot doel tegemoet te komen aan de wensen van medewerkers (mannen en vrouwen) die minder dan fulltime willen werken. (EO paragraph Dutchbank, section 6.8.1)
> (Part-time employment has the aim to meet the wishes of employees (male or female) who want to work less than full-time.)

As we have seen, there has been an increase in part-time work places in both banks, though the extent of part-time working amongst female staff is now significantly greater in Dutchbank. The figures presented above show that part-time employment only increased after 1983; the time when part-time working was also being introduced (on a national level) as a means for 'reallocating available employment' (see chapter 6). The evidence presented here and below supports the idea that part-time working in Britbank has been more directly related to the bank's needs during recessionary years (in line with Humphries and Rubery's claim about a similar trend in the aggregate economy), than to a rising demand by bank women for part-time work.

Other options to combine domestic demands with employment differ markedly between the two banks, and these reflect the aggregate trends I discussed in chapter 6. Britbank now offers its employees (both male and female, though in practice, Britbank's EO advisor explained, only women have made use of this facility so far) the so-called career break. The career break may be regarded as a formalization of a pattern which was already evident in previous years; of women returning to the bank after a number of years' absence. What the career break offered was a period of unpaid leave (at a maximum of 5 years), after which women would be able to return to a job at the same grade level they had left (but without the guarantee that they would return to the same job). Before returning, they could, for a while, work on a part-time basis to gain familiarity with the work again.

Dutchbank's EO policy contained a number of leaves; maternity leave, parent leave, care leave, and unpaid leave. The latter was an offer for leave of a maximum of one year, with regulations similar to Britbank's career break with the exception that it was for one year only. In addition to this leave, Dutchbank now also has a *kinderopvang* (childcare) policy. This aims to make it possible for employees to use existing 'outside' childcare facilities, or where this was necessary, to set up such facilities with other businesses or institutions. The costs for these childcare places were to be shared by the parents and the bank. It would appear, then, that Dutchbank was one step up from Britbank, which did not offer any help with childcare.

Labour supply, employee attitudes and practices

Having discussed these various EO aspects, let us now turn to employee attitudes and practices. A change in attitudes towards work life is evident in my discussions with current bank employees; especially those who started their working lives in the bank in the last 15 years of the research period. However, also in the accounts of older bank employees (who still work in the bank, or those who retired and/or worked in a bank during the 1950s and 1960s) a story is told about the contrasts between then and now. The interweaving of attitudes and practices, and changes therein over time, was evident in the way bank employees responded to questions about career orientation and the combination of home and work life.

Career orientation. According to Sandra, at the end of the 1970s there was a gradual, but noticeable, change in the work attitude of women who were then entering bank work. Whereas she and women of her age-group had accepted the gendered 'status quo' in the bank, the girls who were coming into the bank then were not so ready to do the menial tasks, according to her, and expected more of their work:

> I don't necessarily think it was down to something that occurred in the bank. It was more just the type of people that came in. Their expectancy was different. Their attitude to the job was different ... It was something the banks had to adjust to. (interview Sandra)

Whilst there was recognition amongst my informants that not all bank women who work in banks today are career orientated,[11] there was agreement that more women looked upon their work as a career now than in the past. This assertion needs to be put into perspective.

189

Only a small number of the people I spoke with (whether men or women), said that they had thought of their bank work as a career from the start. The point I am making here is that many new male and new female bank recruits were, in a manner of speaking, 'career-neutral' when they entered the bank. At some point in their future working lives, the notion whether they were or were not following a career - and what that entailed - was constructed as part of their work experience. It is significant here to find how common this position was amongst my male informants. Carl was one example of a male Britbank employee whose work commitment had gradually changed from doing 'a job' to working on a career. In his account, this shift was linked to the time when he was sent to London - after 7 years' work with the bank. By that move, the bank showed him its own expectations about his work with them, and Carl's work orientation changed accordingly.

My informants had quite clear ideas about which women were career orientated, and which women were not. According to Edward (Britbank), for instance, a lot of the women working in his department still looked upon their working lives as 'temporary':

> ... there are a lot of women who, as I say, it's a job, they're just waiting until they get married, ... go away and have children and that. But a few of them come back, but I think it's just really to help with the family and like, money, I suppose a lot of them still do look at it that way.(interview Edward)

In Dutchbank, reference was made to the tiered occupational structure which operates now in identifying non-career women. So especially women who worked at the level of *lager kader* were regarded as non-career women. Paula, who was accountant in one of Dutchbank's branches argued that many of the *lager kader* female employees who worked behind the counter in her branch did not show the interest or willingness to 'progress'. This suggests that the expectations of one's surrounding colleagues as well as those of the employer carry weight in the construction of the work commitment of employees over the years.

Combining home and work life. Talking to bank employees at different stages in their household life-cycle illustrated the different ways in which home and work life have been combined over time. Though my sample was not a representative one, distinct patterns were evident. As we have seen in chapter 5, female employees who worked in the bank during the 1940s and 1950s did not combine home and work life. The interviewees who had started families during the 1970s and early eighties differed from their predecessors in one fundamental way; like Sandra they often returned to the labour market some time after children arrived. During the 1980s, then, the returner-pattern (a pattern called *herintreden* in the Netherlands) was common amongst the women with children who themselves had worked in banks, or who were partners of male bank employees.[12] There was some evidence of a new stage in combination patterns. Bank employees, like Harriet, Chris, Yvonne, Paula and Linda had not, or did not intend to stop work on the arrival of children.

The investigation of attitudes as an indication of social change is often seen as problematic in view of the fact that practices do not always follow suit (Oudijk, 1983). A similar concern may be raised against this study because the informants who were in relationships during the 1980s had not all started families. So what these informants thought and told me about might not ultimately be the practices chosen when the need arose. But it was clear by the way that some went into issues like the combination of childcare and work, that they had, in fact, thought deeply about the possibilities and constraints which faced them. It is in those stories that the contemporary dilemmas still facing (mainly) bank women are reflected.

Because of the lack of childcare facilities more generally, part-time working has virtually been the only way in which Dutchbank women have combined employment with domestic responsibilities, and this combination choice has become increasingly common and acceptable. Unlike their British counterparts, there has been little tradition in the Netherlands where grandmothers, family or close neighbours provide the childcare needed for women to go out to work (de Bruijn, 1989, p.246). Amongst my Dutch informants, there was only one respondent (Chris) who made use of this form of child care. Since publicly funded child care facilities have become more widely available recently, my informants' stories included the increased opportunities which this offered. Reflecting the aggregate trend discussed in chapter 6, female Dutchbank employees now appear to prefer the combination of part-time working with the use - on a part-time basis - of child care facilities. Dutchbank's Paula, for instance, who did not have children during the 1970s, speculated that if she started a family now, she would probably want to work a 3 to 4 day week and use child care the rest of the time. Yvonne, another Dutchbank employee, had put this pattern into practice recently, after the birth of her first baby. Chris, who was a lone parent, would also like to work shorter than a full-time week, but said that this was financially not viable.

Part-time working was not as acceptable in Britbank as a combination option. Harriet, for instance, who had recently come back from her career break to work on a part-time basis, explained at length why this had not been a good experience. Working part-time, she had experienced differential treatment from management as well as from her other colleagues. From the latter Harriet felt she received less respect when she worked part-time, something that has changed since she has started working full-time again. More importantly, there had been a problem in that the grading system changed when Harriet was away, so that when she returned, she was placed in what she regarded as a lower grade. This issue was settled through the union, though Harriet herself interpreted this experience as an example of management trying to get away with something because she was 'only working part-time'. Other combination constraints were also evident in Harriet's account. She would have preferred a full-time childcare arrangement through her employers. However, because this was not forthcoming, she and her husband now used private childcare for part of the week, whilst her husband's mother looked after her daughter the other part of the week. Presumably, buying in full-time private child care was prohibitively costly for their household, even though both partners worked. Given this, one may speculate that the choice constraints on female staff who were financially less well of than Harriet, were even greater.

Part-time working and career progression: Linda's dilemma. Part-time working has become a much used combination option in the Netherlands generally, and in Dutchbank more specifically. However, it seems that the choice to switch to part-time work is more easily achieved by bank employees in lower graded jobs, and becomes increasingly difficult, the higher up the occupational echelon one works. Yvonne, for instance, has continued her work as a secretary on a part-time basis without difficulty. In contrast, Linda, who was branch manager of an *aangevoegd kantoor* (satellite branch), indicated that Dutchbank at the time of research did not allow a branch manager to work less than a full-time week. Even so, she thought that elsewhere in the organization, there would be opportunities for her to work less, at her level, if she wanted this.

Linda made it clear, though, that the request to work part-time carries a particular message. If in the post-war years gender itself, being a woman, was the negation of following a banking career, in the contemporary period part-time working is. In the bank, according to Linda, following a career is not to work part-time:

> Want carriere maken is gewoon 5 dagen werken, 6, 7, maar werken, en niet eh ... daar wat van afknibbelen en 4 dagen gaan werken, om vervolgens 3 dagen voor je kind te kunnen zorgen. Dat is geen carriere maken meer. (interview Linda)
> (Because to make a career is to work 5 days, 6, 7, but work, and not eh ... to nibble away from that time and work 4 days, so that you can then spend 3 days looking after your children. That is no longer making a career for yourself.)

Linda forms part of the small group (13 in total) of management trainees recruited by Dutchbank in 1989. By taking on a 50-50 per cent mix of men and women in her group, Dutchbank had, in contrast to its Dutch counterparts, shown its willingness to change the gender ratio in the higher echelons. Given this, and the anti-career connotations of part-time working, Linda felt that her group of trainees have an example to set. This is to resist reverting to part-time working - because by doing so you showed that you were not fully committed - and to show that a full-time career and children are a possible combination for working women nowadays.

However, Linda realized that this was more easily said than done. She and her husband, like many other couples of similar age, have more or less decided that they do want children in the future, and they were discussing the implications children would have on their working lives. Linda thinks that children should not influence two working lives, and expressed the wish to take on the organizing of tasks around child care, even though her husband had offered to shorten his working week to 4 days.[13] Linda's problem was that, given her intention declaration about not wanting to work part-time, she did not know whether she would, in the end, be able to leave her child, full-time, with a child-minder. And even if she did go part-time, Linda would not be able to stay in her current job. She would have to find another job at her level in the organization where part-time working was permitted.

Contemporary restructuring and gendered employment relations

Above I discussed how two banks, Dutchbank and Britbank, have reacted to a changing economic and technological climate in the contemporary period. I want to come back to a number of the points brought up there, and explore how these relate to current gendered employment relations in banks.

Career breaks and staff reductions

One of the main - and important - differences between the two banks was the emphasis on 'continuity of employment of existing staff'. Dutchbank has followed quite a determined policy of stabilizing its employee numbers over the 1980s. Britbank's reaction in this respect has been quite different. It was cutting staff numbers, at the time of research, and the bank had created an atmosphere of uncertainty about job security. It is here that the first link may be made with gender relations in banks. In principle, Britbank's career break offers its staff extra leeway in their labour supply decisions when domestic circumstances change. One of my informants, Harriet, had made use of this facility in the years prior to the interview. However, she had returned to the bank on a full-time basis fairly quickly, after a short spell of working part-time. In her account, Harriet did not express discontent about her own experience of the career break scheme, but she did wonder whether the bank, having introduced the scheme, was able to honour its agreement with employees:

> I think the bank made a mistake. Because they've introduced it (the career break), but they can't implement it now ...There's been so many people have tried to get back part-time, on a part-time career break, and there's no jobs for them, and they've had to go on full-time career breaks, or come back full-time ... I know of three other people that have tried to get back part-time and there isn't any jobs for them ... (interview Harriet)

This information contradicts with the fact that part-time working amongst Britbank's female staff was still increasing in the early 1990s, as opposed to full-time working, which was declining (see table 7.4). It seems that more Britbank women were working part-time, but that apparently fewer part-time places were available for career break women. Harriet also made the link between job cuts and the career break scheme:

> I mean, now that when you're on a - maternity leave or that, ... I think because of them wanting rid of all these people, they're hoping you don't come back. But ehmm ... you know, a few years ago, they were desperate for you to come back. (interview Harriet)

One conclusion which may be drawn is that Britbank was making the return to work difficult for women on maternity leave and career breaks on purpose, as a means to make job cuts. Whereas the career break is, in principle, a policy designed to hold onto female staff as their personal situation changes, it is not hard to see that under changed circumstances, the policy may in fact be used to achieve the opposite.

Having said that, Dutchbank's *kinderopvang* policy was not without its problems either. For instance, an *ondernemingsraad* (works council) representative told me that the budget the bank had allocated for childcare in 1992, had already run out in February, leaving employees who wanted to make use of the policy for the first time, to find alternative means.

Career bottlenecks and the discouragement factor

If, in the 1970s and early 1980s, banks in both societies experienced a growth in managerial positions, in the last 10 years there has been a decline in such positions. Reorganization has been an important reason behind this decline.

According to Dutchbank employee Peter, the organization has become flatter, and a number of managerial positions have simply disappeared. One example of this development forms the reorganization of the branch-network in both banks discussed here. In the recent past it was the case that all branches had their own managers and accountants. Now, with satellite banking, the responsibility of managers of the smaller branches has declined, and these positions are staffed by lower graded employees than before. This point was succinctly made by Carl, who was himself aspiring to become a branch manager:

> ... every manager of every branch would have been one grade higher than I am now, but now, the majority of them will be a lower grade than I am now, so the opportunities are much much diminished. (interview Carl)

Peter further pointed out that cost savings in head-office meant that some staff had turned to the regional offices and the branch-network to make promotion steps, and in effect, they were taking up promotion opportunities there. Other reasons brought forward for the decline in promotion opportunities were fusion and a decline in staff turnover. No respondents explicitly complained about the fact that women, by staying in bank work longer, competed for promotion jobs.

Was the difficulty of finding promotion opportunities related to labour supply decision taking of career-orientated bank women? Coming back to Linda's discussion is instructive, as she discussed developments around her management-trainee group in some detail. As one of the regulations of the trainee-course was to change work every 2 years, these trainees were constantly confronted with finding new work in the bank, at their grade level. Linda admitted that she had heard that her colleagues were having great difficulty in finding new work, simply because there were no opportunities. Linda herself still had a year to find something for herself. She was interested to find a place in head-office, but at the time of interview, she said, there was a complete stop on entry into head-office.

There was, therefore, a real struggle for places amongst her colleagues, which Linda linked to the changing work commitment amongst the female trainees in her group. In the first instance, these women were choosing this period to have a family:

> Wat ik net schetst, the problematiek rondom het vinden van een nieuwe baan, dat het niet meer zo soepel gaat, en dat je dus ook minder eenvoudig de baan krijgt die je graag ehh ... zou willen. Dat brengt met zich mee dat je al gauw zegt van ehh ... nou het gaat toch niet, ik ben al 32, kinderen moeten er toch een keer komen, laat ik er nu maar mee

beginnen, want op het werk gaat het ook niet meer zo prettig. (interview Linda)

(What I've just described, the problems around trying to find a new job, that everything does not go so easy anymore, and consequently that you don't as easily get the job that you ehh ... would like to do. That carries in its wake that you soon think, ehh ... well things don't go the way I want them to go, I am already 32, children have to come at some point, why not start with that now, because things don't go as well at work anyway.)

In the women who had taken this first step, Linda also saw a greater willingness to work part-time:

Ik denk als het wat minder op je werk gaat, dat je dat al snel als een soort van uitvlucht neemt om eh ... daarmee (met kinderen krijgen) aan te geven dat het gerechtvaardigt is dat je wat minder gaat werken. (interview Linda)

(I think that when things don't go very well at work, that you quickly get that (getting children) is used as an excuse eh ... that you say that by (getting children) you have the right to start to work a bit less.)

Explanations of the relationship between the public sphere of employment and the private sphere of domesticity have often concentrated on the influence which domestic responsibilities have on the labour supply offered by women. Walby (1986) has argued, in contrast, that the employment experiences of women may influence their decision taking regarding the private sphere of the home. The boring and often routine types of work which women are concentrated in, she argues, often make the choice for some kind of domestic life more appealing. The account of Linda would suggest that even women in work of more income, interest and/or responsibility are subject to this tendency. The career bottleneck in Dutchbank has made competition for new jobs so great, that 'career-track' women have become discouraged, the corollary of which has been a slackening of their work commitment in favour of domestic life 'options'.

Externalizing the gender problem

Britbank staff and managers agreed that it was still possible to move from the 'bottom to the top'. In Dutchbank this was no longer the case. There now exist three tiers in this bank, each with its own internal promotion. Entry to these tiers requires attainment of the right external educational credentials. Tijdens

(1989, p.268) has pointed out that this has been a general trend in Dutch banking.

Crompton has argued, in relation to British banking, that multi-tiered recruitment has increased the chances of women to progress into managerial positions, because formal educational qualifications (which women can attain as easily as men) have now replaced the former traditionalist decision taking as the basis for entry into the higher occupational regions. And as the example of Britbank shows, there is also still the opportunity to push through to higher positions from within the bank. The latter, however, is not the case anymore for Dutchbank, and Britbank's manager gave the impression that Britbank might be heading in the same direction. Thinking about the consequences of this for women in banks, it may be argued that multi-tiering has not improved the promotion of women into managerial positions. Tijdens outlines one of the consequences as follows:

> Voor de vrouwelijke personeelsleden van de banken betekent deze trend, dat ze nog steeds niet in aanmerking komen voor doorstroming, hoewel ze steeds meer ervaringsjaren opbouwen. De vrouwelijke personeelsleden met jarenlange ervaring in de administratie of aan de balie van een kantoor kunnen niet meer doorstromen naar beheerdersfuncties. (Tijdens, 1989, p.269)
> (For the female employees of the banks this trend means that they are still not eligible to progress, even though they build up increasing years of experience. The female employees with years of experience in administration or counter work in a branch can not progress anymore to the managerial functions.)

For the majority of women in Dutch banks (and British banks for that matter), there never was much chance for promotion in the past. Today, with the change to multi-tiering, the majority of bank women still have no chance of promotion.

Given this, the question remains whether the 'minority of men and women on career tracks' will, in the future, be evenly divided (Crompton, 1989, p.150)? For a discussion of this, I want to come back here to Dutchbank's management traineeship. It was designed to train university recruits over a period of 8 years for a position in higher management. When this program started in 1987, the bank accepted the demand by the *ondernemingsraad* that the recruits for this program were to be 50 per cent men and women, and consequently it could say with pride in 1991 that of the 106 trainees which had thus far entered the program, 55 were men and 51 were women (*Sociaal Jaarverslag*, 1991, p.17). In this respect, Dutchbank's decision was very much unique amongst the Dutch banks. The others did not have a 50-50 ratio policy. Of course, the reason that Dutchbank was able to follow its policy decision was the fact that it recruited people from a variety of university disciplines. However, since then the bank has changed its trainee program and its recruitment stipulation. Now, only university graduates who have studied organizational economics are recruited. Hence, Linda speculated, it would be impossible for them to continue to recruit on the basis of a 50 per cent gender ratio, by the simple fact that organizational economics is mainly studied by men. The point I am making is that by making educational credentials the basis for entry into managerial positions, Dutch banks have effectively externalized the gender problem that is vertical occupational segregation. Whether British banks will follow this Dutch pattern in the future remains to be seen.

Conclusion

In this chapter, change and continuity in the gender composition of the clerical work forces of Britbank and Dutchbank was investigated in relation to the contemporary period. As was the case with clerical feminization in the 1940-1965 period, a number of similarities were evident between the aggregate and the case-study level of this investigation. At the same time, there were some sector specific themes as well.

The economic uncertainty which characterized the national economies of the Netherlands and Britain, was also felt in the Dutch and British banking sectors, but not until the early 1980s. Prior to that, banks in both societies still enjoyed general growth, which was mirrored in the growth of their staff numbers. Running concurrent to this was a development specific to the banking sectors of the two societies. From the 1960s, which heralded the start of retail banking - itself a response by banks to the changing face of capitalistic enterprise - a seemingly never ending process of reorganization and technological innovation was evident. Whilst the emphasis prior to the 1980s was on coping with a vast expansion in the quantity of work, thereafter the emphasis was on responding to a changing economic climate.

In terms of the ideological-cultural climate within banks, the 1960s also saw a shift away from the patriarchal middle-class culture of the post-war years, towards a more formal-rational culture (Tijdens, 1989, Crompton, 1989). This shift is again comparable to the shift towards liberal thinking at the aggregate level, although it must be clear that bank employers were certainly not at the forefront of this shift. It signalled the end of explicit forms of gendered employment relations, such as the marriage bar and unequal pay scales. I have here examined the contemporary character of the formal inclusion of women in clerical bank work - the third stage in the history of gendered employment relations in British and Dutch banks.

One noteworthy point here is that contemporary patterns of work in Dutchbank and Britbank show similarities with national patterns. The employment statistics of both banks showed an increase in part-time working amongst women. Like the aggregate trend, the rise in part-time working was more significant in Dutchbank than in Britbank, though the ratios of female staff who worked part-time was lower than is the case for the aggregate economy. Similarly, supporting employees with the costs of buying childcare services was unheard of in Britbank, though Dutchbank had started to allocate some resources towards this.

The banking case-study also provided the opportunity to explore how a number of issues relating to women's labour supply were experienced at the level of specific individuals. One question explored was whether the shift to formal inclusion had been accompanied by a change in female bank employees behaving, seeing themselves, and being seen by others, as temporary employees. Various distinct issues relating to work commitment were explored. One of these was whether women's work commitment had changed towards a more permanent association with the employment part of their lives. The bank employees who co-operated in the research seemed to have the unanimous view that although not all female bank employees are career-orientated, more are career-orientated now than in the past. The interviews also indicated that female bank staff were staying longer in bank work than their 1950s predecessors, and it was suggested that this trend was facilitated by the availability - and acceptability - of combination opportunities.

Given the prevailing dominant pattern of the domestic division of labour in both societies, whether women's work commitment can change therefore depends on whether and what combination opportunities are available. I suggested that Britbank and Dutchbank, with some exceptions, now offered different combination opportunities. These were evaluated, partly in the context of the contemporary economic restraints banks in both societies work under. In the first place, there was evidence in Dutchbank that the combination opportunity of part-time working clashed with accepted masculine notions of career-commitment. This suggests that the prevailing notion of the ultimate work commitment in the bank still demands of the employee full-time, undivided attention, and hence negates the notion that employees may also carry domestic responsibilities. Furthermore, and related to the latter, there was some evidence that increased competition for career jobs, due to a flattening of the career hierarchy, was influencing the career commitment of female and male career-track employees differently. Thirdly, I have here suggested that the provision of 'real' combination opportunities may be dependent on the economic climate faced by banks.

Notes

1   The figure for 1988 represented here gives the impression of a slight decline over the eighties. The Department of Employment figures for later years show a rise in the female ratio again. In fact their figures indicate that in 1990, the female ratio amongst bank staff was 62 per cent.

2   Dutchbank only had figures available from 1965 onwards. From that year, Dutch businesses were obliged to provide information concerning their employment by law. Britbank's figures were gathered in a number of ways, but before 1955, I have not been able to find figures.

3   The rise in part-time working in Dutchbank increased as follows: 1970 - 3.2 per cent; 1975 - 9.4 per cent; 1980 - 9.0 per cent; 1985 - 14.1 per cent; 1989 - 14.2 per cent. For the ratio of female employee working on a part-time basis, figures are only available from 1980 onwards. These are presented in table 7.5 below, followed by the ratio of part-time working amongst Britbank's female staff.

Table 7.5
The ratio of women working part-time in Dutchbank and Britbank (percentages)

Year	Dutchbank	Britbank
1980[*]	23.1	8.1
1981	--	--
1982	21.8	--
1983	22.1	--
1984[*]	31.3	18.6
1985	34.3	14.8
1986	35.5	14.7
1987	35.5	14.3
1988	34.0	14.3
1989	33.9	14.5

Sources and notes:
Britbank figures supplied by Britbank.
Dutchbank figures recorded in Dutchbank's Sociale Jaarverslagen 1980-1989.
* The Britbank figures for 1980 and 1984 come from MacInnes (1985:25).

200

4   Britbank did experience a merger in those years, which explains a good proportion of the increase.

5   Dutchbank's branch manager Mr I.'s memories are a good illustration of this. When Mr I. started this branch in 1961, the only other man in the branch had been the *kassier* (cashier clerk). By 1963, this man had been replaced by a female member of the branch's staff, as, according to Mr I., the bank could not find a man to fill the post. Mr I. expresses the feeling that changes were happening so fast on this front. In 1958, when he worked in *Roermond*, girls were not even allowed to work behind the counter. In his branch, the girls did help behind the counter, but to have a woman cashier clerk in 1963, he argues, was an *'unicum'* (*'unique'*).

6   In the Netherlands, the first step in this form of back office automation was the setting up of the *Bankgirocentrale* in 1967 (Tijdens, 1993). Cressey and Eldridge name the Back Office Clearing Systems Ltd. (BACS); the system for bulk processing of direct credits and debits (such as wages) owned by the 5 London clearing banks, and CHAPS (or Clearing House Automated Payment Service) - which is designed to enable same day clearance of larger sums of money - as two forms of back office automation found in British banks.

7   A similar point is made in the *Sociaal Jaarverslag* of Dutchbank (1980, p.34).

8   The profit level of 1981 was 19 per cent below that of 1980 (*Sociaal Jaarverslag*, 1981, p.2).

9   The following quote is a good example of this:
'Het werk verandert, de medewerkers veranderen mee. De trefwoorden voor de komende jaren: aanpassingsvermogen, bereidheid tot verandering en flexibiliteit' (*Sociaal Jaarverslag*, 1987, p.3).
('Work changes, and the employee changes too. The catchwords of the coming years are: adaptability, willingness to change and flexibility'.)

10   Amongst the Britbank informants alone, Sandra has been with the bank for 30 years, and had a break of 3 years, returning to Britbank on a part-time basis (though in a variety of work). June has been with Britbank for 22 years, with a break of 10 years, and Janice has been with the bank for 25 years, with a break of 8 years. Interesting is that both Nancy (who has worked in Britbank for the last 23 years), and Paula (who has worked in Dutchbank since 1963) had no children and also did not have breaks.

11   For an unpacking of the meanings attributed to the concept career see Martens (1994, chapter 7).

12   The presence or absence of children in the household life-cycle was decisive in influencing the outcome of some of these variations;

something which is not surprising. Two of my woman informants (Paula of Dutchbank and Nancy of Britbank) had intended to have children, but had remained childless. Both of them had continued to work in the bank, both of them on a full-time basis. Even so, they both acknowledged that it had been their intention to stop work when they had tried for a baby during the 1970s.

13   Interestingly, none of my informants actually had, or expressed the wish for role reversal; i.e. where the man in the household takes the main responsibility for the tasks involved around child care and domestic work.

8 Conclusion

In this comparative investigation of the gender composition of work forces, and the changes and continuities therein in the recent history of women's economic activity in the Netherlands and Britain, I have directed my attention to those themes and time-periods, which have been indicated as - in some way - significant to the issues at hand. In delineating these themes, I have paid attention to both Dutch and British accounts; particularly those informed by a gender relations perspective. As a consequence, the marriage bar (or marriage bars as I have preferred to refer to these phenomena of women's employment history) featured as a central theme. In addition, the Second World War period, the post-war years, and the contemporary period all featured as central time-periods in the investigation.

Moreover, in the chapters covering these specific time-periods, two separate, though related perspectives on the gender composition of work forces was presented. One involved the aggregate or total work forces of the two societies under investigation. Here, aggregate trends and changes in the gender composition of work forces were considered, and the differences found between the two societies were investigated. These accounts relied on a comparative analysis of relevant secondary sources derived from both societies. In contrast to this macro approach, a more middle-range, case-study investigation of the banking sector was presented. Here too, the gender composition of bank staff was the main theme which shaped the course of the investigations. The investigations were informed by archival materials and accounts from bank employees.

In the conclusion, I want to bring a number of points together which have been made during the course of my discussion. Firstly, each empirical chapter has, in some way, shown the relationship between the culturally specific character of social relations within each society and the extent of women's economic activity. I want to bring these together here. I also want to come back to the peculiarity of bank employment in the two societies. At various time-periods, this case-study has shown, the operations of banks in both societies have been influenced by the demands of the aggregate economy and by aggregate ideological trends. But it is only by acknowledging the interrelation between this and the peculiar employment organization within banks, that comparative differences in the gender composition of bank staff - and changes and continuities in that composition over time - may be understood. Lastly, I shall return to the contemporary time-period, and the controversy with which this discussion started.

Cultural formations and exclusionary measures in remunerated work

In chapters 3 to 7, the specific cultural formations characterizing the two societies under investigation always cropped up as an important aspect underlying the differences found. Here, evidence of this relating to the war and post-war years will be brought together. Crudely speaking, the major cultural difference between the two societies in this period may be characterized as follows. Whilst divisions in social relations in British society were mainly class based, in the Netherlands such divisions were mainly stipulated by the existence of the Catholic, Protestant and Socialist pillars. In the latter, class divisions were evident, but these were not as significant as relations determined within the pillars, and between them. For instance, within the Catholic pillar, one could find Catholic trade unions and employers' federations, both incorporating a Catholic line of thinking. Catholic trade unions, therefore, often took a different position on labour issues than the Socialist unions.

Of interest here is that these different cultural formations incorporated a rather similar 'traditional' gender ideology or gender culture (Pfau-Effinger, 1995). In short, this 'traditional' gender ideology, also termed bourgeois family/gender ideology (Pfau-Effinger, 1995), stipulated gender roles in the private/domestic sphere of the home and the public sphere of employment. In both societies, there were strong tendencies to think of a woman's place as the home, resulting, for instance, in such phenomena as marriage bars. Marriage bars were, taking into account the variations found, institutionalized evidence for the presence of this kind of patriarchal thinking in each society. Even so, given this similarity, the cultural formations which characterized social relations in the two societies was the source for variation in the consequences of this gender ideology. Especially in relation to the presence; timing of the presence; and implementation of marriage bars, this was the case.

This variation is already noticeable in the cross-national variations found in secondary accounts which comment about marriage bars in each society. These have basically emphasized different points. In Britain, commentaries have pointed to the fact that marriage bars appear to have been forgotten as phenomena of women's employment (Walby, 1990a, Glucksmann, 1990, p.300, Roberts, 1988, p.73), the corollary of which has been a call for further investigation of this feature of gendered employment relations. In the Netherlands, almost the opposite is the case. Here, there are quite a number of accounts which trace the variations in time and implementation found in the presence of the bar in State employment (Posthumus-van der Groot, 1977, Schoot-Uiterkamp, 1978, Blok, 1989, and de Bruijn, 1989), although less systematic material is available on other types of work.

This emphasis, then, points to one major difference. This is that in the Netherlands, the State has historically played an important role in the establishment of marriage bars and in their abolition. This, as is pointed out by Schoot-Uiterkamp, for instance, crossed the boundaries of the types of employment which were regulated directly by the State. The State was seen to set the example for other employers in this respect. More importantly, in reasoning why State influence on marriage bars was so significant in the Netherlands, there is a need to recognize the significance of the pillarized character of social relations in Dutch society at the time. Looking upon the State as a process in which the interests of various agents and groups give rise to specific policies and decisions, the influence of the Confessionals at specific historical periods (e.g. during the 1930s, when unemployment was very high) is evident. It was their moral vision on women's employment - which objected specifically to the employment of married women outside the home - which in many cases was decisive in the introduction of bars, in their implementation - and during the 1950s - in their abolition.

In contrast, in Britain, State influence and/or interference in marriage bars has virtually been absent. Though the bourgeois gender ideology just described was clearly evident, it is important to recognize that the British state showed a *laissez faire* attitude where interference in the labour market was concerned. The role of consecutive British governments in the institution, implementation and abolition of marriage bars is therefore negligible. The important exceptions were the war and direct post-war years, when opposition by the government to the marriage bar - related partly to liberal ideology and partly to tightness in the British labour market - resulted in the abolition of marriage bars in the occupations over which it had some control (e.g. teaching, the Civil Service, and the Post-Office). It was argued that this measure was partly related to an attempt by the British Government to influence the stance of private employers. The absence of state interference in marriage bars means that the history of marriage bars in Britain is more difficult to record than is the case for the Netherlands. An attempt to do so was made in chapter 3, where it was argued that marriage bars were probably more common in middle class types of work, signalling the greater 'success' of the institutionalization of bourgeois family/gender ideology in the middle classes than elsewhere.

Cultural formations, gender ideology and socio-economic factors

These same issues return in chapter 4, now in relation to the challenges posed on this familial ideology by an economy seeking 'new' labour supplies. The post-war years in both Britain and the Netherlands may be characterized as a period which sees a gradual decline in the influence of the bourgeois-familial ideology just described. Evidence for this is the increased importance of liberal discourses. These discourses favoured individual freedom and were opposed to the interference of 'outsiders' in matters considered the concern of the individual. Opposition to policies which stipulated whether married women were allowed to work or not, were part of this trend.

The declining influence of bourgeois-familial ideology is, without doubt, accompanied by an unprecedented tightness of the labour market. Of significance here is the difference in the timing at which the 'traditional' familial ideology became challenged in the two societies. In Britain, the Second World War posed a challenge to prevailing attitudes towards employed married women in the preceding years exactly because the demand for labour resources was so pressing. The years following on from the Second World War were years of full employment. This did not allow a relapse to pre-war attitudes. Indeed, the British government to a certain degree tried to stimulate a change in attitudes in this respect, as discussed above. So the post-war state of the labour market was decisive in pushing for permanent change in attitudes towards the employment of certain groups of women.

In the Netherlands, the situation was rather different. Here, the war years had not posed a challenge to pre-war attitudes towards the work - outside the domestic home - of married women, even though the marriage bar in State employment was relaxed as male employees were called to Germany. In the post-war years, as I indicated in chapter 4, evidence suggests that there were a variety of labour resources available. Only during the 1950s, when labour shortage became pressing, was a similar gradual decline in the influence of 'traditional' familial ideology noticeable. For instance in the abolition of the marriage bar in Dutch state employment.

The peculiarity of banking employment

In explaining the different ratios of change in the gender composition of bank staff in the two societies in this period, reference needs to be made to the different aggregate pressures at work on banking employers. One important period in recent history, the Second World War years, shows the way in which banks (and other private firms) can become subject to emergencies arising beyond the boundaries of their own control. The different experiences of the war in the two societies shows the degree to which British banks had to change their traditional employment set-up in order to continue to provide its services during the war. With the exception of the Bank of England and Lloyds Bank, it was uncommon to find female staff employed in the clerical work of British banks prior to the war. The Second World War experience was an 'eye opener' for many British banks, because in the time of a few years, women took over most of the (mainly routine) clerical jobs in the banks. I would argue that the Second World War was therefore a stimulant in the feminization of clerical bank work in Britain. The same can, of course, not be argued for the Netherlands.

Post-war conditions consolidated clerical feminization in British banks for different reasons. On the one hand, British banks suffered from a labour shortage equalling the persistence of this shortage in the aggregate economy. Dutch banks did not face a similar problem, and this again reflected aggregate labour market conditions. On the other hand, and again in contrast to Dutch banks, British banks suffered from an internal labour market problem; the so-called age-bulge problem, which was a direct result of the peculiar organization of employment in banks. One salient consequence of this problem was that British banks were losing control over their internal labour market, because there was a higher than normal turnover amongst male youngsters in the banks, whilst the latter were, on the other hand, increasingly difficult to recruit in the first place. I have argued that the solution which was found signalled the shift in patriarchal gender relations in banking employment from exclusion towards formal/partial inclusion. That is, the recruitment of women in clerical work was speeded up significantly, but this was accompanied by a marriage bar.

So, whilst the extent of clerical feminization was greater in British banks, the form which women's employment took in banks in both societies was similar; i.e. female bank clerks were young and unmarried, and marriage bars were common in banks in both societies. It has been argued that the persistence of the marriage bar in Dutch banks into the 1960s neatly fitted in with the aggregate ideological thinking of the time. Dutch banks did not have to find 'special' reasons to explain the marriage bar. It would, in fact, have been frowned upon if Dutch banks had deviated from an employment pattern which was so common. In Britain, the persistence of marriage bars into the 1950s in various banks contrasted with its abolition in other sectors of work (including middle class types of work) during the 1940s. This persistence has been explained by drawing on three interrelating factors. Firstly, in Dutch and British banks, the marriage bar stemmed well with the middle class/heterosexual family ideal which was seen as befitting the life of a bank employee. Secondly - and specific to the British banking sector - bank employers used the marriage bar, even if symbolically, in the reconstruction of the male career as a 'good' career, and thirdly, they were able to organize their employment in this way because relations in banks were still paternalistic in character.

The significance of the state and cultural formations in gendered employment relations

This investigation on the gender composition of work forces has consciously been a discussion with analysis of gender relations in employment, and relating to it, gender relations in the private/domestic sphere. The interrelation between the public and the private sphere has been of particular significance in the historical time-period considered here, in the sense that the prevailing patriarchal gender relations at the time, as embodied in such phenomena as marriage bars, assigned gender to place; women to the domestic sphere of the home, and men to both. These relations often took forms of exclusion. In Walby's theoretical framework, these relations have been conceptualized as forming part of the historically specific 'private' form of patriarchy, as opposed to the more contemporary form of 'public' patriarchy.

I want here to return briefly to Walby's analysis of comparative variations in the form which patriarchal gender relations have historically taken in industrialized societies, and relate some aspects of my analysis here to her theoretical framework. All industrialized societies, she argues, have gone through a historical period characterized by a private form of patriarchy. Over time, this form has changed; now these societies feature a public form of patriarchy. Within the latter, cross-national variations are apparent. A three-fold distinction is made by Walby, based on whether the State or the market has been decisive in 'bringing women into the public sphere' (Walby, 1990a, p.95). The variations in the public form of patriarchy, Walby argues, are stipulated by the 'introduction of the level of the State as a new element' (1990a, p.95). As discussed in chapter 2, Walby then provides an account of the comparative differences in public patriarchal relations, in which East European societies are contrasted with West European societies, and in turn with the United States. What we get is an emphasis on these differences, and an implied uniformity in the public form which patriarchy takes in West European societies. As I commented in chapter 2, Western Europe is said to have a 'mixed state/market' form of public patriarchy.

This analysis of the gender composition of two national work forces spans the period in which one could argue, using Walby's terminology, there has been a shift from a private form to a public form of patriarchal gender relations. More specifically, in part 2 of the book, I looked in some detail at, what Walby calls, 'the second moment' in the shift from private to public patriarchy in which women have gained 'effective access to paid employment' (1990a, p.96). Walby's account, if anything, implies the similarity of private patriarchal gender relations in industrialized societies, and the State only becomes important as a differentiating factor in patriarchal relations in the contemporary period.

This comparison of Dutch and British work forces suggests that some refinement of this theoretical model of private patriarchy would be appropriate. I have argued that both societies have seen the influence of a bourgeois-familial ideology, opposed to the presence of women in the public sphere. Chapter 3 also provides sufficient evidence that this ideology generated institutionalized forms ensuring the closure of women's access to employment. But the cultural structures which intermediated between ideology and institutional outcomes in fact generated different outcomes. Given the above discussion on cross-national differences in the institutionalization of the bourgeois-familial ideology, it seems to me that the state/market dimension is important in identifying the different modes in which the closure of women's access to employment was operationalized in Britain and the Netherlands.

Moreover, in understanding why this is so, the cultural formations specific to the two societies are important. Dutch pillarization entailed a strengthening of Confessional interests at State level during the first half of the 20th century. Through their power on State level - as well as at a local and regional level - Dutch Confessionals were relatively successful in enforcing their ideological thinking, including the distinct thinking on women and work outside the home, to a significant degree, on Dutch society at large. Maybe in this respect, the outcome of a private form of patriarchy should also be seen as a manifestation of the:

> ... difference in state policy, which itself is an outcome of various struggles between opposing forces on both gender and class issues. (1990a, p.95)

The exception being that in the Netherlands class issues intermediated with religious/cultural manifestations, whilst the latter were, if anything, more significant than the former. In Britain, with the absence of state interference, the marriage bar form of employment closure was orchestrated by employers and trade unions.

Given the linkage I have made here between bourgeois-familial ideology and cultural manifestations, it seems appropriate to return to another commentary on cross-national differences in women's remunerated work patterns. Plantenga's thesis on the peculiarity of Dutch women's economic activity, based on a comparison of Germany and the Netherlands over this century, is a combination of two interrelated themes. As discussed in chapter 2, she has suggested that a bourgeois-familial ideology was present in both Germany and the Netherlands, and that this can hence not serve as a causal factor in the explanation of cross-national differences in women's remunerated work. However, she argues (as I have argued here) that the different cultural structures through which this ideology was operationalized did generate different outcomes. Dutch pillarized sociality, Plantenga argues, entailed that Dutch society was vertically layered, and this provided the cultural structure through which a gender ideology could pervade large sections of Dutch society. Germany - like Britain, but in contrast to the Netherlands - was a horizonally layered society, which made the penetration of a bourgeois-familial ideology to all layers of society more difficult. It is clear that there are obvious similarities in our two studies in this respect.

Plantenga's thesis is developed by the inclusion of a socio-economic facet in the explanation. Based on a comparison of national productivity statistics over time, she argues that the Netherlands was a relatively prosperous country, and that it could hence afford its low female activity rate. That is, Dutch women were economically able to live a life according to the ideal, in contrast to their German sisters. This is an ingenious argument, the relevance of which I would be ready to adopt, were it not for the fact that - as Plantenga herself shows in relation to her local study of Tilburg - hidden forms of employment amongst Dutch women were widespread. Why, if Dutch women could afford not to engage in remunerated work, was hidden home-work so widespread? An answer to this question could be that, given the ideological climate, and Dutch women's need to help finance their households, hidden forms of home-work were the most acceptable means through which to earn an income, and - given the evidence of the prevalence of marriage bars in Dutch society - often the only means through which to do so.

I pointed out in chapter 2 that the research aims of Plantenga's study differ from this one, and that this had consequences for the investigation. More specifically, my concern with the later rise in Dutch women's economic activity after W.W.II suggests that the relative tightness of the labour markets in the respective countries is an important socio-economic factor of this aspect of social change. Lastly, Plantenga discounts a third facet of possible causal significance; political-institutional factors. After an historical investigation of three policy themes through which the German and Dutch states could have influenced the access of women to remunerated work; care leaves; childcare and fiscal arrangements, she concludes that Dutch and German state policy has historically been one of intervention. This similarity again raises doubts as to the significance of political-institutional factors in the explanation of differences in German and Dutch women's paid work. As discussed above, my investigation suggests that there was a distinct difference in British and Dutch state intervention concerning exclusionary measures in employment. Consecutive British governments have shown a *laissez faire* attitude towards married women's remunerated work, whereas the opposite is true for Dutch governments of the 1920s till the 1950s.

Cultural formations and inclusion in remunerated work

There can be no doubt that in order to understand change and continuity in the gender composition of the aggregate work forces in the last 25 years, and some of the features - like part-time employment - which have accompanied this, one needs to recognize the legacy of the 'traditional' bourgeois-familial ideology which characterized patriarchal gender relations in the past. Illustrating this point is the fact that similar solutions were found to the contradictions which arose, between these 'traditional' discourses and the demands of the economies in both societies. The legacy is evident, thus, in the existence of a relatively large degree of part-time working amongst economically active women. In Britain, the use of part-time employment had been pioneered in the Second World War, and had expanded significantly amongst female workers in the post-war years. In the Netherlands, part-time working was experimented with for the first time during the 1960s, and this form of employment expanded rapidly during the 1970s and 1980s.

The persisting influence of 'traditional' bourgeois-familial ideological discourses is also evident in the persistence of part-time working (and the significant increase in part-time working in the Netherlands) in the last 20 years, and the relatively slow shift in the social acceptance of publicly provided child care facilities. The presence of childcare facilities for young children, directed at facilitating the employment of their mothers, was as good as absent in both societies over the whole period investigated. For instance, whilst there was a more widespread agreement in the Netherlands that women (even women with children) had a right to work during the 1970s, this agreement did not extend to include the provision of childcare facilities. The other apt example of how 'traditional' gender discourses recurred is evident in both societies during the early 1980s depression, when politicians in both societies drew on this discourse to justify state withdrawal from a number of service provisions.

The continued relevance of cultural specificities

From the post-war years into the contemporary period there has been change in the cultural constitutions specific to the Netherlands and Britain. The salience of the pillarized organization of Dutch society has declined significantly, though it would be rash to say that aspects of it have disappeared altogether. At the national political level, for instance, we find that the *CDA* -

the political party in which the Confessional parties of the pillarization period have come together - is the largest political party during the 1980s. Equally, it would be wrong to argue that social divisions based on class differences have disappeared in Britain. More accurate, probably, is to argue that the character of these divisions has changed somewhat over time.

My discussion on the respective changes in the recorded economic activity rate of women in Britain and the Netherlands in the contemporary period, shows that society specific cultural formations continue to be relevant. One of these is the different State systems in the two societies; consensus politics in the Netherlands and a two-party system in Britain. In my discussion, this difference was related to developments around part-time working, as well as child care facilities.

State action has facilitated the rise in part-time employment in both societies, but in different ways. In Britain, the rise in part-time working in the last 20 years is related to neo-conservative economic policies, which have effectively generated a low-waged economy. British employers have enjoyed more freedom in creating low wage jobs, and consequently, increasingly poorer part-time employment has been on the increase in Britain, particularly during the severe recessions of the early eighties and early nineties. It is not difficult to see the connection between the degree and form in which neo-conservatism was adopted in Britain, and the class constitution of society. But one of my arguments here has been that neo-conservatism was able to develop in this way because Britain's state system, which is basically a two party state in which governments are one party governments, facilitated this shift.

New conservatism has not directed Dutch politics to the same degree. One significant facet of this difference is that Dutch governments have remained of the opinion that the state has a regulating role where unemployment is concerned. The Dutch State has also encouraged the creation of part-time employment over the last 20 years, but for different reasons. During the 1980s, part-time employment was part of a policy package which aimed to reduce unemployment. During the 1970s, as Morée (1992) has argued, the Dutch government was involved in setting up a system of subsidy provision to encourage private sector employers to create part-time work. The reasoning behind this was to provide the possibility for Dutch mothers to go out to work. Why did neo-conservatism not develop in the same way in the Netherlands? I have suggested here that one reason was the consensus politics which characterize the Dutch state system.

The degree and form of neo-conservatism has also been relevant for the different ways in which childcare service provision has developed in the two societies. In Britain, policies of a redistributory nature have been out of fashion, and childcare services are only available to those who can afford it, on a private basis. Redistribution has not been as unpalatable in the Netherlands,

212

and the government finally agreed to allocate public resources to this service at the end of the 1980s.

The different state systems may also be related to the manner in which feminists have lobbied for the public provision of childcare services, and consequently, in the relative successes of campaigns. Dutch consensus politics has been relatively open to the influence of feminism, and Dutch feminists have targeted national politics. This meant that in 1982, parliament passed an act calling upon the government to make resources available for the provision of publicly funded childcare. British feminists have not targeted national politics in the same way, the reason being that the two-party system of government is also a fairly closed system. Instead, British feminists have targeted local governments, the implications of which have been that the successes have been varied, and dependent on the whims of national government.

This last point, coming back to Walby's state/market form of public patriarchy, would suggest that in the last 15 years, Britain has relied more on the market as a means to make the combination of employment and children possible for British women. In the Netherlands, the State has been mobilized into financing these services - and in stimulating part-time working - and hence the state has played a role in making employment more accessible for Dutch women. Lastly, I have argued that the character of feminist campaigning has itself been an indicator of the different cultural realities in the two societies. In Britain, class oppositions have certainly been evident in divisions in the women's movement. Childcare campaigns are one instance where these divisions have led to differences in aims and priorities. In the Netherlands such divisions are less obvious, in contrast to the variety of collaborations between diverse women's groups which have taken place.

Modernizing discourses and Dutch women's labour supply

We may here, shortly, come back to the contradiction which I mentioned in the introduction. This was, you will remember, the curious mixing of the image of Dutch 'progressiveness' with women's emancipation, which in turn clashed with the relatively low Dutch average participation rate of women. This contrasted with British 'conservativeness'; a 'low' women's emancipation and a high average rate of women's economic activity. Looking back to the themes and issues brought up in this book, I would like to make a few additional comments here.

Firstly, the research has shown that history in part explains the currently comparatively low average participation rate for Dutch women (and the comparatively high rate for British women). I have also argued that an awareness of this history has itself been instructive in changing Dutch women's labour supply. The cultural changes discussed above were heralded by 'modernizing' discourses, of which second wave feminism(s) were one example. I have further speculated that the 'modernizing' discourses addressing the 'gender order' (Connell, 1987), were directly related to the low economic activity of women in the Netherlands, whereas in Britain, this was not the case. The 'catching-up' process which has occurred in the Netherlands since the early 1970s, even if this has been accompanied by a high ratio of part-time working, is therefore to a significant degree due to Dutch women wanting to engage in paid work.

Secondly, the 'progressive' image many Dutch people no doubt have of themselves, and which they purvey to the outside world, is also part and parcel of their own peculiar history, and the meanings which have subsequently been given to this. In this respect, cultural change in the post-war period, conceptualized as a 'modernization push' (Pfau-Effinger, 1995), has involved the juxtaposition of the 'traditional' (i.e. the 'old' Confessional pillarized order and the values and ideas it stood for) with the 'modern' (i.e. the 'new' secular and non-pillarized order). In Britain, with its rather different cultural reality, this was rather different. Even so, change does not happen overnight. Certainly in relation to the gender composition of the Dutch aggregate work force, I have indicated how 'traditional' voices remained in evidence, and probably slowed down a process of change, which has in any case been rather quick.

The peculiarity of banking employment

In the post-war period, banks in both societies developed a gendered employment set-up - of young female staff working in a job and male staff working in a career - the salience of which has been commented on in Britain by Crompton (1989), MacInnes (1986, 1988) and Heritage (1983) and in the Netherlands by Wierema (1979) and Tijdens (1989). However, from the 1960s onwards, various aspects of this explicitly gendered organization of employment were relaxed. A continued tight aggregate labour market eventually required bank employers to look for 'alternative' labour supply sources. Marriage bars disappeared, and gradually the profitable aspects of employing married women and providing part-time employment, became emphasized. Overt gender differences in wages also disappeared. I have suggested that this change has signalled a second shift in patriarchal employment relations in banks; from partial inclusion to formal inclusion. Gender and marital status have ceased to be grounds for the exclusion of women, though in reality, this has not meant the end of gender differences in clerical bank employment.

Investigating the gender composition of bank staff in the contemporary period has involved a number of different questions and issues than was the case for the war and post-war years. In the earlier research period the attention was directed towards comparing and contrasting the increased employment of women in clerical bank work. In the contemporary period, aspects which contribute to change and continuity in the gender composition of bank staff have been at issue. The contemporary period contrasts with the post-war years in other ways too. Whilst the latter were characterized by continuity in the operations within banks, the former are characterized by significant changes which have taken place - and which are still taking place - in the banking sectors of the two societies. These changes may be brought together under the concept 'restructuring', and have included such change as concentration; the step-by-step introduction of new technology; the centralization followed by the decentralization of operations; the expansion of the branch network followed by its contraction and reshaping, and so on. It is these changes and the influence of second wave feminism which I have here considered in an effort to point out the salient features of formal inclusion in banking employment. However, given the concern with the gender composition of bank staff, my efforts have concentrated on labour supply and labour demand related themes, instead of a direct concern with occupational segregation.

I have argued here that part of the influence of second wave feminism has been that more women who have entered bank work in the last 15 years have a different attitude towards their work than their predecessors. More contemporary bank women look upon their employment as a permanent feature of their life and more of these women are also career-orientated. The time when bank managers could predictably influence the gender composition of their staff (on the certainty that there was a predictable turn-over amongst women staff) has now gone. Bank employers have paid lip-service to these changes by accompanying them with policies to facilitate women's labour supply. In Dutchbank, the combination options available include part-time working, various leaves, and assistance with the payment of childcare services. Britbank's main combination policies centred on part-time working and the career break scheme.

However, as these policies have developed during the 1980s, banks have indicated the need to change the 'old' conditions and understandings around the employment they offer. In both Britbank and Dutchbank, employees have been called upon to become more flexible, more market orientated, and to take responsibility for their own productivity. In both banks, too, the traditional single-tiered internal labour market has shifted towards a multi-tiered set-up, where entry requirements are linked to external educational credentials, and where movement between the tiers is increasingly difficult to achieve. But whilst Dutchbank has - up until now - worked within the context of holding onto existing staff, Britbank has heralded job cuts (in accordance with many other British banks), a policy from which they have not retracted subsequently.

In this context, the increased seniority of female employees does not necessarily lead to the promotion rewards which their male colleagues in past times enjoyed (see also Tijdens, 1989). Britbank's managers in fact expressed the view that seniority was going be valued less in the future. In the context of job cutting, one may also wonder about the effectiveness of their combination policies. In Dutchbank, in contrast, the attempt to hold onto existing staff in addition to reorganization had generated a career bottleneck. There was some evidence to suggest that in this situation, notions of work commitment favoured masculine notions of the career and what it stood for. The combination option of working part-time clashed with such notions, and enhanced the idea that part-time workers - who are mostly women - are less committed workers.

Appendix

The semi-structured interviews conducted to inform the banking case-study in this book were held with a variety of people (see table A.1 for an overview). I set out to speak to a diverse group of people, and did not set myself specific targets. Under the category 'employer' are included my conversations with personnel managers of different banks, and at different levels of the organization (some in head-office; some regional). Under the employee (now) category, I spoke to equal numbers of Britbank and Dutchbank employees (male and female). In the Netherlands, I also spoke to a number of employees from two other Dutch banks, but these are not recorded in table A.1.

Table A.1
Overview of the interviews held in the banking sector

Type	Britain			The Netherlands		
	Male	Female	Total	Male	Female	Total
Employer	1	2	3	4	3	6
EO-ideas		1	1		2	2
Employee (now)	7	8	15	7	8	15
Employee (former)	5	3	8	8	7	15

Below, information - about work title, grade, and the year when these employees started work in Britbank and Dutchbank - has been presented for a number of the interviews held. Information about the domestic circumstances of these respondents is included.

Current Britbank employees

Sandra: Bank Officer; branch (grade 4). Has worked in the bank since 1963. Until 1979 she worked full-time, when she left to have her baby. After a 3 year break, she started to work again on a part-time basis, and has done so ever since. Is married to another Britbank employee.

Janice: Clerical Officer; department (grade 5). Started work in 1967, and has taken approximately 8 years out for child care reasons, after which she returned on a part-time basis. Is currently lone parent of her two children, and works full-time again.

Nancy: Head Typist; branch (grade 6). Has worked in the bank since 1969. Is married and lives in dual earner household with husband. Had intended to leave work when they tried for children during the 70s.

Carl: Manager; department (grade 10). Has worked in the bank since 1970. Is married and started a family during the 1980s. His wife subsequently gave up her employment, and has since been full-time housewife.

June: Senior systems programmer; department (grade 10). Has worked in the bank since 1970, stopped work in 1977 and had a break out for 10 years to have children and look after them. When June had children, working part-time was not an option, and there was no career break scheme (which she would have used if available). June has worked full-time since returning to the bank in 1988.

Bill: Group manager (grade 12). Started work in the bank in 1976. Is married, and wife stopped work when they had children. Wife has not resumed work since.

Paul: Administration manager (grade 7). Has worked in the bank since 1977. Is married with two children, and his wife is full-time housewife.

Graham: Trust manager (grade 9). Has worked in the bank since 1978. Is married to another bank employee (who is in a lower grade), and they possibly will try for children in the future. Sees his wife as taking on the main childcare responsibilities, possibly making use of the bank's career break scheme.

Sheila: Suboffice supervisor; branch (grade 5). Started work in the bank in 1979. Is single.

Malcolm: Senior bank officer (grade 5). Started work in the bank in 1980. Has been married three years, and his wife also works in the bank (at grade 4, though she started two years before Malcolm). They were planning to have children, and for his wife to take on the main responsibilities for childcare.

Harriet: Senior Bank Officer; department (grade 5). Has worked in the bank since 1981. Left a number of years ago on the bank's official career break scheme to have her first baby. Worked part-time for a short period and now works full-time again. Is married and lives in dual earner household with husband and daughter.

Edward: Clerical officer; department (grade 3). Has worked in the bank since 1987. Is single.

Current Dutch employees

Mies: Branch manager (*moederkantoor*) (grade 12). Has worked in the bank since 1957. Is single and employs a cleaner.

Peter: Branch manager (*aangevoegd kantoor*) (grade 8). Has worked in the bank since 1962. Is married and has children. Wife is full-time housewife.

Paula: *Chef particulieren* (grade 8). Has worked in the bank since 1963. Intended to have children in the 1970s, and to stop work. Housework is shared between partners and they employ a cleaner.

Jan: Branch manager (*aangevoegd kantoor*) (grade 11). Has worked in the bank since 1969. Is married with children. Wife does housework and childcare, and combines this with part-time work.

Ellie: *Chef Particulieren* (grade 6). Has worked in the bank since 1979. Cohabits with a partner, there are no children, and they do the housework together.

Margaret: Telephonist/receptionist (grade 4). Has worked in the bank since 1980. Cohabits with a partner, but there are no children, and there is some sharing of domestic work.

Geert: Branch manager (*moederkantoor*) (grade 13). Has worked in the bank since 1980. Is part of a dual career household with three children. Domestic work and childcare work are bought in.

Yvonne: Secretary (grade 5). Has worked in the bank since 1982, and currently works a half-time week. Is married and takes the main responsibility for her daughter, who goes into a nursery two and a half days a week.

Chris: Secretary (management) (grade 6). Has worked in the bank since 1984. Went on maternity leave last year, and has been a lone parent since the birth of her son. She works a full-time week, and her son goes three days in the week to a nursery and two days a week to Chris's mother.

Andre: *Adviseur bankzaken* (grade 9). Has worked in the bank since 1986. Is married, with one child, and his wife is full-time housewife.

Tim: *Huismeester* (caretaker) (grade 5). Has worked in the bank since 1986. Is married, both partners work and they have made a conscious choice not to have children.

Linda: Branch manager (*aangevoegd kantoor*) (grade 9). Has worked in the bank since 1989. Is married to another Dutchbank employee, and they plan to have children in the future. She would like both partners to continue work full-time, and to buy in full-time childcare. They employ a cleaner and share the domestic work that is left.

Former bank employees

Discussions were held with former bank employees, both male and female, in the Netherlands and in Britain. These employees differed according to which bank(s) they had worked in, how long they had been bank employees, when they had worked in a bank, and what their reasons were for leaving when they did. Former Dutch bank employees were invited to collaborate with the research through advertisements in Dutch newspapers and through Dutchbank's society for former bank employees *'Nog Mijn Bank'*. Recruiting British former bank employees proved somewhat more difficult, particularly with respect to women, and this is reflected in the number of former female bank employees who co-operated with the research. Information about when the informants worked in a bank, what their last position was, and why they left bank employment are recorded in tables A.2 and A.3.

Table A.2
Former and retired bank employees: British banks

Name	When worked	Last position	Reason for leaving
Mr T.	1941-1985	General Manager HO	retirement
Mr Z.	1947-1985	General Manager Region	retirement
Mr H.	1940-1982	Branch Manager	retirement
Mr G.	1950-1990	Branch Manager	retirement
Mr Q.	1936-1980s	General Manager Region	retirement
Mrs B.	1969-1992	Manager HO	early retirement
Mrs H.	1948-1959	Typist	marriage (bar)
Mrs C.	1941-1945	Clerkess	other work

Table A.3
Former and retired bank employees: Dutch banks

Name	When worked	Last position	Reason for leaving
Mr R.	1946-1988	General Manager Region	retirement
Mr I.	1951-1990	Branch Manager	retirement
Mr B.	1945-1988	Branch Manager	retirement
Mr F.	1941-1947	Clerk	other work
Mr A.	1937-1961	Manager HO	other work
Mr S.	1939-1962	Branch Manager	other work
Mr L.	1959-1979	Accountant	other work
Mr D.	1959-1965	Lawyer	other work
Mrs V.	1953-1960	Clerkess	marriage (bar)
Mrs F.	1943-1951	Clerkess	marriage (bar)
Mrs J.	1949-1953	Clerkess	other work
Mrs R.	1963-1970	Clerkess	pregnancy
Mrs J.	1969-1973	Insurance	pregnancy
Mrs K.	1960-1992	Accountant	early retirement
Mrs T.	1947-1957	Clerkess	1- marriage (bar) 2- pregnancy

Bibliography

Acker, J. (1989), 'The Problem with Patriarchy', *Sociology*, Vol. 23, May.

Acker, J. (1992), 'Gendered Organizational Theory', in Mills, A.J. and Tancred, P. (eds.), *Gendering Organizational Theory*, Sage: London.

Adlam, D. (1981), 'The Case Against Capitalist Patriarchy', *m/f*, pp. 83-102.

Aglietta, M. (1979), *A Theory of Capitalist Regulation*, New Left Books: London.

Anderson, G. (ed.) (1988), *The White Blouse Revolution, female office workers since 1870*, Manchester University Press: Manchester.

Alexander, S. and Taylor, B. (1982), 'In Defence of "Patriarchy" ', in Evans, M. (ed.), *The Woman Question. Readings on the subordination of women*, Fontana Paperbacks: Oxford.

Alexander, S. (1990), 'Women, Class and Sexual Differences in the 1830s and 1840s. Some reflections on the writing of a feminist history', in Lovell, T. (ed.), *British Feminist Thought. A reader*, Basil Blackwell: Oxford.

Anthias, F. (1980), 'Women and the Reserve Army of Labour. A critique of Veronica Beechey', *Capital and Class*, Vol. 13, pp. 50-63.

Arnhem, C. van (1985), ' "Beter nú de vrouwen geweerd dan straks zelf het huishouden geleerd". Enkele opmerkingen over het belang van betaald werk voor vrouwen', *Socialisties-Feministiese Teksten 9*, Amboboeken: Baarn.

Atkinson, J. (1984), 'Manpower Strategies for Flexible Organisations', *Personnel Management*, August, pp. 28-31.

Atkinson, J. (1985), *Flexibility, Uncertainty and Manpower Management*, Report No. 89, Institute of Manpower: Studies Brighton.

Bakker, I. (1988), 'Women's Employment in Comparative Perspective', in Jenson, J., Hagen, E. and Reddy, C. (eds), *Feminization of the Labor Force. Paradoxes and promises*, Oxford University Press: New York.

Bakker, N. (1982), 'Een mooi beroep voor een meisje, onderwijzeressen tijdens het interbellum', *Jaarboeken voor Vrouwengeschiedenis*, SUN: Nijmegen, pp. 105-128.

Barratt, M. (1980), *Women's Oppression Today. Problems in marxist feminist analysis*, Verso: London.

Beechey, V. (1979), 'On Patriarchy', *Feminist Review*, Vol. 3, pp. 66-82.

Beechey, V. (1982), 'Some Notes on Female Wage Labour in Capitalist Production' in Evans M. (ed.), *The Woman Question. Readings on the subordination of women*, Fontana Paperbacks: Oxford.

Beechey, V. (1989), 'Women's Employment in France and Britain. Some problems of comparison', *Work, Employment and Society*, Vol. 3, No. 3, pp. 379-402.

Beechey, V. and Perkins, T. (1987), *A Matter of Hours. Women, part-time work and the labour market*, Polity Press: Cambridge.

Berg-Wink, A.J. van de, Jong, A.M. de, and Zwart, A. de (1983), 'De Vrouw en het Personeelsbeleid', *Bank- en Effectenbedrijf*, Februari, Vol. 270, pp. 46-54.

Bernoux, P., Cressey, P., Eldridge, J. and MacInnes, J. (1990), *New Technology and Employee Relations in a Scottish and French Bank*, Research Project Report, Glasgow University, internal paper.

BIFU, (1985), *Jobs for the Girls? The impact of automation on women's jobs in the finance industry*.

Blackburn, R.H. (1967), *Union Character and Social Class*, Batsford: London.

Blok, E. (1985), *Uit de Schaduw van de Mannen. Vrouwenverzet 1930-1940*, Feministiese Uitgeverij Sara: Amsterdam.

Blok, E. (1989), *Werkende Vrouwen in de Jaren Veertig en Vijftig*, Sara/Van Gennep: Amsterdam (previously published in 1978 as *Loonarbeid van Vrouwen in Nederland 1945-1955*, SUN: Nijmegen.).

Blonk, A. (1929), *Fabrieken en Menschen. Een Sociografie van Enschede*, van den Loeff: Enschede.

Boston, S. (1980), *Women Workers and the Trade Union Movement*, Davis-poynter: London.

Bottero, W. (1992), 'The Changing Face of the Professions? Gender and explanations of women's entry to pharmacy', *Work, Employment and Society*, Vol. 6, No. 3, pp. 329-346.

Bradley, H. (1989), *Men's Work, Women's Work. A sociological history of the sexual division of labour in employment*, Cambridge: Polity Press.

Brand, W. (1937), *Eindhoven, Sociografie van de Lichtstad*, N.V. J. Emmering's uitgevers mij: Amsterdam.

Braverman, H. (1974), *Labor and Monopoly Capitalism*, Monthly Review Press: New York.

Braybon, G. (1981), *Women Workers in the First World War. The British experience*, Croom Helm: London.

Braybon, G. and Summerfield, P. (1987), *Out of the Cage. Women's experiences in two world wars*, Pandora: London.

Brouns, M. (1990), *The Developments of Women's Studies. A report from the Netherlands*, STEO.

Bruijn, J. de (1981), 'Vrouwen en de Arbeidsmarkt. De waarde van een tweetal arbeidsmarkttheorieën voor het verklaren van de achtergestelde positie van vrouwen op de arbeidsmarkt', *Kongresbundel Zomeruniversiteit Vrouwenstudies*, Amsterdam.

Bruijn, J. de (1986), 'Kwaliteit van Vrouwenarbeid', *Tijdschrift voor Politieke Ekonomie*, Jrg. 10, Nr. 1, pp. 85-100.

Bruijn, J. de (1988), 'Functiewaardering en Sekse', *Tijdschrift voor Arbeisvraagstukken*, Jrg. 4, Nr. 2, pp. 75-83.

Bruijn, J. de (1989a), *Haar Werk. Vrouwenarbeid en arbeidssociologie in historisch en emancipatorisch perspectief*, SUA: Amsterdam.

Bruijn, J. de (1989b), 'Rationalization of the Labour Process and Participation Rates of Sexes in Firms', *Gender and Class Conference*, University of Antwerpen.

Bruijn-Hundt, M. (1988), *Vrouwen op de Arbeidsmarkt. Nederlandse situatie in de jaren tachtig en negentig*, Spectrum: Utrecht.

Burns, T. and Stalker, G.M. (1961), *The Management of Innovation*, Tavistock Publications: London.

Checkland, S. (1975), *Scottish Banking. A history, 1695-1973*, Collins: Glasgow.

Clerkx, L. (1985), 'Vermaatschappelijking of Privatisering van de Kinderopvang', *Socialisties-Feministiese Teksten 9*, Amboboeken: Baarn.

Cockburn, C. (1983), *Brothers. Male dominance and technological change*, Pluto Press: London.

Cockburn, C. (1986), 'Relations of Technology. What implications for theories of sex and class?', in Crompton, R. and Mann, M. (eds.), *Gender and Stratification*, Polity Press: Oxford.

Coe, T. (1992), *The Key to the Men's Club. Opening the doors to women in management*, Institute of Managers, Im Bodis: Burston.

Cohn, S. (1985a), *The Process of Occupational Sex-Typing. The feminization of clerical labour in Great Britain*, Temple University Press: Philadelphia.

Cohn, S. (1985b), 'Clerical Labour Intensity and the Feminisation of Clerical Labour in Great Britain, 1857-1937', *Social Forces*, Vol. 62, pp. 1060-8.

Collinson, D. (1987), 'Banking on Women. Selection practices in the finance sector', *Personnel Review*, Vol. 16, No. 5, pp. 12-20.

Collinson, D., Knights, D. and Collinson, M. (1990), *Managing to Discriminate*, Routledge: London.

Connell, R.W. (1985), 'Theorising Gender', *Sociology*, Vol. 19, No. 2, pp. 260-272.

Connell, R.W. (1987), *Gender and Power. Society, the person and sexual politics*, Polity Press: Cambridge.

Couvee, D.H. and Boswijk, A.H. (1962), *Vrouwen Vooruit! De weg naar gelijke rechten*, Bert Bakker/Daamen NV: Den Haag.

Coward, R. (1983), *Patriarchal Precedents. Sexuality and social relations*, Routledge and Kegan Paul: London.

Cressey, P. and Eldridge, J.E.T. (1987), *Industrial Relations in the British Clearing Banks of Issue*, End of project Report, Glasgow, Internal paper.

Cressey, P. et al. (1985), *Just Managing. Authority and democracy in industry*, OUP: Milton Keynes.

Cressey, P. and Scott, P. (1992), 'Employment, Technology and Industrial Relations in UK Clearing Banks. Is the honeymoon over?', *New Technology, Work and Employment*, Vol. 7, No. 2.

Crompton, R. (1986), 'Women and the "Service Class" ', in Crompton, R. and Mann, M. (eds.), *Gender and Stratification*, Polity Press: Cambridge.

Crompton, R. (1988), 'The Feminisation of the Clerical Labour Force Since the Second World War' in Anderson, G. (ed.), *The White-Blouse Revolution. Female office workers since 1870*, Manchester University Press: Manchester.

Crompton, R. (1989), 'Women in Banking. Continuity and change since the Second World War', *Work, Employment and Society*, Vol. 3, No. 2, pp. 141-156.

Crompton, R. and Jones, G. (1984), *White-Collar Proletariat. Deskilling and gender in clerical work*, Macmillan Press: London.

Crompton, R. and Sanderson, K. (1987), 'Where Did All the Bright Girls Go?', *Quarterly Journal of Social Affairs*, Vol. 3, No. 2, pp. 135-147.

Crompton, R. and Sanderson, K. (1990), *Gendered Jobs and Social Change*, Unwin Hyman: London.

Davidoff, L. and Westover, B. (1986), *Our Work, Our Lives, Our Words. Women's history and women's work*, Macmillan: London.

Devine, F. (1992), 'Gender Segregation in the Engineering and Science Professions. A case of continuity and change', *Work, Employment and Society*, Vol. 6, No. 4, pp. 557-575.

Dex, S. (1984), *Women's Work Histories. An analysis of the women and employment survey*, Research Paper No. 46, Department of Employment.

Dex, S. (1985), *The Sexual Division of Labour*, Wheatsheaf Books: Brighton.

Diemer-Lindeboom, Dr F.F. (1948), 'Aan het Thuisfront', in Schenk, Dra M.G. (ed.), *Vrouwen van Nederland 1898-1948. De vrouw tijdens de regering van Koningin Wilhelmina*, Amsterdam.

225

Dohrn, S. (1988), 'Pioneers in a Dead-End Profession. The first women clerks in banks and insurance companies', in Anderson, G. (ed.), *The White-Blouse Revolution. Female office workers since 1870*, Manchester University Press: Manchester.

Doorman, J.C. (1948), 'Industrie en Bedrijf', in Schenk, Drs M.G. (ed.), *Vrouwen van Nederland 1898-1948. De vrouw tijdens de regering van Koningin Wilhelmina*, Amsterdam.

Drew, E. (1992) 'The Part-Time Option? Women and part-time work in the European Community', *Women's Studies International Forum*, Vol. 15, No. 5/6, pp. 607-614.

Duguenin, A. (1984), 'Who doesn't Marry and Why?', *Oral History*, Vol.12, No.1, Spring.

Dunk, H.W. van der, et al. (1986), *Wederopbouw, Welvaart en Onrust. Nederland in de jaren vijftig en zestig*, De Haan: Houten.

Dyhouse, C. (1989), *Feminism and the Family in England, 1880-1939*, Basil Blackwell: Oxford.

EC Childcare Network (1990), 'Childcare in the European Communities: 1985-1990', *Women of Europe*, Supplement No. 31, Commission of the European Communities: Brussels.

EC Childcare Network (1996), *A Review of Services for Young Children in the European Community*, Equal Opportuntities Unit, Commission of the European Community.

Edholm, F., Harris, O. and Young, K. (1977), 'Conceptualising Women', *Critique of Anthropology*, No. 9/10, pp. 101-130.

Egan, A. (1982), 'Women and Banking. A study of inequality', *Industrial Relations Journal*, Vol. 13, No. 3, pp. 20-31.

Eldridge, J., Cressey, P. and MacInnes, J. (1991), *Industrial Sociology and Economic Crisis*, Harvester Wheatsheaf: London.

Fagan, C., Plantenga, J. and Rubery, J. (1994) 'Part-Time Work and Inequality. Lessons from the Netherlands and the UK' in *A Time For Working, A Time For Living*, Conference publication by ETUC and ETUI (December).

Glucksmann, M. (1990), *Women Assemble. Women workers and the new industries in inter-war Britain*, Routledge and Kegan Paul: London.

Graaff, B. de and Marcus, L. (1980), *Kinderwagens en Korsetten. Een onderzoek naar de sociale achtergrond en de rol van vrouwen in het verzet 1940-1945*, Bert Bakker: Amsterdam.

Gros Clark, F. le, (1962), *Women, Work and Age*, Nuffield Foundation: London.

Hagen, E. and Jenson, J. (1988), 'Paradoxes and Promises. Work and politics in the postwar years', in Jenson, J., Hagen, E. and Reddy, C. (eds.),

Feminization of the Labor Force. Paradoxes and promises, Oxford University Press: New York.

Hakim, C. (1979), *Occupational Segregation. A comparative study of the degree and pattern of the differentiation between men's and women's work in Britain, the United States and other countries*, Department of Employment Research Paper, Department of Employment: London.

Hakim, C. (1993), 'Notes and Issues: The myth of rising female employment', *Work, Employment and Society*, Vol. 7, No. 1, pp. 97-120.

Halford, S. and Savage, M. (1995), 'Restructuring Organisations, Changing People. Gender and restructuring in banking and local government', *Work, Employment and Society*, Vol. 9, No. 1, pp. 97-122.

Hamilton, M.A. (1941), *Women at Work*, The Labour Book Service: London.

Hartmann, H. (1981), 'The Unhappy Marriage of Marxism and Feminism. Towards a more progressive union' in Sargent, L. (ed.), *Women and Revolution. The unhappy marriage of marxism and feminism*, Pluto Press: London.

Hennessey, E. (1992), *A Domestic History of the Bank of England, 1930-1960*, Cambridge University Press: Cambridge.

Heritage, J. (1983), 'Feminisation and Unionisation. A case study from banking' in Gamarnikow, E., et al. (eds.), *Gender, Class and Work*, Heinemann: London.

Higgs, E. (1987), 'Women, Occupations and Work in the Nineteenth Century Censuses', *History Workshop*, Vol. 23, Spring, pp. 57-78.

Hoffmann, H. (1971), 'Het Nederlandse Bankwezen 1960-1970', *Bank en Effectenbedrijf*, pp. 477-489.

Holtmaat, R. (1987), 'Flexibele Arbeid en Economische Zelfstandigheid', *Socialisties-Feministiese Teksten 10*, Amboboeken: Baarn.

Holt-Taselaar, A.M.J. ten, (1954), 'Vrouwen en Meisjes in het Verzet' in Bolthuis, J.J. van, Brandt, L.D.J. and Randwijk, H.M. van (eds.) *Onderdrukking en Verzet. Nederland in Oorlogstijd (deel drie)*, Amsterdam/Arnhem.

Huijgen, F., Riesewijk, B.J.P. and Conen, G.J.M. (1983), *De Kwalitatieve Structuur van de Werkgelegenheid in Nederland. Bevolking in loondienst en functieniveaustructuur in de periode 1960-1977*, Staatsuitgeverij: Den Haag.

Humphries, J. and Rubery, J. (1988), 'Recession and Exploitation. British women in a changing workplace, 1979-1985', in Jenson, J., Hagen, E. and Reddy, C. (eds.), *Feminization of the Labor Force. Paradoxes and promises*, Oxford University Press: New York.

Hunt, A. (ed.) (1988), *Women and Paid Work*, Macmillan: London.

Inman, P. (1957), *Labour in the Munitions Industries*, Longmans, Green and Co.: London.

International Labour Review, (1962), *Reports and Inquiries. Discrimination in employment or occupation on the basis of marital status I and II*, No. 85, pp. 262-82 and pp. 368-89.

Jager, J. L. (1989), *De Bank van de Gulden. Organisatie en personeel van de Nederlandse Bank, 1814-1989*, De Nederlandsche Bank NV: Amsterdam.

Jenkins, R. (1988), 'Discrimination and Equal Opportunities in Employment. Ethnicity and "race" in the United Kingdom', in Gallie, D. (ed.), *Employment in Britain*, Basil Blackwell: Oxford.

Jenson, J., Hagen, E. and Reddy, C. (eds.) (1988), *Feminization of the Labor Force. Paradoxes and promises*, Oxford University Press: New York.

Jephcott, P. et al. (1962), *Married Women Working*, Allan Unwin: London.

Jong, A.M. de (1983), *Gelijke Behandeling en het Personeelsbeleid. De positie van de vrouw in de arbeidsorganisatie*, Kluwer: Deventer.

Jong, A.M. de (1985), *De Positie van Vrouwen bij een Grote Bank. Een onderzoek naar de achtergronden van het verschil in positie tussen mannen en vrouwen*, unpublished Thesis, Erasmus Universiteit: Rotterdam.

Jong, B. de and Sjerps, I. (1987), 'Zweven in de Breedte. Vier jaar breed platform vrouwen voor ekonomische zelfstandigheid', *Socialisties-Feministiese Teksten 10*, Amboboeken: Baarn.

Joshi, H. and Owen, S. (1987), 'How Long is a Piece of Elastic? The measurement of female participation rates in British censuses, 1951-1981', *Cambridge Journal of Economics*, Vol. 11, pp. 55-74.

Kooij, G. and Pley, G. (1984), 'Drie Kwesties Rond Vrouwenarbeid in de Nederlandse Sigarenindustrie Tijdens het Interbellum', *Jaarboeken voor Vrouwengeschiedenis*, 1984, SUN: Nijmegen.

Knijn, T. (1990), 'Terug van Weggeweest? Theorievorming en onderzoek naar de relatie tussen sekse en klasse', *Tijdschrift voor Vrouwenstudies*, Jrg. 11, pp. 445-451.

Knijn, T. (1994) 'Social Dilemmas in Images of Motherhood in the Netherlands', *The European Journal of Women's Studies*, Vol. 1, pp. 183-205.

Kroon, L. (1983), *Voetstukken en Valkuilen. De hardnekkigheid van een vrouwbeeld*, Informatiereeks 7, Feministische Uitgeverij Sara: Amsterdam.

Kuhn, A. and Wolpe, A.M. (eds.) (1978), *Feminism and Materialism. Women and modes of production*, Routledge and Kegan Paul: London.

Kuipers, A. (1984), *Vrouwenarbeid in de Dertiger en Seventiger Jaren*, unpublished doctoral dissertation, Universiteit van Nijmegen: Nijmegen.

Kulsdom, D. and Westeringh, M. van de (1983), 'Postbank en Particuliere Banken, kan een staatsbedrijf overleven?', *Tijdschrift voor Politieke Ekonomie*, Jrg. 7, Nr.1, pp. 88-102.

Lane, C. (1988), 'Industrial Change in Europe. The pursuit of flexible specialisation in Britain and West Germany', *Work, Employment and Society*, Vol. 2, No. 2, pp. 141-68.

Lane, C. (1993) 'Gender and the Labour Market in Europe. Britain, Germany and France', *The Sociological Review*, Vol. 41, No. 2, pp. 274-300.

Lash, S. and Urry, J. (1987), *The End of Organized Capitalism*, Polity Press: Cambridge.

Leser, C.E.V. (1952), 'Men and Women in Industry', *Economic Journal*, No. 62, pp. 330-344.

Lever-Tracy, C. (1983), 'Immigrant Workers and Post-War Capitalism. In reserve or core troops in the front line', *Politics and Society*, Vol. 12, No. 2, pp. 127-157.

Lewenhak, S. (1977), *Women and Trade Unions. An outline history of women in the British trade union movement*, Ernest Benn Ltd: London.

Lewenhak, S. (1980), *Women and Work*, London: Macmillan.

Lewis, J. (1984), *Women in England 1870-1950. Sexual divisions and social change*, Wheatsheaf Books: Sussex.

Lewis, J. (ed.) (1986), *Labour and Love. Women's experience of home and family, 1850-1940*, Basil Blackwell: Oxford.

Lewis, J. (1988), 'Women Clerical Workers in the Late Nineteenth and Early Twentieth Centuries', in Anderson, G. (ed.), *The White Blouse Revolution. Female office workers since 1870*, Manchester University Press: Manchester.

Lewis, J. (1992), *Women in Britain since 1945. Women, family, work and the state in the post-war years*, Basil Blackwell: Oxford.

Lipietz, A. (1987), *Mirages and Miracles*, Verso: London.

Llewellyn, C. (1981), 'Occupational Mobility and the Use of the Comparative Method' in Roberts, H. (ed.), *Doing Feminist Research*, Routledge and Keagan Paul: London.

Lovenduski, J. (1986), *Women and European Politics. Contemporary feminism and public policy*, Harvester Press: Brighton.

Lovenduski, J. and Randall, V. (1993), *Contemporary Feminist Politics. Women and power in Britain*, Oxford University Press: Oxford.

Lowe, G. (1987), *Women in the Administrative Revolution. The feminisation of clerical work*, Polity Press: Cambridge.

Lown, J. (1990) *Women and Industrialization*, Cambridge: Polity Press.

MacInnes, J. (1986), *New Technology in Scotbank. Trade unions, new technology and industrial democracy*, paper presented to the EGOS Colloquium.

MacInnes, J. (1987), *Thatcherism at Work. Industrial relations and economic change*, Open University Press: Milton Keynes.

MacInnes, J. (1988a), 'New Technology in Scotbank. Gender, class and work', in Hyman, R. and Streeck, W. (eds.), *New Technology and Industrial Relations*, Basil Blackwell: Oxford

MacInnes, J. (1988b), 'The Question of Flexibility', *Personnel Review*, Vol. 17, No. 3, pp. 12-15.

Marchebank, J. (1994), *Skirting the Issue. Agenda setting, policy development and the marginalisation of women*, Unpublished PhD Thesis, Strathclyde University: Glasgow.

Martens, L. (1994), *A Comparative Study of the Gender Composition of Work Forces in Britain and the Netherlands, 1940-1990. With special reference to banking*, Unpublished PhD Thesis, Glasgow University, Glasgow.

Martin, J. and Roberts, C. (1984), *Women and Employment. A lifetime perspective*, Department of Employment: London.

Marwick, A. (1968), *Britain in the Century of Total War. War, peace and social change*, The Bodley Head: London.

Marwick, A. (1974), *War and Social Change in the Twentieth Century. A comparative study of Britain, France, Germany, Russia and the United States*, The Macmillan Press: London.

Mass-Observation, (1987), *War Factory*, The Cresset Library: London.

McDonough, R. and Harrison, R. (1978), 'Patriarchy and Relations of Production', in Kuhn, A. and Wolpe, A. (eds.), *Feminism and Materialism. Women and modes of production*, Routledge and Kegan Paul: London.

Merton, R.K. (1957), *Social Theory and Social Structure*, The Free Press: New York.

Messing, F. (1981), *De Nederlandse Economie 1945-1980. Herstel, groei, stagnatie*, Fibula- van Dishoeck: Haarlem.

Meurs, P., Röhling, M. and Weggelaar, M. (1982), *Micro-Elektronika en Vrouwenarbeid, Deel 1: Literatuurstudie*, Ministerie van Sociale Zaken en Werkgelegenheid: Den Haag.

Middelton, C. (1988), 'The Familiar Fate of the Famulae. Gender divisions in the history of wage labour', in Pahl, R.E. (ed.), *On Work. Historical, comparative and theoretical approaches*, Basil Blackwell: Oxford.

Miles, R. (1987), *Capitalism and Unfree Labour. Anomaly or necessity?*, Tavistock Publications Ltd: London.

Millett, K. (1971), *Sexual Politics*, Sphere: London.

Molen, G. van der (ca. 1938), *De Beroepsarbeid van de Gehuwde Vrouw*, NV Drukkerij: Hoorn.

Morée, M. (1982), 'Waarom de Apothekers voor Vrouwen Kozen. De transformatie van het apothekersassistentenberoep in de periode 1865-1900', *Jaarboeken voor Vrouwengeschiedenis*, SUN: Nijmegen.

Morée, M. (1986), 'Vrouwen en Arbeidsmarktbeleid 1950-1985' in Schuyt, K. and Veen, R. van der (eds.), *De Verdeelde Samenleving. Een inleiding in de ontwikkeling van de Nederlandse verzorgingsstaat*, Stanfert Kroese Uitgevers: Leiden/Antwerpen.

Morée, M. (1992), *'Mijn Kinderen Hebben Er Niets Van Gemerkt'. Buitenshuis werkende moeders tussen 1950 en nu*, Jan van Arkel: Utrecht.

Morée, M. and Schwegman, M. (1981), *Vrouwenarbeid in Nederland, 1870-1940*, Elmar Vorspel BV: Tilburg.

Mourby, K. (1983), 'The Wives and Children of the Teeside Unemployed: 1919-1939', *Oral History*, Vol. 11, No. 2.

Mudde, J.M. (1974), 'Werken in een Bank. Hand- en hoofdwerk met nieuwe gereedschappen', *Informatie*, Jrg. 16, Nr. 2, pp. 148-153.

Myrdal, A. and Klein, V. (1956), *Women's Two Roles*, Routledge and Kegan Paul: London.

Nederlands Economisch Historisch Archief (NEHA) (1992), *Historische Bedrijfsarchieven. Bankwezen, een geschiedenis en bronnenoverzicht*, NEHA: Amsterdam.

Oram, A. (1983), 'Serving Two Masters? The introduction of a marriage bar in teaching in the 1920s' in London History Group (ed.), *The Sexual Dynamics of History*, Pluto: London.

O'Reilly, J. (1992), *'Banking on Flexibility. A comparison of the use of flexible employment strategies in the retail banking sector in Britain and France'*, Paper presented at the BSA 1992 conference.

Outshoorn, J. (1975), 'Loondruksters of Medestrijdsters? Vrouwen en vakbeweging in Nederland 1890-1920', *Te Elfder Ure 20*, Feminisme 1, Jrg. 22.

Owen Jones, S.(1987), 'Women in the Tinplate Industry, Llanelli 1930-1950, *Oral History*, Vol. 15, No. 1, Spring.

Paukert, L. (1985), *The Employment and Unemployment of Women in OECD Countries*, OECD: Paris.

Pennington, S. and Westover, B. (1989), *A Hidden Workforce. Homeworkers in England 1850-1985*, Macmillan: London.

Pfau-Effinger, B. (1993) 'Modernization, Culture and Part-Time Employment. The example of Finland and West Germany', *Work, Employment and Society*, Vol. 7, No. 3, pp. 383-410.

Pfau-Effinger, B. (1995) 'Social Change in the Gendered Division of Labour in Cross-National Perspective', paper presented to 2nd ESA conference, Budapest.

Piore, M. and Sabel, C. (1984), *The Second Industrial Divide: Possibilities for prosperity*, Basic Books: New York.

Plantenga, J. (1987), 'Structurele Veranderingen en de Beroepsarbeid van Vrouwen', *Zomeruniversiteit Vrouwenstudies: Werken*, Groningen.

231

Plantenga, J. (1992), 'De Kantelende Tijd. Opvattingen over vrouwenarbeid in de jaren vijftig', *Tijdschrift voor Vrouwenstudies*, Jrg. 13, Nr. 2, pp. 140-161.

Plantenga, J. (1993) *Een Afwijkend Patroon. Honderd jaar vrouwenarbeid in Nederland en (West-) Duitsland*, Uitgeverij SUA: Amsterdam.

Plantenga, J. and Doorne-Huiskes, A. van (1993), 'Verschillen in Arbeidsmarktposities van Vrouwen in Europa', *Tijdschrift voor Arbeidsvraagstukken*, Jrg. 9, Nr. 1, pp. 51-62.

Pollert, A. (1988), 'The "Flexible Firm". Fixation or fact?', *Work, Employment and Society*, Vol. 2, No. 3, pp. 281-316.

Posthumus-van der Groot, Dr W.H. et al. (1977), *Van Moeder op Dochter. De maatschappelijke positie van de vrouw in Nederland vanaf de franse tijd*, SUN: Nijmegen (reprint from 1948).

Pott-Buter, H. (1993) *Facts and Fairy Tales about Female Labor, Family and Fertility. A seven-country comparison, 1850-1990*. Amsterdam: Amsterdam University Press.

Power, M. (1983), 'From Home Production to Wage Labour. Women as a reserve army of labour', *Revue of Radical Political Economy*, pp. 71-91.

Reinalda, B. (1981), *Onze Strijd. Beknopte geillustreerde geschiedenis van de vakbeweging van handels- en kantoorbedienden in Nederland tussen 1859-1942*, SUN: Nijmegen.

Reinalda, B. (1985), *De Dienstenbonden. Klein maar strijdbaar*, AMBO: Baarn.

Rex, J. and Tomlinson, S. (1979), *Colonial Immigrants in a British City*, Routledge and Kegan Paul: London.

Roberts, E. (1988), *Women's Work 1840-1940*, Macmillan: London.

Romme, A.G.L. (1987), 'Het macro-Economisch Arbeidsaanbod van Vrouwen, Een verklaring voor de periode 1971-1985', *Maandschrift Economie*, Jrg. 51, pp. 53-66.

Rowbotham, S. (1982), 'The Trouble with "Patriarchy" ', in Evans, M. (ed.), *The Woman Question. Readings on the subordination of women*, Fontana Paperbacks: Oxford.

Rubery, J. (ed.) (1988), *Women and Recession*, Routledge & Kegan Paul: London.

Rubery, J. and Tarling, R. (1988), 'Women's Employment in Declining Britain', in Rubery, J. (ed.), *Women and Recession*, Routledge & Kegan Paul: London.

Rubery, J. and Fagan, C. (1994) 'Does Feminization Mean a Flexible Labour Force?', in Hyman, R. and Ferner, A. (eds), *New Frontiers in European Industrial Relations*, Basil Blackwell: Oxford.

Sabel, C. (1982), *Work and Politics. The division of labour in industry*, Cambridge University Press: Cambridge.

Savage, M. (1992a), 'Gender and Career Mobility in Banking 1880-1940', in Miles, A. and Vincent, D. (eds.), *Building European Society*, Manchester University Press: Manchester.

Savage, M. (1992b), 'Women's Expertise, Men's Authority. Gendered organization and the contemporary middle classes', in Savage, M. and Witz, A. (eds.), *Gender and Bureaucracy*, Blackwell Publishers: Oxford.

Schenk, Dra. M.G. (1948), 'Vrouwen in Dienst', in Schenk, Dra M.G. (ed.), *Vrouwen van Nederland 1898-1948. De vrouw tijdens de regering van Koningin Wilhelmina*, Amsterdam.

Schilstra, W.N. (1940), *Vrouwenarbeid in Landbouw en Industrie in Nederland in de 2e Helft der 19e Eeuw*, Amsterdam.

Schoot-Uiterkamp, A. (1978), 'Terug naar het Paradijs? Akties tegen de beperking van vrouwenarbeid in de jaren dertig', *Jaarboeken voor de Geschiedenis van Socialisme en Arbeidsbeweging in Nederland*, 1978, SUN: Nijmegen.

Schwegman, M. (1979), *Het Stille Verzet. Vrouwen in illegale organisaties Nederland 1940-1945*, SUA: Amsterdam.

Siltanen, J. (1981), 'Theories of Female Wage Labour', in CWSC (ed.), *Women in Society*, Virago Press: London.

Silverstone, R. (1976) 'Office Work for Women. An historical review', *Business History*, Vol. 18, pp. 89-100.

Silverstone, R. and Ward, A. (eds.) (1980), *Careers of Professional Women*, Croom Helm: London.

Smith, H. (1981), 'The Problem of "Equal Pay for Equal Work" in Great Britain during World War II', *Journal of Modern History*, No. 53, pp. 652-672.

Smith, H. (1986), 'The Effect of the War on the Status of Women', in Smith, H. (ed.), *War and Social Change. British society in the Second World War*, Manchester University Press: Manchester.

Sociaal Cultureel Planbureau (1988), *Sociaal en Cultureel Rapport 1988*, Staatsuitgeverij: Den Haag.

Soldon, N. (1978), *Women in British Trade Unions 1874-1976*, Gill and Macmillan Ltd: Dublin.

Spender, D. (1984), *Time and Tide Wait for No Man*, Pandora Box: London.

Strachey, O. (1934), 'Married Women and Work', *Contemporary Review*, CXLV.

Strachey, R. (1937), *Careers and Openings for Women*, Faber Ltd: London.

Stuurman, S. (1981), 'Verzuiling en Klassestrijd in Nederland', *Jaarboeken voor de Geschiedenis van Socialisme en Arbeidersbeweging in Nederland*, SUN: Nijmegen.

Stuurman, S. (1984), 'Het Zwarte Gat van de Jaren Vijftig', *Kleio*, 8, pp. 6-13.

Sullerot, E. (1979), *Geschiedenis en Sociologie van de Vrouwenarbeid*, SUN: Nijmegen (reprint from the French 1968 publication *Histoire et Sociology du travail feminin*).

Summerfield, P. (1984), *Women Workers in the Second World War. Production and patriarchy in conflict*, Croom Helm: London.

Summerfield, P. (1988), 'Women, War and Social Change. Women in Britain in World War II', in Marwick, A. (ed.), *Total War and Social Change*, The Macmillan Press: London.

Taylor, S. (1977), 'The Effect of Marriage on Job Possibilities for Women and the Ideology of the Home: Nottingham 1890-1930', *Oral History*, Vol. 5, No. 2, pp. 46-61.

Thom, D. (1978), 'Women at the Woolwich Arsenal 1915-1919', *Oral History*, Vol. 6, No. 2, pp. 58-73.

Tijdens, K. (1989), *Automatisering en Vrouwenarbeid. Een studie over beroepssegregatie op de arbeidsmarkt, in de administratieve beroepen en in het bankwezen*, Jan van Arkel: Utrecht.

Tijdens, K. (1990), *Veroudering en Doorstroming. De invloed van demografische ontwikkelingen op het personeelsbestand bij de vier grote banken*, Research Memorandum No. 9018, Faculteit der Economische Wetenschappen en Econometrie, UVA: Amsterdam.

Tijdens, K. (1991), 'Veroudering van Personeel. Ontwikkelingen in het personeelsbestand bij de 4 grote banken', *Tijdschrift voor Politieke Ekonomie*, Jrg. 13, Nr. 4, pp. 16-33.

Tijdens, K. (1991), 'Arbeidsparticipatie en bedrijfskinderopvang', in Tijdens, K. and Singer, E., (eds.), *Uit en Thuis. Wetenschapsters over kinderopvang in Nederland*, Jan van Arkel: Utrecht.

Tijdens, K. (1993), '25 jaar Produktinnovatieprocessen van het Binnenlandse Girale Betalingsverkeer in het Bankwezen. De ontwikkeling van informatietechnologie in de dienstensector', *Tijdschrift voor Politieke Ekonomie*, Jrg. 15, Nr. 3, pp. 67-89.

Tilly, L. and Scott, J. (1989) *Women, Work, and Family*, London: Routledge.

Troberg, P. (1975), *Het Bankwezen in de Europese Gemeenschap*, NIBE: Amsterdam.

United Nations (1979), *Labour Supply and Migration in Europe. Demographic dimensions 1950-1975 and prospects*.

Veerman, H. and Verheijen, C. (1984), *Beroepsarbeid en Gezin. Vrouwen in een spanningsveld?*, Van Loghum Slaterus: Deventer.

Veld-Langeveld, H.M. in 't (1969), *Vrouw-Beroep-Maatschappij. Analyse van een vertraagde emancipatie*, Uitgeverij Bijlenveld: Utrecht.

Vossen, H., Plantenga, J. and Volman, M. (1992), 'Omstreden Consensus en Onbetwiste Strijd. Sekse en sekseverhoudingen in de periode 1947-1973.

Inleiding op het thema', *Tijdschrift voor Vrouwenstudies*, Jrg. 13, Nr. 2, pp. 133-139.

Vries-Bruins, A.E.J. de (1948), *Uit Spuit - De Bocht Weer Uit?*, Comité tot Verdediging van de Vrijheid van de Arbeid van de Vrouw.

Walby, S. (1986), *Patriarchy at work. Patriarchal and capitalist relations in employment*, Polity Press: Cambridge.

Walby, S. (1989), 'Theorising Patriarchy', *Sociology*, Vol. 23, No. 2, pp. 213-234.

Walby, S. (1990a), 'From Private to Public Patriarchy. The periodisation of British history', *Women's Studies International Forum*, Vol. 13, No. 1/2, pp. 91-104.

Walby, S. (1990b), *Theorising Patriarchy*, Basil Blackwell: Oxford.

Walker, J. (1988), 'Women, the State and the Family in Britain. Thatcher economics and the experience of women', in Rubery, J. (ed), *Women and Recession*, Routledge & Kegan Paul: London.

Weggelaar, M. and Boer, K. de, (1984), *Micro-elektronika en Vrouwenarbeid, Deel 2: Gevolgen van de invoering van micro-elektronika voor de arbeid van vrouwen*, Ministerie van Sociale Zaken en Werkgelegenheid: Den Haag.

Westergaard, J. and Resler, H. (1975), *Class in a Capitalist Society*, Heinemann: London.

Wierema, H. (1979), *Arbeidsverhoudingen in het Bankwezen. Een kritische analyse*, SUN: Nijmegen.

Wiener, M.S. and Verwey-Jonker, H. (1952), *Wat Hebben We Gedaan? En Wat Staat Ons Te Doen?*, Nederlandse Vereeniging voor Vrouwenbelangen, Vrouwenarbeid en Gelijk Staatsburgerschap, Den Haag.

Wigham, E. (1980), *From Humble Petition to Militant Action. A history of the civil and public services association: 1903-1978*, The Civil and Public Services Association.

Winton, J. (1982), *Lloyds Bank: 1918-1969*, Oxford University Press: Oxford.

Williams, G. (1945), *Women and Work*, Nicolson and Watson: London.

Wilson, E. (1980), *Only Halfway to Paradise. Women in postwar Britain 1945-1968*, Tavistock: London.

Witz, A. (1992a), *Professions and Patriarchy*, Routledge: London.

Witz, A. and Savage, M. (1992b) 'Theoretical Introduction. The gender of organizations', in Savage, M. and Witz, A. (eds.), *Gender and Bureaucracy*, Blackwell Publishers: Oxford.

Wright, G. (1968), *The Ordeal of Total War, 1939-1945*, Harper & Row Publishers: London.

Wood, S. (ed.) (1989), *The Transformation of Work? Skill, flexibility and the labour process*, Routledge: London.

Young, I. (1981), 'Beyond the Unhappy Marriage. A critique of the dual systems theory', in Sargent L. (ed), *Women and Revolution. The unhappy marriage of marxism and feminism*, Pluto Press: London.

Archival Sources

Bank en Effectenbedrijf
The Banker
The Bankers' Magazine
The Scottish Bankers' Magazine
The Bank Officer
The Bank of England Archive
Britbank's Archive
Dutchbank's Archive
Sociale Jaarverslagen Dutchbank
Archive Twentsche Bank
Mercurius
The Committee of Scottish Clearing Bankers' Archival Materials
Werkgeversvereeniging voor het Bankbedrijf Archival Materials
Institute of Bankers' Annual Reports
Sidney Checkland's Working Papers

Parliamentary papers

Parliamentary paper, Cmd. 3508, (1930), *Women in Industry*.
Parliamentary paper, Cmd. 6402, (1942), *Kennett Committee Report on Man-Power in Banking during the War*.
Parliamentary paper, Cmd. 6886, (1946), *Marriage Bar in the Civil Service*.
Parliamentary paper, Cmd. 7047, (1947), *Economic Survey*.

Statistical sources

British Census from 1931-1981.
Centraal Bureau voor de Statistiek: *Volkstelling van 1930, 1947, 1960 en 1971*.
Centraal Bureau voor de Statistiek: *Tachtig jaren statistiek in tijdreeksen, 1899-1979*.
Centraal Bureau voor de Statistiek: *Arbeidskrachtentelling, 1973-1985*.
Centraal Bureau voor de Statistiek: *Statistiek Werkzame Personen, 1973-1987*.

Eurostat, *Labour Force Survey*.
Eurostat (1985), *Labour Force Survey - Methods and Definitions*.
OECD, *OECD Labour Force Statistics*.

Index